07-BPW-125

D0122534

ON EVERY FRONT

Other Books by Thomas G. Paterson

IMPERIAL SURGE: THE UNITED STATES ABROAD, 1890s–EARLY 1900s
(with Stephen G. Rabe)

EXPLAINING THE HISTORY OF AMERICAN FOREIGN RELATIONS
(with Michael J. Hogan)

THE ORIGINS OF THE COLD WAR
(with Robert J. McMahon)

AMERICAN FOREIGN POLICY: A HISTORY
(with J. Garry Clifford and Kenneth J. Hagan)

A PEOPLE AND A NATION: A HISTORY OF THE UNITED STATES
(with Mary Beth Norton et al.)

KENNEDY'S QUEST FOR VICTORY: AMERICAN FOREIGN POLICY, 1961–1963

MAJOR PROBLEMS IN AMERICAN FOREIGN POLICY

MEETING THE COMMUNIST THREAT: TRUMAN TO REAGAN

SOVIET-AMERICAN CONFRONTATION: POSTWAR
RECONSTRUCTION AND THE ORIGINS OF THE COLD WAR

CONTAINMENT AND THE COLD WAR: AMERICAN FOREIGN POLICY SINCE 1945

AMERICAN IMPERIALISM AND ANTI-IMPERIALISM

COLD WAR CRITICS: ALTERNATIVES TO AMERICAN
FOREIGN POLICY IN THE TRUMAN YEARS

ON EVERY FRONT

THE MAKING
AND UNMAKING OF
THE COLD WAR

Revised Edition

Thomas G. Paterson

W·W·NORTON & COMPANY

New York   London

The text of this book is composed in 11.5/13.5 Bodoni Book
with the display set in Onyx
Composition and Manufacturing by the Haddon Craftsmen, Inc.
Book design by Margaret M. Wagner

Library of Congress Cataloging-in-Publication Data
Paterson, Thomas G., 1941–
On every front : the making and unmaking of the Cold War / by
Thomas G. Paterson.—Rev. ed.
p.   cm.
Includes index.
1. United States—Foreign relations—1945–1992.   2. Soviet Union-
Foreign relations—1945–   3. United States—Foreign relations-
Soviet Union.   4. Soviet Union—Foreign relations—United States.
5. World politics—1945–   6. Cold War.   I. Title.
E744.P312   1992
327.73047—dc20   92–1174

ISBN 0-393-03060-1
W.W. Norton & Company, Inc.
500 Fifth Avenue, New York, N.Y. 10110
W.W. Norton & Company Ltd.
10 Coptic Street, London WC1A 1PU
1 2 3 4 5 6 7 8 9 0

For Stephen W. C. Paterson

CONTENTS

PREFACE

WHY and how the Cold War *ended* became the question of the day after the Berlin Wall came down in 1989. To people whose lives had long been circumscribed, if not terrified, by Cold War–related events, the remarkable disintegration of the Soviet Union, the collapse of communism in Eastern Europe, and the reunification of Germany signified the end of one era and the beginning of another. Any explanations for the demise of the Cold War depended, of course, upon answers to another fundamental question: Why and how did the Cold War *begin?* People had to fathom the past—what the Cold War *had been*—before they could sensibly interpret the end of a "war" that had bedeviled world history for nearly a half century.

Like a huge glacier, the Cold War had imposed a distinct topography on international relations; its retreat exposed a scarred, debris-littered landscape much in need of repair and redefinition. Historical memories of the Cold War era guided the creation of a new world order. Past, present, and future, as always, fused.

This book explores the past, the world that Winston S. Churchill called "bewildered, baffled, and breathless."[1] The story of the rise and fall of the Cold War is told and analyzed from voluminous archival records, oral histories, memoirs, published government documents, the popular press, historical scholarship, and international relations literature in the United States and abroad. These many materials suggest that the Cold War derived from three closely intertwined sources: the conflict-ridden international system; the divergent fundamental needs, ideas, and power of the major antagonists, the United States and the Soviet Union; and the diplomatic conduct and domestic political systems—the tactics—of American and Soviet leaders. International, national, and individual elements intersected to produce a world divided into competing spheres of influence.

The first chapter introduces the world of 1945, reeling from the dislocations of global war. Chapter 2 plumbs the international system to identify those features that guaranteed conflict among the major postwar nations. The third chapter studies the great powers' building of spheres of influence and then accounts for the embittering events that generated the Cold War before 1947. Chapter 4 takes the story into 1950 and the Korean War, when the characteristics of the Cold War hardened.

Subsequent chapters explain why the two powers acted as they did. Chapter 5 searches for the wellsprings, or fundamentals, of American foreign policy that induced the United States to undertake an activist, global diplomacy. Chapters 6 and 7 investigate the "tactics" of President Harry S. Truman and other American leaders: how they conducted their diplomacy, made their decisions, and maneuvered within the boundaries of their national politics. The eighth chapter, with necessary speculation because reliable Soviet sources remain scarce, probes the fundamental and tactical ingredients of Joseph Stalin's foreign policy in order to explain why the Soviets behaved in such a way as to arouse fears that they were ruthless aggressors in a fierce global contest with the United States.

Beginning with Stalin's death, Truman's retirement, and armistice in Korea, the altogether new Chapter 9 takes a sweeping view of the Cold War to the mid-1980s and links the decline of the two major powers with their pursuit of détente. Weakened by the tremendous economic costs of the Cold War, unrelenting challenges from allies, and the diffusion of power in the international system that accompanied the rise of the Third World, the United States and the Soviet Union welcomed accommodation in order to halt their slide and restore their power. The new last chapter considers the concrete steps Moscow and Washington took to end the Cold War in the late 1980s and early 1990s and the consequences of their decisions.

Although the structure and argument of this revised edition remain much the same as in the first version, I have thoroughly rewritten the text to include representative examples from recent scholarship and my own ongoing research, to engage new interpretations and reaffirm old ones through more persuasive cases, and to apply concepts from other disciplines that historians of American foreign relations have increasingly found useful. I have also learned from international perspectives based upon declassified documents in other nations. The promising but still modest opening of the Soviet record and the freer expression Soviet historians began to enjoy in the late 1980s permitted me to study afresh Soviet foreign policy. The impressive work of both foreign and American scholars has encouraged me to expand discussion of such subjects as the impact of nuclear weapons on world politics, Israel and Palestine, conflict and cooperation in U.S.-Western European relations, decolonization in the Third World, Stalin's diplomacy, and the Central Intelligence Agency as an instrument of American foreign policy.

I thank the many scholars cited in the notes for continuing to rethink the history of the Cold War era. Readers interested in moving beyond this book are invited to use these notes as an instructive bibliography.

My writing has always benefited from the advice and help of others. My special friend and colleague at the University of Connecticut J. Garry Clifford read the manuscript in its entirety. He has long been my best critic; I continue to marvel at his talents in turning a phrase, cutting to essentials, finding nuance, and discovering flawed cases. I thank Garry for his counterarguments and good counsel and for his enviable ability to convey frank criticism in a manner that encourages. My colleagues in the Department of History—especially my chairs, Bruce M. Stave, Edmund S. Wehrle, and Richard D. Brown—have over the years created a fine environment for teaching and research. Ed Wehrle deserves particular mention as a stimulating intellectual companion; we have taught side by side in courses on postwar international history, but more, for years we have talked over just about every global issue in just about every way possible just about every day. Professor Elizabeth Mahan of the University of Connecticut's Center for Latin American and Caribbean Studies marked up the manuscript, urged more clarity, and questioned generalizations. She will see her excellent touches throughout the book. Elizabeth has also become my wise and caring friend whose good influence on me, hence on this book, has been considerable.

The generous librarians and archivists who facilitated my research and thus helped shape this book are too numerous to name here. But their libraries and archives are cited in the notes, and they should know that they are deeply appreciated. I also thank Debra Crary and Carol Roberts for typing the manuscript and for solving word-processing problems. The Research Foundation at the University of Connecticut has often funded my research and writing; directed by Hugh Clark and Thomas Giolas, the foundation has served the university well. Bradley Hale and Shane Maddock served as research assistants, and their contributions are greatly appreciated. Shane Maddock, LeeAnna Keith, Margaret Robinson, and Stephen Armstrong helped me puzzle through the issues in Chapters 9 and 10. My thanks also go to Benedict Maciuika, Melvyn P. Leffler, and Ronald Pruessen for sharing materials with me. My resilient department secretaries, Lisa Ferriere, Diedra Gosline, and Roberta Lusa, deserve gratitude for keeping the faculty on course and for giving me essential assistance.

Let me once again thank those people who provided help for the first edition: Jean-Donald Miller, James Gormly, Eduard M. Mark, Thomas G. Smith, Stephen Rabe, Robert McMahon, Thomas Zoumaras, Holly Izard, Jane Lebow, Mary Pain, Robin Beveridge, Charlton Brandt, and Harold Hyman. The Harry S. Truman Institute, Eleanor Roosevelt Institute, University of Connecticut Research Foundation, and National Endowment for the Humanities provided initial financial support.

ON EVERY FRONT

1

RUBBLE
The World in 1945

WINSTON S. CHURCHILL wore his usual bulldog visage. The ever-present cigar and hunched gait, other familiar trademarks of the British prime minister, also drew the crowd's attention on that very hot day of July 16, 1945. He was surveying the dusty remains of the Nazi capital—"That rubble heap near Potsdam," murmured one Berliner.[1] This time a preoccupied Churchill evinced little interest in his curious onlookers. What captured Churchill's attention in Berlin was the grisly aftermath of heavy Allied bombing and artillery fire and stout German resistance. He and the passengers in his motorcade grew sick, utterly stunned by the stark display of carnage in the humbled German city.

The prime minister entered what was left of Adolf Hitler's Chancellery. The Führer's marble-topped desk lay in a thousand pieces. Iron Crosses, military ribbons, and papers littered the floor. The British visitors picked up souvenirs; one pocketed a fragment of Hitler's world map. The descent into the damp hideaway carried great moment for Churchill, who, uncharacteristically, said little. Shaken by what he saw, General H. L. Ismay hurried away to his villa to take a hot bath and a strong drink.[2] That night Churchill finally talked about his visit to the Chancellery. "It was from there that Hitler planned to govern the world," he mused. "A good many have tried that; all failed."[3] Savoring the Allied victory, the prime minister smiled contentedly and went to bed.

The president of the United States, Harry S. Truman, surveyed Berlin that same day. After reviewing the American Second Armored Division, the president led his entourage down the Wilhelmstrasse to the Chancellery of the Third Reich, all the while growing more awestruck by the destruction of the city. "That's what happens," he remarked, "when a man overreaches himself." For two hours Truman rode through Berlin's streets. "I was thankful," he noted later, "that the United States had been spared the unbelievable devastation of this war."[4]

At the time 65 to 75 percent of Berlin was leveled or damaged.[5] General Lucius Clay, who was soon to become the military governor of the American zone, found that "the streets were piled high with debris which left in many places only a narrow one-way passage between mounds of rubble, and frequent detours had to be made where bridges and viaducts were destroyed. . . . It was like a city of the dead."[6] The once-prized chariot of victory on the Brandenburg Gate had been reduced to a gnarled mass of molten metal, the Reichstag to a hollow shell. Some NICHT FÜR JUDEN signs remained, ugly reminders of the Nazi extermination of European Jews. Factories that had escaped bombing raids now stood hulllike, stripped as war booty by the conquering Soviets, who tore industrial equipment from their foundations.

"There is nothing to do here," sighed a dispirited Berliner.[7] Old men, women, and children trudged along, aimlessly pushing wheelbarrows. More than a million people lived in cellars, ruins, and makeshift suburban shacks, trading what they could for precious scraps of food to support their meager diets. In the western zones of Germany alone, two million crippled people hobbled about. Thirty-four percent of the Germans born in 1924 were badly mutilated in some way by 1945. "The people seem so whipped," wrote an American official to a friend back home, "that you can never believe that they had nursed Storm Troopers among them."[8] Partially buried corpses lay rotting in the sun. As Berliners, under the stern guidance of Soviet and other Allied soldiers, began to stack bricks and shovel ashes, thousands of bodies were unearthed. The American diplomat Robert Murphy smelled "the odor of death" everywhere. Indeed, "the canals were choked with bodies and refuse."[9] Lord Moran, who traveled with Churchill through Berlin, "felt a sense of nausea." Worse, "it was like the first time I saw a surgeon open a belly and the intestines gushed out."[10]

From urban center to rural village, Germany looked charred and ravaged. Bomb-gutted Cologne and Nuremberg were hardly recognizable. Ninety-three percent of the houses in Düsseldorf were totally destroyed. Hamburg, Stuttgart, and Dresden had been laid waste by fire bombs and fire storms. In Dresden mounds of bodies had to be bulldozed into mass graves or burned on huge makeshift grills, so great was the toll and the fear of epidemic disease. An American army air corpsman flying low over the country at the end of the war could not spot streets or homes in Mannheim—only tossed dirt. "Aachen," he observed, "lay bleaching in the sun like bones on a desert." A disbelieving companion gazed at the pulverized land below and asked, "Where do the people live?"[11]

Hospitals, schools, and churches throughout Germany felt

the war's fury. Fourteen of the nation's twenty-three universities were severely damaged. Transportation and communication systems were disrupted. Untreated sewage flowed into waterways, spreading disease. Traffic on the Rhine River, which before the war had been greater than that of the Suez or Panama Canal, slumped to negligible numbers because demolished bridges and sunken vessels blocked the artery. Industrial plants, once the marvel of Europe, lay prostrate. The Ruhr, which had once produced four hundred thousand tons of coal a day, could manage only a paltry twenty-five thousand in 1945. "If we had then realized the confusion and chaos which existed," General Clay wrote five years after the war, "we would indeed have thought ours a hopeless task."[12]

In Churchill's once-mighty island nation the war also claimed a frightful toll. Some observers after V-E Day grimly observed that the Germans looked better fed and less ragged than many British. The air blitz, which struck London, Coventry, and other cities in 1940–1941 and then subsided, began anew in 1944 with German V-1 and V-2 rockets that indiscriminately pounded buildings and people. Major districts of London were badly mangled, turning that regal city into a shabby, battered replica of itself. The Foreign Office building lost most of its windows and doors, and the prime minister's residence at No. 10 Downing Street looked racked as well. After one attack it took workmen six hours to free a woman from a tumbled row house on Stepney High Street. The rescuers asked her if she had a husband. "Yes," she snapped. "He's at the front, the dirty coward."[13]

Few Europeans escaped the marauding armies and death-dealing bombers of the Second World War.[14] In Greece in 1945 a million people were homeless; one-quarter of the nation's buildings were damaged or destroyed. In addition, 80 percent of railway rolling stock and three-quarters of the Greek ocean shipping fleet were incapacitated. Before leaving Greece, the Germans had blasted the walls of the Corinth

Canal, filling it with nine hundred thousand cubic yards of earth. The modern port facilities of Piraeus lay in ruins. Farm yields were down by 50 percent, in part because 80 percent of the nation's tractors had been wrecked. Lost were 65 percent of all cattle, sheep, and goats. Famine, disease, and unemployment (50 percent in the cities) plagued Greece. Gravely undernourished people found hospitals overcrowded. Five hundred thousand registered cases of tuberculosis spelled epidemic. An American doctor who tried to work at the Athens Red Cross Hospital, during an outbreak of civil war in early 1945, found that the "operating room had been blown up with all the glass gone and even the surgical instruments had been melted by the magnesium bombs and were lying around in heaps of molten metal."[15]

In neighboring Yugoslavia the retreating Germans had devastated the countryside, causing starvation in some regions. Upon liberation only one of Yugoslavia's seven large power stations was operating, and the rails running through the Danube Valley, which linked the nation to other European states, were inoperable. In the Hungarian capital of Budapest, the splendor of the Hapsburgs had given way inelegantly to the specter of death. All the bridges over the Danube were demolished, houses were flattened, and the 860-room royal palace of Maria Theresa and Franz Josef survived only as a maze of walls. During the winter of 1944–1945, near the war's end, the cold, hungry people of Budapest huddled in basements as Soviet bombs pummeled suspected German positions. One citizen described his apartment as a "ghostly castle, inhabited by a few scarcely living shadows."[16] In Austria, German fires and Allied bombs had gutted 70 percent of the center of Vienna, not even sparing the seven-hundred-year-old St. Stephen's Cathedral. Women searched for sticks in the Vienna Woods, there being no coal for fuel. Elderly Viennese men and women looked pallid; listless young people begged for GI rations.

In Czechoslovakia and Italy, Prague and Rome had merci-
fully escaped large-scale devastation, but such blessings were
rare in those otherwise-trampled nations. Italy's agricultural
production was down 50 percent, and the government lacked
foreign currency to pay for essential imports of food and raw
materials. People in Naples clawed like cats through garbage
cans for tidbits of food. Before abandoning that city, the
Germans had wrecked the gas, electric, and water systems
and put the torch to the university. In the Netherlands, 540,-
000 acres were flooded and Rotterdam was battered. As for
France, Paris had largely been spared, but almost 20 percent
of the buildings in the entire country were destroyed—twice
the number demolished in the First World War. As many as
90 percent of French trucks were out of action, and much of
the French fleet rested on the bottom of the harbor at Tou-
lon.

John Hersey, whose book *Hiroshima* (1946) reported the
ghastly details of the Asian atomic holocaust, also witnessed
the tragedy of Warsaw, Poland, which the Germans had "destroyed, systematically, street by street, alley by alley, house
by house. . . . Nothing is left except a mockery of architec-
ture." Hersey watched as desperate Poles scratched at the
flesh of a fallen army horse, quickly leaving a steaming skele-
ton. "God, my God, God," whispered a horrified Polish officer who was returning from battle to his native city.[17] One
American journalist saw "rows of roofless, doorless, window-
less walls" that "might have been dug out of the earth by an
army of archaeologists."[18] Almost six million Poles died in
World War II. Polish Jews had been deliberately exter-
minated, with the Auschwitz concentration camp setting bar-
baric records in human cremation. The cities of Gdynia, Dan-
zig, and Stettin were mauled. In this predominantly
agricultural nation, one-sixth of the farms were inoperable,
70 percent of the horses gone, and one-third of the cattle
dead.[19] American Ambassador Arthur Bliss Lane flew into

Warsaw on an Army C-47 in July 1945. The seven-mile trip from the airport to the center of the city chilled him. "The smoky smell of long-dead fires hung in the air. The sickening sweet odor of burned human flesh was a grim warning that we were entering a city of the dead. . . ." But, he went on, "the most terrible sight of all was that of the one-legged children."[20]

To the east, the Union of Soviet Socialist Republics tallied the greatest losses of all. More than 21 million soldiers and civilians had died—one-ninth of the total population.[21] More than 30,000 industrial plants and 40,000 miles of railroad track were destroyed. Thousands of towns and cities had been leveled. Agricultural production was half of what it had been in 1940. Coal mines were flooded; bridges were down. The oil industry suffered shortages of steel pipe. As if the war had not done damage enough, a killer drought struck farming regions in 1946.[22] The Ukraine ranked high in the gruesome record of war losses. Before the war a mainstay of the Soviet economy, with its large production of coal, pig iron, steel, and manganese, as well as farm goods, the region now lay denuded by the Soviet scorched earth policy and the German rampage. Mines were blown up and flooded, the Dnieper Dam blasted, whole farm villages razed, tractors wrecked, and livestock massacred or driven off. The modern Zaporozhal steel plant near the Dnieper Dam was reduced to acres and acres of tangled debris. Famine and starvation hit the Brovary district, where 12,099 out of 16,000 prewar farm buildings were destroyed. The Soviet Socialist Republic of Byelorussia fared no better. Outside Minsk, thirty-four pits held the corpses of 150,000 people murdered and buried by the Germans. The much-fought-over province of Vitebsk counted 300,000 dead.

Elsewhere in the Soviet Union, correspondent Harrison Salisbury called Sevastopol "a city of the dead." Of the city's fifteen thousand houses, only five hundred remained standing after the German retreat. "If a room has three walls and a ceiling," the mayor told Salisbury, "we count it in good shape."[23] As for Stalingrad, American Ambassador W. Averell Harriman viewed "a desert of broken brick and rubble, the survivors huddling in cellars or tar-paper shanties."[24] Another reporter, Alexander Werth, passed through Istra, west of Moscow, and saw nothing but a "forest of chimney-stacks."[25] The people of Moscow looked haggard as they piled their rubble. Shortly after the war British visitors entered a Moscow trade school and began asking students about their economic problems. Did their homes have heat and water? The school's director interrupted. There were more important questions. He asked pupils who had lost fathers at the front to stand up. All but one rose. The lone student who remained seated explained that his father had also fought against the Germans but had lost both his legs rather than his life.[26]

The Second World War claimed the lives of some 55 million—*55 million*—people, and at least 35 million of them were Europeans. The grisly statistical gallery ranked the Soviet Union an uncontested first. The exact numbers are not known, but Poland and Germany (and Austria) shared second place with about 6 million dead each; Yugoslavia lost at least 1.6 million; France, 600,000; Rumania, 460,000; Hungary, 430,000; Czechoslovakia, 415,000; Italy, 410,000; Britain, 400,000; and the Netherlands, 280,000. C. Day Lewis's "War Poem" read:

> They lie in the Sunday Street
> Like effigies thrown down after a fête
> Among the bare-faced houses frankly yawning revulsion,
> Fag ends of fires, litter of rubble, stale
> Confetti sprinkle of blood. . . .[27]

As for the living, they had to endure food shortages, closed factories, idle fields, cold stoves, currency inflation, festering wounds. Displaced persons (DPs) provided another picture. "The wind will tell you what has come to us; / It rolls our brittle bones from pole to pole," went "The Refugees' Testament."[28] Many dazed refugees wandered helplessly through Europe, searching for relatives, for friends, for a livelihood, for a ride home. One account has noted:

> [T]he people in parts of Europe seemed a population of cripples, of women and children and the very old. Some were starving; some were sick with typhus or dysentery. . . . The survivors, gray-faced ghosts in parodies of clothing, trundled their salvaged belongings in homemade handcarts—rugs, threadbare overcoats, a kettle, an alarm clock, a battered toy. They waited at standpipes for a dribble of brown water; they queued for bread and potatoes; they rummaged for sticks and scraps. For them, this waste land of rubble, rags, and hunger was a prison without privacy or dignity; and like all prisons, it smelled. It smelled of dust, oil, gunpowder, and greasy metal; of drains and vermin; of decay and burning and the unburied dead.[29]

Asia had its own sobering chronicle of the living and the dead. As the imperial Japanese went down to stubborn defeat, they took other Asians down with them. The lush vegetation of the Philippines and numerous Pacific islands was singed and burned, whole jungles disappearing. Some 120,-000 Filipinos died, and Manila lay in ruins. Nobody counted exactly, but probably 4 million Indonesians died under Japanese occupation. In 1945, 1 million Vietnamese died of starvation; the war also took the lives of 150,000 natives of Okinawa, 70,000 Koreans, 40,000 Indians, and 30,000 Australians.[30]

China had known population pressure, hunger, and epidemics before the war. But Japanese plunder, destruction of cities, and disruption of vital agricultural production increased the burdens that the Chinese had to bear in the postwar period.[31] The provinces of Hunan, Guangxi, and Guangdong, like others, were visited by famine; millions suffered malnutrition and outright starvation. Cholera, plague, tuberculosis, smallpox, and malaria struck a population that had only twelve thousand physicians—one for every forty thousand people. In 1938 the Japanese had blown up the key dikes along the Huang Ho (Yellow) River—"China's Sorrow"—killing thousands and flooding three million acres of fertile land. China's rivers now rampaged in the spring and summer through vulnerable villages. Manchuria's industrial plants were destroyed or dismantled, and China's small railroad network hardly functioned.

The Chinese counted ten million war dead, many of them in 1945–1946 from starvation or disease caused by Japan's end-of-the-war devastation of rice-producing areas. People in Harbin suffered a peculiar calamity: In 1947 thirty thousand of them died from bubonic plague; two years earlier, at war's end, Japanese military researchers experimenting with germ warfare techniques had released infected rats into the city. Kiang Ling's "The Chinese Refugee" captured the troubled times:

> Weeping I left my loved hills;
> Now by this flat long river
> Wandering, homeless, fleeing, fearing . . .
> Wandering till what time?
> Fleeing to what clime?
> Today's riches are ashes tomorrow;
> In a moment joy turns into sorrow.
> How call this yours or mine,
> How rich and poor define?
> In the eyes of death and flame
> Rich and poor are all the same.[32]

For defeated Japan, the bitter results of imperial dreams could be measured in the loss of 2.5 million lives.[33] American

planes had dropped napalm-filled bombs on Tokyo, engulfing residential districts in fire storms which generated intense
temperatures that reached 1,800° F. The odor of burning
flesh drifted upward, sickening the pilots who delivered the
horrible punishment. After a savage March 1945 raid that
killed 84,000 people in what observers described as a mass
burning, a Japanese reporter wrote that Tokyo was "like a
desert, in a drab and monotonous panorama of hopeless-
ness."[34] The fifteen-mile stretch between Yokohama and
Tokyo, remarked an American officer who accompanied
American General Douglas MacArthur to Japan, had become
a "wilderness of rubble."[35] A light dust hung in the air, stain-
ing visitors' clothing. Wood and paper houses had been reduced to powdered ashes, factories to twisted metal. A shan-
tytown of rusted, corrugated sheets and other junk ringed the
capital city, its inhabitants reminding some observers of the
Okies who trekked to California during the Great Depression—except that the Japanese scene was more shocking.
One of the first American naval officers to arrive in Tokyo
wrote to a friend that "I feel like a tramp who has become
used to sleeping in a graveyard."[36]

Hiroshima and Nagasaki became special cases, sharing and
enduring a special fate, giving unique meaning to the most
familiar postwar word: "rubble." Hiroshima was Japan's
eighth-largest city, a residential, commercial center of 250,-
000 people. But until 8:15 A.M. on August 6, 1945, Hiroshima
had not witnessed large-scale American bombing raids. On
that cloudless day the crew of the *Enola Gay*, a custom-
outfitted B-29, unleashed "Little Boy," an atomic device
packing the power of twenty thousand tons of TNT. The
bomb fell for fifty seconds and exploded about two thousand
feet aboveground. A blinding streak of light raced across the
sky; a tremendous boom punctuated the air. Then a huge
purplish cloud of dust, smoke, and debris shot forty thousand feet into the atmosphere. At ground level the heat be-

came suffocating, the winds violent. Buildings instantly disintegrated. Shadows were etched in stone. Trees were stripped of their leaves. Fires erupted everywhere, and the sky grew dark. Survivors staggered toward water to quench their intense thirst. Skin peeled from burned bodies.[37] A maimed resident, Dr. Michihiko Hachiya, noted that "no one talked, and the ominous silence was relieved only by a subdued rustle among so many people, restless, in pain, anxious, and afraid, waiting for something else to happen."[38]

The toll: 140,000 dead, tens of thousands wounded, and 81 percent of the city's buildings destroyed. Three days later the nightmare was repeated in Nagasaki, where at least 70,000 died.[39] Two weeks before the slaughter President Truman told his diary that the atomic bomb "seems to be the most terrible thing ever discovered, but it can be made the most useful."[40] Upon hearing of the success of the world's first nuclear destruction of a city inhabited by "savages," as the president had recently called the Japanese, he allowed that "this is the greatest thing in history."[41] Truman's words did not necessarily mean that he was pleased that so many Japanese civilians had been killed but rather that he was marveling over the new, spectacularly deadly weapon in America's possession—a weapon that might bring the long war to a close and boost U.S. power in the postwar era.

The Hiroshima tragedy was but one chapter in the story of massive, war-induced destruction. This story, with all its horrid details, must be recounted not because it shocks or sensationalizes but because it illustrates how massive and daunting were the problems of the postwar world, how shaky the scaffolding of the international order. Hitler had once said about his warmongering pursuits that "we may be destroyed, but if we are, we shall drag a world with us—a world in flames."[42] Because he largely satisfied his prophecy, the Second World War, like any war of substantial duration, served as an agent of conspicuous international changes. The conflagration of

1939–1945 was so wrenching, so total, so profound, that a world was overturned—not simply a material world of crops, buildings, and rails, not simply a human world of healthy and productive laborers, farmers, merchants, financiers, and intellectuals, not simply a secure world of close-knit families and communities, not simply a military world of Nazi storm troopers and Japanese kamikazes, but all that and more. The war also unhinged the world of stable politics, inherited wisdom, traditions, institutions, alliances, loyalties, commerce, and classes.

When Acting Secretary of State Dean Acheson surveyed the fragile condition of the postwar world and identified the primary problems that faced American foreign policy in the postwar era, he saw "social *disintegration,* political *disintegration,* the loss of faith by people in leaders who have led them in the past, and a great deal of economic *disintegration.*"[43] How could this alarming condition be reversed? The question preoccupied people in all countries; they worried that the war-induced dislocations would perpetuate rather than diminish the extremism that had led to the Second World War. American leaders asked themselves in particular how safe the United States could be in such a disorderly world. How secure would be America's core values of liberal capitalism and political democracy and its global economic and strategic interests—all of which in the past had guaranteed most Americans a comparatively high standard of living and national security?[44]

Leaders of all political persuasions, as they witnessed the immensity of the destruction, spoke of a new age without knowing its dimensions. "The world was fluid and about to be remade," remembered the American journalist Theodore H. White.[45] The normal way of doing things now seemed inappropriate, although as creatures of the past the survivors remained attached to ideas and institutions that seemed to provide security through familiarity. They sensed the seriousness and the enormity of the tasks of cleaning up the rubble, of putting the broken world back together again, of shaping an orderly international system. But imponderables abounded. Would peoples in the long-restive colonized countries, for example, rebel against their foreign masters at the very time that the once-mighty imperial nations themselves suffered internal political upheavals? Few people could say with confidence that they knew the configuration of the postwar world. What lay ahead was a tortuous time of experimenting, of trial and error, of stumbling and striving, of realized and dashed hopes, of contests among competing formulas for a stable world order.

Few nations or individuals had the material resources, talent, and desire—the sheer energy, guts, and money—to mold a brave new world out of the discredited and crumbled old. If the reconstruction tasks seemed Herculean, however, the opportunities appeared boundless for the ambitious, the hearty, and the caring. One vigorous, optimistic, well-intentioned, competitive voice sounded above the rubble that constituted London, Berlin, Warsaw, Minsk, and Tokyo. That voice echoed with power from the United States, the wartime "arsenal of democracy."

At war's end President Truman declared a two-day national holiday.[46] Horns, bells, and makeshift noisemakers sounded across the nation. Paraders in Los Angeles played leapfrog on Hollywood Boulevard; farther north, jubilant sailors broke windows along San Francisco's Market Street. In New York City office workers tossed tons of paper from the windows of skyscrapers on cheering crowds below. Stock market prices shot up. A five-year-old boy recorded the August 1945 moment: "This is the best year. The war is over. Two wars are over. Everyone is happy. Tin cans are rolling. Everything is confused. And little pieces of paper."[47] Not only had the dying subsided, but also the United States had emerged from the global conflict in the unique position of an unscathed belligerent. No bombs had fallen on American cities. No armies had ravaged the countryside. No American boundaries had been redrawn. Factories stood in place, producing goods at an impressive rate. In August, at the General Motors plant in Moraine, Ohio, shiny new Frigidaire refrigerators and airplane propeller blades moved along parallel assembly lines. Farm fields were rich in crops, and full employment during the war years had buoyed family savings. "The American people," remarked the director of the Office of War Mobilization and Reconversion, "are in the pleasant predicament of having to learn to live 50 percent better than they have ever lived before."[48]

Whereas much of Europe and Asia confronted a massive task of "reconstruction," the United States faced "reconversion"—adjusting the huge war machine to peacetime purposes. Automobile plants had to convert production from tanks to cars, a delightful prospect for auto manufacturers, who knew that Americans were eager to spend their wartime earnings on consumer goods once again. With great pride Americans applauded their good fortune. They were different. They had no rubble to clear. The Soviets knew, said Joseph Stalin in a grand understatement, that "things are not bad in the United States."[49]

Actually Americans had worries. Some feared that the sparkling prosperity of the war years would dissipate in a postwar economic disaster. They remembered that military production, not Franklin D. Roosevelt's New Deal reform program, had pulled the United States out of the Great Depression of the 1930s. Would there be enough jobs for the returning GIs? Americans also suffered temporary shortages of many goods, sugar and gasoline among them, and resented the rationing that limited their economic freedom. "Hey, don'tcha know there's a war on?" said clerks to anxious consumers. There were not enough houses to meet the needs of an expanding and mobile American population, which grew from 131 million to 140 million during the war years and was entering a "baby boom" period. The national debt skyrocketed from $37 billion to $269 billion. The war cost the federal government $664 billion. Inflation threatened economic stability. At least 10 million American families still lived in poverty in this land of plenty. Although these national pains aroused grumbles, they seemed bearable and soluble, were played down, or were ignored. As *Fortune* magazine commented two months after V-J Day: "August 14, 1945, marked not only the war's end but the beginning of the greatest peacetime industrial boom in the world's history."[50]

Americans read charts brimming with impressive data that justified such enthusiasm. The gross national product of the United States expanded from $90.5 billion (1939) to $211.9 billion (1945). Steel production jumped from fifty-three million tons in 1939 to eighty million tons at the close of the war. Cut off from rubber imports from the Dutch East Indies during the war, Americans developed synthetic rubber, launching a new industry. New aluminum plants went up, and the aircraft industry, in infancy when Germany attacked Poland, became a major new business as well. In 1939 only 5,856 military and civil airplanes were turned out, but in 1945 the figure reached 48,912, a decline from the peak of more than 95,000 in 1944. All told, more than 300,000 aircraft rolled from American factories during the war—a figure far surpassing that of any other nation, including Germany and Japan combined. Employment in the aircraft industry swelled 1,600 percent. With its numerous aircraft factories, Southern California bustled, becoming a mecca for dreamers of wealth and adventure. During the war 444,000 people moved to Los Angeles.

Workers' wages kept up with inflation during the war years. Women took jobs once held by men who were called to military duty. Unable to spend their abundant incomes on the shrinking supply of consumer items during the war, many Americans visited their banks. Total personal savings increased from $6.85 billion to $36.41 billion. Americans continued to spend for pleasure as well. The baseball World Series played on, and films whirred at local theaters. Beaches beckoned vacationers. In the summer of 1944, as Europe and Asia reeled from the blasts of war, Americans flocked to resorts and racetracks. Betting on horse racing totaled a record-breaking $1.4 billion in 1945, even though the tracks were closed from January to May. Farmers enjoyed some of their best years of the twentieth century. Whereas in 1939 they counted sixty-six million head of cattle, by 1945 that figure had reached eighty-three million. Agricultural output rose 15 percent. American universities also made wartime advances. Government contracts for scientific research went to the California Institute of Technology for rocket studies; Princeton University received grants for ballistics research. In mid-1945 the Massachusetts Institute of Technology held government contracts worth $117 million. The GI Bill, which offered money to veterans for their college educations, promised higher enrollments. Wartime musicals like *Oklahoma!* and *Carousel* caught the optimistic mood, and sluggers Joe DiMaggio and Ted Williams were heading home to reclaim their baseball fame. Despite uncertainties about the future, life looked good to Americans, and after the hardships and setbacks of the depression decade, "the old self-confident America is coming into its stride again."[51]

When foreign delegates journeyed to San Francisco for the United Nations Conference in April 1945, many crossed the territorial United States and could not help noticing the stark contrast with war-torn Europe and Asia. Soviet Foreign Minister V. M. Molotov once referred to statistics in the *World Almanac* to remind Americans about their uniqueness as prosperous survivors of the Second World War.[52] During a conversation with Stalin in 1944 the president of the United States Chamber of Commerce, Eric A. Johnston, citing the

American example, lectured the Kremlin leader on the need for a better distribution of goods in the Soviet Union. No doubt wondering how so knowledgeable a man as Johnston could be misreading reality, Stalin replied that "in order to distribute, there must be something to distribute."[53] Months before, at the Teheran Conference, Stalin had toasted the United States as a "country of machines," applauding its great productive capacity for delivering victory to the Allies.[54] Truman's words also bear repeating: "I was thankful that the United States had been spared the unbelievable devastation of this war."[55] Even the death count for Americans in uniform, about four hundred thousand, appeared merciful when compared with staggering figures elsewhere. Indeed, the *Saturday Evening Post* editorialized in 1945 that "we Americans can boast that we are not as other men are."[56] The war had overturned a world, and many Americans believed that they were now on top of it. A new international system for the postwar era was in the making, and the United States intended to be its primary architect.

2

CONFLICT
The Postwar International
System

IN THE rubble-strewn postwar world, international relations changed markedly from prewar interactions. Any historical period, such as the Cold War, is identified by a particular structure of relationships among the world's leading nations—by, in short, the international "system." Bipolarism, for example, characterized the Napoleonic era of the late eighteenth and early nineteenth centuries; Great Britain and France vied for world mastery, established alliances with lesser powers, frequently clashed in war, and managed far-flung empires. The period between the Congress of Vienna in 1815 and the outbreak of World War I in 1914 was multipolar, with a number of leading actors on the international stage who preferred diplomatic negotiations to military combat and who deliberately set about to create a balance of power for the maintenance of a conservative, imperial, antirevolutionary world. Systems are always in flux, and they change dramatically when shocked by brash newcomers, devastating wars, and economic depressions.

Any international system in any age is conflict-ridden. Anarchy more than peace is a system's most consistent feature, and this characteristic in turn compels most governments to worry about insecurity and to strive for security. The attempts that nations have made to reduce the anarchy constitute our diplomatic history. Conflict is inherent in any international system simply because peoples and countries seldom share common goals, interests, cultures, and ideologies. "This is a lawless world," University of Chicago Professor Herman Finer told a postwar radio audience, "because it is a world without a common morality or a common superior. Nationalisms and moralities collide."[1] The ways that politics, economies, and societies are organized, and the ideas that sustain them, are different from one corner of the world to the other. Core values clash. A few nations are ruled by monarchs; some suffer under dictators; others enjoy popularly elected governments. Some people prefer public ownership of property; others champion private enterprise. Some societies are centered on simple, rural, peasant life; others are marked by mass-production industries located in sprawling metropolises. Buddhist, Christian, Jewish, Muslim, Hindu, and countless other religions contend for followers in holy crusades that accentuate the fragmentation of the international system. Intense ethnic and racial differences—witness the Turks and the Armenians or the white and black South Africans—disturb the peace as well. Civil wars, social revolutions, new technologies, economic recessions, famines, natural disasters, environmental abuses—they, too, push the international system toward disorder.

Some nations are more powerful or influential than others and flaunt their superiority. Strong nations tend to expand; large and small countries alike will resist. Historical examples

abound of peoples who fervently believe they possess superior ideas and institutions that must be exported to the less
fortunate—in essence, that they must replicate their domestic systems at the international level. Some nations have what
others want—territory, food, water, minerals, labor, and a
multitude of things over which peoples have squabbled for
centuries. Great nations are always looking for friends who
will join them in formal or informal alliances to check the
growth of those states they consider unfriendly or potentially
so. Small nations have to be wary of the major actors, who
may cast longing eyes on them and exploit their vulnerability. Some countries become dependent upon others for their
prosperity and security, and the dependent inevitably develop resentments against the metropole that profits from the
dependency relationship. Nations wishing to remain "neutral" or unaligned are wooed or cajoled.

The leading powers, whether aligned or at loggerheads,
watch one another suspiciously, on the assumption that in
international politics, as in business, one can supposedly
trust friends seldom, enemies never. Slight shifts in the distribution of power—of resources—arouse concern. What one
government considers defense, another labels "offense." The
construction of a military base, the testing of a new weapon, a
request to alter a boundary, the signing of a treaty—all may
be defined as both defensive or offensive, depending upon
one's point of view. A rifle is a defensive weapon if seen from
the butt, but it is a weapon of attack if one is staring into the
muzzle. Suspicion and fear undermine trust and prompt
countermeasures. Leaders may assume evil intentions on the
part of other nations and then, playing it safe, plan for the
worst. Governments feel compelled to match the decisions of
their adversaries. Failure to develop a new weapon, for example, might entail risk, for an enemy might gain some advantage by producing it.

Leaders also fear falling dominoes, chain reactions, collid-

ing rows of bowling pins, mud slides, rising tides, the snow-
balling effect, or the spread of contagious diseases—to name
some oft-heard metaphors—that begin far from their homes
but that may come cascading toward them through momentum. Economic chain reactions—tariff wars, economic down-
turns, competition for raw materials—also prompt alarm.
Military interventions abroad or the political manipulation of
another nation seem imperative to break the momentum of
such calamities. For great powers, the containment of foreign
threats ranks high, and therefore, lines need to be drawn far
from home. In such a threatening and disorderly world, leaders often exaggerate danger and thus escalate chances for war.
The degree and kind of conflict may vary, but there is always
conflict.

Higher degrees of conflict are reached when the international system undergoes significant change, when it transforms into a new or revised system. Such was the case after
World War II. Change, by definition, is destabilizing. Some
postwar leaders, even though immersed in day-to-day decision making, pondered the general characteristics of the international system. They knew that significant changes had
altered the configuration of power. As participants in and
shapers of a new age they were "present at the creation."[2] But
the outline of the new system was only vaguely evident. The
process of creating a new system out of the ashes of the discredited prewar system intensified the conflict inherent in
any international structure.

In this chapter a macroanalytic view of the international
system will enable us to identify the opportunities and constraints which faced the major actors. Like a menu, this systemic level of analysis outlines the choices available, as well
as the limits of choice. It sketches the "big picture," so that
the disparate components of the postwar system may be ex-
amined in proper relationship. Exploration of the broad international context reveals which nations held real or poten-

tial power and why, ultimately, they jettisoned international cooperation and moved toward a divided world of competing spheres of influence.[3]

Yet analysis of the characteristics of the international system alone does not go far enough to explain the origins of the Cold War. While it is true that a nation's foreign policy responds to the prevailing features of the international system, each nation will react differently according to its peculiar domestic order. If the Soviet-American confrontation were simply the inevitable product of the conflict-ridden international system, there would be little purpose in studying the leaders, ideas, policies, economics, politics, or societies of particular nations because, this logic would have it, events would be largely beyond their control. Under this interpretation the system would dictate antagonistic relations, leaving few alternatives for reconciling differences. It would not matter whether different personalities or different national policies existed. But of course, leaders make choices, even if they only dimly understand their consequences, and they choose policies they think will protect their nations' interests. Franklin D. Roosevelt, Harry S. Truman, Winston Churchill, Clement Attlee, Joseph Stalin, Ho Chi Minh, Mao Zedong, and many others helped create the international system to which they had to react. To fathom the beginnings of the Cold War, then, we must discuss not only the traits of the international system but also the dynamics of particular nations and the individuals who led them. Later chapters will develop these ingredients of conflict. Here we will explore the birth and nature of the postwar international system.

The Second World War visited wrenching changes upon the old international system and spawned new characteristics that produced conflict. One conspicuous characteristic was the redistribution of power. The defeat of Germany, Italy, and Japan left power vacuums. Britain, nearly bankrupt, dependent, and unable to police its empire, was reduced to a resentful second-rate power; France, much of whose territory had been occupied by the Germans during the war, continued to suffer from unstable politics and no longer mustered international respect. In the colonial world nationalist insurgencies bargained for power with these weakened imperial states and fought to make the world less Europe-centered. In short, many of the nations which had wielded authority in the multipolar system of the 1930s had fallen from their elevated status.

Two nations with quite different ideologies emerged from the rubble of World War II to claim high rank. The United States and the Soviet Union, eager to realize their universalist visions of the postwar world and to seize opportunities for extending their respective influence, tried to fill vacuums of power. With the old barriers to American and Soviet expansion gone, Washington and Moscow clashed over occupation policies in Germany, Italy, Japan, Austria, and Korea. They squabbled over which political groups should replace the Nazi regimes in Eastern Europe. The competitive interaction between the United States and the Soviet Union—"like two big dogs chewing on a bone," said Senator J. William Fulbright—shaped the bipolarism or bipolarity of the immediate postwar years.[4] "Not since Rome and Carthage," Dean Acheson claimed, "had there been such a polarization of power on this earth."[5] This new bipolar structure replaced the multipolar system of the 1930s, wherein at least six nations had been active, influential participants. By the late 1940s decisions made in the imperial capitals of Washington and Moscow often determined whether people in other nations voted, where they could travel, how much they ate, and what they could print.

To say that the world was bipolar, however, is not to suggest that the two poles were equal in power. They were not. An asymmetry—not a balance—of power existed. In fact, the United States held preponderant power and flexed its multidimensional muscle to build even more power. As the only major nation not devastated by the war, the United States so outdistanced other nations in almost every measurement of power—from industrial production to domestic political stability—that it enjoyed hegemony.[6] Hegemony exists when one nation possesses superior economic, military, and political power in the world system. The first ingredient is a prerequisite for the other two. No nation can aspire to hegemony or achieve that Olympian status unless its economy is strong—and stronger than any other's. More than statistics established American supremacy. World conditions did so. The United States was powerful because almost every other nation was war-weakened.

Both the United States and the Soviet Union emerged from the war as powers, but only one at that time was a superpower—the United States. The Soviet Union was certainly not weak. Although handicapped by its economic wreckage, the huge nation held predominant postwar power over its neighbors in Eastern Europe. Still, the Soviet Union was a regional, not a global, power before the early 1950s. The characteristic of hegemony meant that the United States had more opportunities and resources than other nations to shape the postwar system. By exercising their preponderant global power—through military occupations, foreign aid and loans, and domination of the World Bank and United Nations Organization, for example—U.S. officials pushed the world toward the American postwar goal of a nonradical, capitalist, free trade international order in the mold of domestic America.

The United States, as we shall see, did not get all that it wanted (hegemonic powers seldom do) because a host of obstacles thrown up by allies and foes alike sometimes obstructed American hopes and plans, and resources were finite. "We cannot scatter our shots equally all over the world," Acheson remonstrated. "We just haven't got enough shots to do that. . . ."[7] American power, however superior, had limits and suffered failures. More serious, in the long run, any hegemon like the United States risks traveling a path toward decline because it cannot afford to be both global economic master and global policeman. The latter, a very expensive role, strains the domestic economy, undermines the infrastructure (by underfunding education and technological research, for example), and ultimately diminishes the nation's competitiveness in the international marketplace. A globe-circling superpower ultimately experiences insecurity because it becomes a worldwide target.[8] "Imperial overstretch" undercuts hegemonic power.[9] But this theme of decline jumps ahead of the story here. However circumscribed, American hegemony was conspicuous in the international system of the early Cold War period.

Another prominent characteristic of the international system that unleashed conflict was the destruction of economies in many parts of the world.[10] The war cut an ugly scar across Europe and Asia. "If Hitler succeeds in nothing else," mused Office of Strategic Services officer Allen Dulles, "like Samson, he may pull down the pillars of the temple and leave a long and hard road of reconstruction."[11] The postwar task was forbidding. Not only did cities have to be rebuilt, factories opened, people put back to work, rails repaired, rivers and roads made passable, and crop yields increased, but the flow of international commerce and finance had to be reestablished if nations were to raise through exports the money needed to buy the imports required for recovery. Many old commercial and financial patterns had been broken, and given the obstacle of economic disarray, new exchanges were difficult to establish. Where would Germany's vital coal and steel go? Would industrial Western Europe and agricultural Eastern Europe re-create old commercial ties? Would the restrictive trade practices of the 1930s, especially the tariff barriers, continue into the 1940s? Would colonies continue to provide raw materials to their imperial lords? Could international cooperation and organizations like the General Agreement on Tariffs and Trade (1948) curb economic nationalism? Would trade be conducted on a multilateral, "open door" basis, as the United States preferred, or by bilateral or preferential methods, as many others, such as Britain and the Soviet Union, practiced? Would the economic disorders spawned by the Great Depression be repeated to produce political chaos, aggression, and war?

The answers to these questions helped define the international system of the post-1945 era. The new international system, it was hoped, would enjoy stable economic conditions to ensure pacific international relations. Yet the very effort to reconstruct economies and create economic order engendered conflict because different models and formulas— Communist? socialist? capitalist? mixed economy?—competed to define the future. At the same time the asymmetrical distribution of power persuaded weaker nations that they faced the danger of economic coercion.

The Second World War also bequeathed domestic political turmoil to the new international system.[12] The governments of the 1930s, now discredited, vied with insurgent groups for governing power in many states. Socialists, Communists, and other varieties of the political left, many of whom had fought in the underground resistance movements and had thus earned some popular respect and following, challenged the more entrenched, conservative elites, many of whom had escaped into exile when the German armies goose-stepped into their countries. In Poland the Communist, Soviet-sponsored Lublin Poles successfully undercut the political authority of the Poles who had fled to London. The conservative Dutch government-in-exile watched warily as leftist resistance groups gradually rallied political support. Political confusion in the Netherlands was heightened by the wartime loss of voting lists. In Greece a coalition of leftists in the National

Liberation Front (EAM) fought the return to power of a British-created government and the unpopular Greek monarchy of King George. The civil war that rocked Greece until fall 1949 claimed some 158,000 lives and ended in an American-backed conservative government. In France Charles de Gaulle gained ascendancy after vying for power with the Communists. The Chinese civil war, which had raged for years between the Communists of Mao Zedong and the Nationalists of Jiang Jieshi (Chiang Kai-shek), flared up again at the close of the war. That internecine struggle ended in a Communist victory in 1949. Yugoslavia was also the scene of political battle between Josip Broz Tito's ultimately successful Partisans and a group headed by Dr. Ivan Šubašić of the London émigré government, which in turn suffered strained ties with King Peter. In the occupied nations of Germany, Austria, and Korea, moreover, the victors created competitive zones, postponing the formation of central governments. In the defeated countries of Japan and Italy, American officials decided who would rule, whereas in parts of Eastern Europe, Soviet officials placed Communists in strategic positions of power.

The major powers, in short, intervened abroad to exploit the political opportunities created by the destructive scythe of World War II. The stakes seemed high. A change in a nation's political orientation might presage a change in its international alignment. The great powers tended to ignore local conditions, especially nationalism, which might and often did mitigate against alignment with an outside power. Americans nonetheless feared that a leftist or Communist Greece would look to the East and permit menacing Soviet bases on Greek territory or open the door to a Soviet naval presence in the Mediterranean. Moscow dreaded a conservative anti-Soviet Polish government led by the London faction, for it might prove so weak and so hostile to Moscow as to permit a revived Germany to send storm troopers once again through the Polish corridor into the heart of Russia or block the Soviet Union's efforts to contain a resurgent Germany. A Communist China, thought Americans, might align with the Soviet Union; a Nationalist China would remain in the American camp. All in all, the rearranging of political structures within nations drew the major powers into competition, accentuating the conflict inherent in the postwar international system.

Just as the war threw politics into chaos, so it hastened the disintegration of empires.[13] The Japanese movement into French Indochina and drive for Dutch East Indies oil had led to Pearl Harbor in 1941. The initially successful Japanese expansion demonstrated to many Asian nationalists that their white imperial masters could be defeated. In a spirit of Pan-Asianism, some nationalists collaborated with Tokyo during the war. The Japanese, in need of administrators to manage occupied areas, trained and armed some indigenous leaders. Japan granted Burma considerable autonomy in 1942, for example, and after the war the Burmese became determined to push the British out. Other nationalists gained organizational unity, élan, and experience by battling the Japanese invaders. At the end of the war the European powers, exhausted and financially hobbled, had to struggle to reestablish mastery over rebellious colonies. The appeal of the self-determination principle, still echoing from the days of Woodrow Wilson and given new emphasis by the Atlantic Charter (1941) and the United Nations Charter (1945), became far-reaching. The long process of "regime collapse" in what became known as the Third World gained momentum.[14] "There are many peoples who are clamoring for freedom from the colonial powers," American Undersecretary of State Sumner Welles remarked during the war. He predicted "trouble" unless these peoples got what they wanted. Failure to plan for the transfer of power to them, he warned, "would be like failing to install a safety valve and then waiting for the boiler to blow up."[15] There were too many boilers and too few safety valves.

No empire was immune to decolonization. The United States granted the Philippines independence in 1946, but that new nation became a client state where U.S. officials helped the government resist a peasant revolt led by the Huks. The British, worn low by the war and by the challenges of nationalist groups demanding independence, retreated in 1947 from India, which then descended into civil war between Hindus and Muslims. The two new nations of India and Pakistan were thus born amid massacres and a massive uprooting of people. The following year Britain also relinquished Burma (Myanmar) and Ceylon (Sri Lanka). Israel, carved out of British-governed Palestine, became a new independent state in 1948. The British also found it difficult to maintain their sphere of influence in Iran, Greece, and Egypt and began retreats from those politically unsteady states. The French clung to Indochina, where nationalist forces led by Ho Chi Minh had declared an independent Vietnam by quoting the American Declaration of Independence. "If those gooks want a fight," boasted French General Étienne Valluy, "they'll get it."[16] Bloody battle ensued, ultimately forcing French withdrawal in 1954. The French empire also came under siege in Africa; in early 1947 Malagasy insurgents in the island colony of Madagascar rebelled. Ninety thousand people died as French troops crushed the insurrection the next year (France finally granted the Malagasy Republic independence in 1960). The Dutch also decided to fight, but after four debilitating years of combat they pulled out of Indonesia in 1949. The defeated Japanese were forced to give up their claims to Formosa and Korea, as well as to Pacific island groups. Italy departed from Ethiopia and lost its African colonies of Tripolitania (Libya) and Eritrea. In the Middle East, Lebanon, Syria, and Jordan, areas once managed by Europeans, gained independence in 1943, 1944, and 1946 respectively.

The world map, as after World War I, was redrawn. The emergence of so many new states, and the instability associated with the transfer of authority, shook the very foundations of the international system. Power was being redistributed. In varying degrees the United States and Soviet Union competed for the allegiance of the new governments, meddled in colonial rebellions, and generally sought to exploit opportunities for an extension of their influence. In the case of Vietnam the powers supported different sides: Washington, without relish, backed the ruling French, and Moscow endorsed the Vietminh insurgency. The stakes seemed high. President Roosevelt told an adviser near the end of the war that more than one billion "brown people" yearned for independence—and "1,100,000,000 potential enemies are dangerous."[17] The emerging nations could serve as strategic bases, markets for exports, sources of vital raw materials, sites for investments, and votes in international organizations; conversely, they could deny powerful nations such assets. As a Central Intelligence Agency report emphasized, the resource-rich Third World and the reconstruction of hobbled Western Europe were intricately linked: "The continuance of unsettled conditions [in colonial or former colonial areas] hinders economic recovery and causes a diversion of European strength into efforts to maintain or reimpose control by force."[18]

To the angry frustration of the great powers, some new nations, like India, chose nonalignment in the developing Cold War. Asian countries, asserted Indian nationalist leader Jawaharlal Nehru, "can no longer be used as pawns by others; they are bound to have their own policies in world affairs. . . . We do not intend to be the playthings of others."[19] To U.S. officials, neutralism meant not only that some nations were not with them but also that they stood against them—that the nonaligned countries were forming "a power bloc against us," as the American ambassador to Burma put it.[20] Indeed, Americans feared that Nehru championed a "third force" that, if it developed to the stage of a bloc of like-minded states, could shift the world from bipolar to tripolar form.[21] Avowedly neutral states thus ultimately became targets for Cold War conversion through American and Soviet foreign aid, subversion, and propaganda campaigns.

As one U.S. government study noted, the disintegration of empires, especially the withdrawal of the British from their once-vast domain, created an "over-all situation of near chaos" in the international system. In some areas, such as Southeast Asia, it meant a "new balance of power." The upheaval was fundamental: "Old values are being changed and new ones sought. New friendships are being formed."[22] The international system creaked and swayed under this unsettled burden.

Conflict over and within the new United Nations Organization also disturbed the system. At the Dumbarton Oaks Conference in 1944 the Allies initiated plans for a United Nations Organization to replace the defunct League of Nations. The United States, Britain, and Soviet Union became its chief architects, and the institution they helped create at the San Francisco Conference of April–June 1945 reflected their insistence on big-power domination. They instituted a veto power for the five "permanent members" of the Security Council (the United States, Britain, USSR, France, and China) and assigned the General Assembly, the forum for smaller nations, a subordinate status. Because each member recognized that the new international body could become an instrument, through bloc voting, of one nation's foreign policy, they feuded. Churchill crudely complained that China, hardly a "great" power, would be a "faggot vote on the side of the United States," and the Soviets protested that France would simply represent a British vote.[23] "China was a joke," remarked State Department veteran John Hickerson, "a FDR joke."[24] For a time Roosevelt pushed Brazil as a veto power member; Brazil, he said, was "a card up his sleeve."[25]

Because Britain could marshal the votes of several of its Commonwealth countries and the United States could muster most of the Latin American nations, the conferees at the Yalta Conference of early 1945 acknowledged the glaring imbalance by granting the Soviet Union three votes in the General Assembly.

At the San Francisco Conference membership applications from Argentina and Poland produced heated differences. Against vehement Soviet objections, Argentina, which had declared war against Germany only at the last minute and which some critics considered a "fascist" nation, gained membership after the United States backed its application and the nations of the Western Hemisphere voted yes as a bloc. Yet when Lublin-led Poland, not yet reorganized according to the American interpretation of the Yalta accords, applied for entry, the United States voted no, and the conference denied Poland a seat. Moscow railed at this rebuff, charging a double standard. The United Nations Organization, which held its first session in January 1946, thus made its debut amid controversy. Rather than serve as a stabilizing force in the postwar international system, the largely U.S.-dominated United Nations early became a source of conflict, a competitive arena of power brokers, a verbal battleground for the allegiance of world opinion, a vehicle for condemnatory resolutions, a graveyard for idealistic hopes—in short, part of a "masquerade peace."[26]

The new atomic bomb and the ensuing nuclear arms race further destabilized the postwar international system. As the two bickering major powers groped for ways to deal with "the bomb" and spurred their atomic development programs, people everywhere held their breaths, harboring thoughts about doomsday. Nuclear weapons were not simply dangerous to enemies; they threatened apocalypse for humankind. Cartoonists sketched pictures of uncontrollable monsters that the scientists had created. "All the scientists are frightened—frightened for their lives—and frightened for *your* life," a Nobel Prize-winning chemist wrote in early 1946 in a popular magazine.[27] About the same time a French radio station broadcast a make-believe story about an atomic storm engulfing the earth after radioactive atoms had escaped from a U.S. research laboratory. Many Parisians thought they heard truth and panicked.[28] One observer suggested that a Soviet-American war "might not end with *one* Rome but with *two* Carthages."[29]

The atomic bomb, uncontrolled, envied, copied, and brandished, became a major obstacle to a peaceful postwar international system. The "most terrible weapon ever known in human history," Secretary of War Henry L. Stimson quietly told the president, unsettled the world community, for it was an agent of massive human destruction, and "in a world atmosphere already extremely sensitive to power, the introduction of this weapon has profoundly affected political considerations in all sections of the globe."[30] Nations that possessed *the* bomb seemed to hold an advantage in international politics, for it could serve as a deterrent against an adversary as well as a means to annihilate an enemy. When combined with air power and a long-range delivery capability, the atomic bomb also hurdled geographical boundaries, rendering them useless as protective elements in a nation's security shield. With the perfecting of air warfare in World War II, "the roof blew off the territorial state."[31]

The question that dogged the peacemakers was: How were they to control the development, spread, and use of atomic energy? There had been arms races before, and disarmament conferences in the 1920s and 1930s, but the postwar nuclear race moved at a far different and more dangerous level. The atomic bomb was the "absolute weapon," not only more violent but also capable of speedy delivery, rapid retaliation, immediate cataclysm, and lingering death-dealing radioactivity.[32] Americans worried that they would lose their monopoly—that nuclear proliferation would leave them vulnerable, too. Such fears intensified when the Soviet Union success-fully produced its own bomb in 1949. While from the start some people appealed for a world government to put the atomic genie back in the bottle—"world state or world doom"—others began to marvel over the new armament's potential value as a diplomatic weapon to pry concessions from adversaries or as a deterrent to keep them at bay.[33]

Some scholars have argued that the advent of nuclear weapons, because of their deterrent role, as well as the bipolarity of the Cold War, served to stabilize the postwar international system.[34] But this interpretation suffers from a narrow definition of peace and stability, concentrates almost solely on Soviet-American relations, and confines itself to the strategic-military realm. Because the militaries of the United States and the Soviet Union did not directly clash or because the two nations did not destroy each other in a nuclear holo-caust, "peace" prevailed. Such an assumption discounts too much history, a history hardly peaceful or stable.

One of the reasons why the Soviets kept their troops in Eastern Europe—conceivably ready to pounce on America's European allies if necessary—was the immediate postwar U.S. atomic monopoly and "atomic diplomacy"; in short, the Soviet Union deployed conventional forces in its sphere to deter superior American nuclear and air power.[35] Since the much-disputed presence of the Red Army in Eastern Europe contributed considerably to the coming of the Cold War and the division of the continent, American atomic weapons ac-centuated instability, not stability. In addition, numerous wars fought by the client or dependent states of the two pow-ers, as well as great-power military interventions and covert activities, repeatedly disturbed the peace for decades after 1945. And they took the lives of millions of people in Korea, Vietnam, Guatemala, Hungary, Czechoslovakia, Angola, and Afghanistan, among many others. It would come as a surprise to most world leaders in the period since 1945, furthermore, that they presided over a "long peace." Many of them knew anxious moments of a "long war"—severe crises, nuclear brinkmanship, events spinning out of control, accidents, missed signals, poor communications, and stress, as the confrontations in Berlin and Cuba attest.

Huge economic costs are also neglected in the "long peace" argument. Nuclear weapons and their delivery systems, military establishments, and interventions consumed trillions of dollars. The spending of such monumental sums on armaments and wars meant that the money was not spent on economic development, environmental protection, education, medical research and health, famine relief, and a host of other undertakings that might better have served international stability. No, as Stimson suggested, nuclear weapons brought neither peace nor stability to the postwar international system, and certainly not in the early years of the Cold War.

Any exploration of the causes of the Cold War must give prominence to another new characteristic of the international system: the shrinkage of the globe and the related emergence of a global outlook for most peoples and nations. Geography had not changed, but ways of moving across it and of thinking about it had.[36] Observers began to speak not only of an "atomic age" but of an "air age" and a "global age." Remarkable advances in communications and transportation, especially in aviation, brought nations closer to one another. "We are for all time de-isolated," noted one analyst.[37] The world seemed more compact and accessible. President Truman described a "much smaller earth—an earth whose broad oceans have shrunk and whose national protections have been taken away by new weapons of destruction."[38]

People had to think now not only in traditional land miles but also in flying hours. "Starvation and over-production, bloated wealth and extreme poverty on a national scale cannot co-exist, only hours apart, without developing pressures far more intense than those of other days when time and distance served as safety valves," General Dwight D. Eisenhower told a postwar meeting in New York City.[39] In a popularization for schoolchildren, N. L. Englehardt, Jr., urged his young readers to think "air thoughts" and titled one of his chapters "How the World Has Shrunk."[40] Because the Atlantic Ocean could be traversed easily and quickly by flying over it, that once-prominent barrier between the Old and New worlds disappeared. The Canadian minister of national defence noted, too, that "only the top of the world separates us [Canada and the USSR], and that means we're next-door neighbors in this modern flying age."[41] The British also recognized the significant change; sea power, they regretted, no longer served to defend their island fortress, now vulnerable to air attack.[42] Stimson perceived that the United States could never again "be an island to herself. No private program and no public policy, in any sector of our national life can now escape from the compelling fact that if it is not framed with reference to the world, it is framed with perfect futility."[43] Geographical isolation was gone with the past. In a world contracted by science, events in lands once considered distant or tangential now held greater significance than ever before for all peoples.

Because frontiers had been extended, because nations were brought nearer one another, and because the world had shrunk, the major powers coveted bases far from home, much as the United States had sought and acquired bases in the Caribbean in the early twentieth century to protect the Panama Canal. By drawing peoples and nations closer to one another, by making some fearful of surprise attack and others concerned that their security was threatened by faraway events, the airplane drew the great powers into confrontations as never before. The shrinkage of the world and the globalist perspective and interdependence that followed this phenomenon ensured international conflict.

Such was the postwar international system—with its opportunities and constraints, with its many characteristics that generated conflict. The makers of the postwar order grappled with immense, new problems, and they strove to reduce the systemic instability. Their decisions, however, exacerbated conflict. The reason why the leaders of the postwar world made bad conditions worse is clear: Sensing danger from the volatile international system to their domestic systems, they sought to build their nations' power, to enlarge their spheres of influence. The conflict inherent in any international system, especially one struggling to make the transition from full-scale war to postwar peace, hardened into a four-decade-long Cold War.

3

SPHERES
The Quest for Influence to
1947

PORTLY, bespectacled British Foreign Secretary
Ernest Bevin had been puzzling over the characteris-
tics of the postwar international system for several
months—ever since his Labour party had won a national election in July 1945 and ousted Churchill's
Conservatives from office. In a private meeting on
December 16, 1945, with American Secretary of State
James F. Byrnes, Bevin ruminated that the postwar
world was "drifting into the position of 'three
Monroes.' " Like Great Britain in the Mediterranean
and Middle East and the Soviet Union in Eastern
Europe, the United States had its "Monroe," or
sphere of influence, in the Western Hemisphere and
was now "extending it to the Pacific." Byrnes perked
up, alert to any suggestion that his nation was behav-
ing like other great powers in coveting a sphere of
influence. The United States, retorted the American

secretary, "only wished to establish bases for security purposes in [Pacific] islands many of which were uninhabited."[1] That lame answer certainly did not separate the United States from other great nations; if anything, Byrnes's reply demonstrated that the United States was seeking to expand and secure its sphere of influence.

Bevin certainly thought so. As he had been telling his Foreign Office colleagues and others who would listen, because "this sphere of influence business" seemed irreversible, it was prudent to set some rules. Each of the three powers— Bevin still hoped that weakened Britain would exercise influence, although he knew it ranked last among his three— "would be responsible for maintaining international order within its own sphere." The powers would agree not to interfere in the internal affairs of the other spheres and would "allow freedom of access" to their spheres for trade.[2] As the Soviets and Americans expanded into Eastern Europe and Asia respectively, Bevin grumbled that Britain was "dealing with power politics naked and unashamed." British social democracy, he concluded, stood between "the red tooth and claw of American capitalism and the Communist dictatorship of Soviet Russia."[3] Another British leader saw more hegemony than balance. "These Americans," Harold Macmillan was heard to say, "represent the new Roman Empire. . . ."[4]

Yet Americans believed they were different, not like imperialists of the past, not like the great-power sphere builders of yesterday, definitely not like Europeans. In 1823 the Monroe Doctrine itself had striven to distinguish between the crass, monarchical Old World and the superior republicanism of the New, suggesting that the latter practiced a higher morality in international relations. Monroe's message held that the United States would not interfere in the affairs of Europe and that Europe must keep its hands off the Western Hemisphere. "The trouble with these people," Lord Halifax remarked about Americans in early 1945, "is that they are so much the victim of labels: 'Power Politics, Spheres of Influence, Balance of Power, etc.' As if there was ever such a sphere of influence agreement as the Monroe Doctrine!"[5] The point was well taken: The Monroe Doctrine had become invested with self-interest on behalf of a supreme U.S. position in the Western Hemisphere. Still, American diplomats like Byrnes in the first few postwar years seldom admitted the self-interest of their own expanding global sphere of influence. They spoke instead in broad terms about their selfless pursuit of an open international system. By 1947, however, they had become more frank and more public about the existence of spheres and the importance of enlarging and protecting an American sphere of influence.

As the two major protagonists of the postwar era, the United States and the Soviet Union, became ensnared in the instability of the new international system and increasingly clashed over the making of the peace, they did what countries had done for centuries: They built competing spheres of influence. They sought friends; they pressed neighbors; they built alliances; they put up fences; they drew lines; they charged each other with trying to foul the peace by meddling in the other's sphere. Gradually, beginning soon after V-E Day, nations gravitated toward or were pulled toward one sphere or the other. Countries that did not choose sides felt the constant pressure of the great powers. Two camps came to dominate global politics, and the Cold War assumed "the character of position warfare."[6]

A "sphere of influence" usually refers to a grouping of states and territories over which a major power wields authority or hegemony.[7] A powerful nation does not even have to intend to build a sphere in order to acquire one. " 'Influence,' or 'power,' or 'empire' automatically accrues to those states which are sufficiently wealthy, sufficiently strong, and sufficiently self-confident," the British scholar Michael Howard has pointed out.[8] Although the dominant power seeks to create policies that benefit all sphere members to reduce chances for disorder, the hegemonic nation builds a "sphere of action," as Churchill called it, to serve its own national interest: to provide itself with security, to gain economic advantages through trade, investment, and raw materials exploitation, or to satisfy nationalistic or ideological ambitions.[9] The dominating power might act unilaterally in its sphere, resisting or avoiding international sanctions and the protestations of sphere members who might have to sacrifice some degree of their sovereignty. The hegemonic power exercises its authority through defense pacts, selection or imposition of local officials, positioning of troops, naval demonstrations, development of military bases, assignment of advisers to local institutions, commercial links, trade treaties, loans, and finally, threats designed to force conformity. In short, influence may be exerted directly or indirectly. A sphere is in essence posted with a "keep out" sign, a warning to others that the major power has claimed special interests. Spheres may be tightly closed, or they may be porous, permitting other powerful nations to conduct reasonable, but not exploitative, relations within the sphere.

Small-nation sphere members often have to make concessions to the hegemonic power. They might have to give up self-determination and endure subordination, or at best, they might be permitted codetermination, because the dominant power might be willing to share decision making in order to deflect criticism, keep members satisfied, and sustain hegemony without having to use force. Sphere nations are often organized according to the hegemonic power's economic principles and trade arrangements. Sometimes the members of a sphere share security goals, economic objectives, or an ideology, or they believe that they need and must accept the help of the dominant power. Then the hegemon's exercise of influence does not have to be hardfisted but rather light, even invisible. Such cases of willing compliance and quiet persuasion—the Western European-United States relationship after the Second World War is often cited as an example—represent "consensual" hegemony.[10] Spheres can have long reaches because some members are colonial rulers. Thus, because Western Europe sat within America's early Cold War sphere, the Third World colonies of Britain and France became members, too.

Spheres of influence, of course, have had a long history. In the twentieth century, for example, the United States created a sphere in Latin America through the Monroe Doctrine, political interferences like the Platt Amendment in Cuba and the Roosevelt Corollary in the Caribbean, military interventions in Haiti and Nicaragua, among others, lucrative trade and investment ties, and Pan-Americanism. The lecture that American Secretary of State Richard Olney delivered to the British during the Venezuelan controversy in 1895 typified great-power thinking: "Today the United States is practically sovereign on this continent, and its fiat is law upon the subjects to which it confines its interposition." The United States was "master of the situation and practically invulnerable as against any or all other powers."[11] The British themselves held sway over an elongated sphere of influence that stretched through the Mediterranean to the Persian Gulf and into Asia. In the 1930s Japan declared a "Greater East Asia Co-Prosperity Sphere" and cut a path through China into the East Indies and Indochina. Also during the depression decade, Hitler's Germany drew the Eastern European states— the "satellites"—into its orbit. The Nazi-Soviet Pact of 1939, which partitioned Poland, also reflected the evident prewar politics of spheres.

During the Second World War President Franklin D. Roosevelt began to plan for a postwar system of loose spheres based on great-power cooperation, with the United States the dominant partner. At the same time his public rhetoric, laced with Wilsonian references, cast doubt on the practices of the past. The Atlantic Charter, which he and Churchill wrote in 1941, reiterated Woodrow Wilson's lofty appeal for self-determination, the open door, and disarmament. Secretary of State Cordell Hull, who seemed to embrace these principles more deeply than did Roosevelt, stood foursquare against the creation of spheres of influence. Upon his return from the Moscow Conference in 1943, for example, Hull told Congress that with a new postwar international organization, "there will no longer be need for spheres of influence, for alliance, for balance of power. . . ."[12] Roosevelt himself at times echoed Hull's position, as when the president asked Churchill in mid-1944 to remember "that we are not establishing any postwar spheres of influence."[13]

Yet Roosevelt was in fact envisioning a world of spheres, of "four policemen" (United States, Soviet Union, Great Britain, and China) or "sheriffs" who would manage the international system.[14] The contrast between his rhetoric against spheres and his decisions for them is stark. Roosevelt recognized that spheres were a fact of international life that the United States could not change and would have to accept. In early 1944 he informed Churchill that the United States would not "police" postwar France because "France is your baby"; Britain must "discipline your own children" in Europe.[15] He also lectured Hull about Germany: "We have to remember that in their occupied territory [the Soviets] will do more or less what they wish. We cannot afford to get into a position of merely recording protests on our part unless there is some chance of some of the protests being heeded."[16]

President Roosevelt intended big-power guardianship of the postwar world, and he insisted that the United States become the prime guardian. His four policemen were not going to be equal partners; the United States was poised to be chief of police—as well as premier banker and trader. The key question for the postwar world, Roosevelt thought, "was one of power among the victors. How would they use their power."[17] He anticipated that through American leadership, based upon the emergence of the United States as the most powerful nation in the world, and through power sharing, he would ensure postwar cooperation and world stability.

The president sought Soviet participation in this consortium of power to keep order in Eastern Europe and to help deter peacebreakers. There could be no postwar peace, he reasoned, if the Soviets remained isolated and hostile. Through cooperation Roosevelt also hoped to co-opt the Soviets into an American-dominated postwar system so that they could be contained by the other policemen. In short, he both courted and contained the Soviets. He always hoped that the Soviet Union's influence among its Eastern European neighbors could be dressed up, if not camouflaged, perhaps through contrived elections, so that critical public opinion could be blunted. Roosevelt kept the Atlantic Charter alive through his famous oratorical generalities so that he could mollify sentiment that expected a principled peace, while at the same time he could always invoke the charter as a tool to check unacceptable Soviet behavior.[18] France's Charles de Gaulle bluntly concluded that Roosevelt's "will to power cloaked itself in idealism"; this American, the Frenchman wrote even less kindly, was an "artist" and a "seducer."[19]

In the spring of 1944 the British, surely sensing Roosevelt's proclivities but acting upon their own interests, asked the United States to approve a scheme wherein London would "take the lead" in Greece and Moscow would do likewise in Rumania. Ambassador to the United States Lord Halifax saw no reason why the United States should object, for "we follow the lead of the United States in South America as far as possible."[20] Hull strongly dissented, but Roosevelt accepted the scheme on a trial basis. In October Churchill journeyed to Moscow. Spheres of influence very much on his mind, he struck a bargain with Joseph Stalin. In Rumania, they agreed, the Soviet Union would hold 90 percent predominance; in Greece Britain would enjoy 90 percent influence; in Bulgaria the Soviets would have 75 percent; and in both Yugoslavia and Hungary Britain and the USSR would share authority on a 50-50 basis.[21] This frank if unenforceable division threw Hull into a funk, but Roosevelt did not protest. Churchill and Stalin had taken a precaution: They had deleted any mention of "dividing into spheres" because the Americans might be "shocked." The British prime minister assured the Soviet marshal that he "could explain matters" to the American president.[22] Churchill never really did explain fully to Roosevelt what happened at Moscow, but he did not need to. The American observer at the talks, W. Averell Harriman, kept the president informed about the emphasis on, if not the details of, spheres making. And Roosevelt acquiesced. He told Harriman that he accepted "practicable" steps to "insure against the Balkans getting us into a future international war."[23] At the end of the conference Roosevelt even wrote to Stalin (with the text of the letter also sent to Churchill) in such optimistic tones about the "success" of the meeting in helping to secure and maintain "a satisfactory and a durable peace," that the other two Allied leaders could only have concluded that the United States endorsed their handiwork.[24]

The term "spheres" did not receive much currency at the Yalta Conference in February 1945, but the results bespoke it. With the spirit of compromise prevailing, the British, American, and Soviet conferees, seeking to perpetuate their wartime cooperation, dismembered Germany into four zones, giving one to France. The Soviets received some Asian territory, partial control of Chinese railroads, and virtual recognition of their handpicked Communist Polish government (Lublin). The United States earned a pledge from the Soviet Union that it would sign a treaty of friendship and alliance with America's client, Jiang. Churchill, Stalin, and Roosevelt also agreed to establish a new world organization which also smacked of spheres of influence. The five "permanent" members of the Security Council alone possessed the veto, giving them unequal power in the institution. Frankly recognizing that the Soviet Union would be outvoted by two groups, the U.S.-dominated Latin American nations and the British Commonwealth, the leaders at Yalta granted the Soviet Union three votes in the General Assembly. Under a provision for "territorial trusteeship," it became evident that former League of Nations mandates and areas detached from the losers of World War II would fall under the authority of the large-power victors. As created at San Francisco in April, then, the United Nations Organization reflected the trend toward spheres; indeed, Articles 51 and 52 of the charter permitted regional defense pacts. Perhaps through great-power cooperation, thought Roosevelt, the United Nations would become a peacemaker that could "pull the fangs of the predatory animals of the world."[25]

Although the Declaration of Liberated Europe, a grand restatement of the Atlantic Charter and a call for free elections, also emerged from Yalta, Roosevelt did not consider it a denial of spheres. He knew full well that elections in Eastern Europe would produce the friendly governments the Soviets sought. Perhaps the declaration constituted a mere sop to American public opinion or one of the few tools available to Roosevelt to restrain the Soviets in Eastern Europe. In any case, Churchill, as Roosevelt knew well, never intended the principles of the Atlantic Charter or the declaration to be extended to the British Empire.[26] Two months after the conference Ambassador to the Soviet Union Harriman summed up Soviet views: "Stalin and Molotov considered at Yalta that by our willingness to accept a general wording on the declarations on Poland and liberated Europe, by our recognition of the need of the Red Army for security behind its lines, and of the predominant interest of Russia in Poland as a friendly neighbor and as a corridor to Germany, we understood and were ready to accept Soviet policies already known to us."[27] As for Asia, historian Akira Iriye has suggested that a new "Yalta system" emerged to replace "the long period of Anglo-Japanese domination, which had been followed by Japan's determination to establish a new order, with a situation in which the United States and the Soviet Union divided the region into spheres of predominance. . . ."[28]

Other wartime decisions contributed to the creation of spheres of influence. The armistice agreements in Eastern Europe placed Soviet officers in command of the Allied Control Commissions—in Rumania and Hungary, for example; British and American officials exercised authority in Italy; in Japan the United States took the leadership role. At the Potsdam Conference in July 1945 the great powers took another step toward distinctive spheres. Unable to agree on a reparations bill for defeated Germany, they decided that reparations would largely be taken from their respective zones. Would not the agreement "mean that each country would have a free hand in their own zones and would act entirely independently of others?" asked Molotov. Byrnes answered that that was essentially true.[29] The chargé d'affaires in Moscow, George F. Kennan, described the arrangement as "catch as catch can."[30]

Although for most Americans "sphere of influence" was an "unpopular term," as Harriman noted, some analysts argued that spheres of influence were a reality of international politics that ought to be recognized.[31] "Spheres of influence do in fact exist," concluded a State Department report in mid-1945, "and will probably continue to do so for some time to come."[32] To those who endorsed this view, spheres simply seemed inevitable. Such analysts embraced Robert Frost's principle that good fences make good neighbors. So thought Secretary of War Henry L. Stimson, who complained that "some Americans are anxious to hang on to exaggerated views of the Monroe Doctrine and at the same time butt into every question that comes up in Central Europe." He counseled that the United States should not try to challenge the Soviets in the Balkans; peace was possible because "our respective orbits did not clash."[33] Secretary of Commerce Henry A. Wallace thought that "whether we like it or not, the Russians will try to socialize their sphere of influence just as we try to democratize our sphere of influence. . . ." He favored "regional internationalism."[34]

Some State Department officers also foresaw and recommended a frank acceptance of a spheres of influence configuration to the international system. Cloyce K. Huston, chief of the Division of Southern European Affairs, argued for a restrained American policy toward the Soviet sphere. American "barkings, growlings, snappings and occasional bitings," he concluded, only irritated the Soviets without dislodging them.[35] H. Stuart Hughes of the Division of Research for Europe reported later that the "spheres-of-influence concept survived in the State Department's bureaucratic underground." He recalled that "our contention had been that if each side would stay out of the other's sphere, then each could tolerate substantial dissent within the sphere." Thus "one could find an intermediate course between armed antagonism and a cordial *modus vivendi.*"[36] Kennan, who, like the others, did not condone the repressive Soviet behavior in Eastern Europe, believed that the United States had insufficient power to roll back Soviet authority there. He urged that Europe be partitioned, that the United States build up a sphere of influence in Western Europe, and that we "keep ourselves out of the Russian sphere and keep the Russians out of ours."[37] Otherwise the United States would be in "danger of losing, like the dog standing over the reflecting pool, the bone in our mouth without obtaining the one we saw in the water."[38]

A venerable and widely respected American journalist,

Walter Lippmann, also viewed the postwar world as a system of spheres. He predicted and advocated the growth of "regional constellations of states" with a great power presiding over each. Thus the United States would be the most important partner in the "Atlantic Community," the Soviets would dominate the "Russian Orbit," and China would oversee the "China Orbit." Within each "regional grouping" the major power's security would be ensured, and global peace would be guaranteed if each power refrained from reaching into another's region for allies.[39] A British diplomat who read Lippmann's exposition of these ideas in the columnist's *U.S. War Aims* told his Foreign Office colleagues that the book "runs directly counter to the trends of American popular mythology, which tends toward universalism and is sharply critical of anything remotely resembling a sphere of influence."[40]

Although most Americans did indeed tend toward "universalism"—a vague term meaning the American fulfillment of an open economic and political world—and did reject spheres of influence in principle, the United States nonetheless sought to build an ever-larger sphere of its own. Although the U.S. sphere had nations and territories throughout the world, it could be measured in more than geographical terms. Economically its reach was global—a capitalist order based upon multilateral trade agreements and the open door and sustained by U.S. trade, investment, and foreign aid. Politically the American sphere included decisive U.S. authority in the many new postwar international organizations.

How could Americans square their universalist rhetoric with their hardnosed sphere building? They did so in part by not acknowledging the contradiction and in part by making a distinction between "open" and "exclusive" spheres. An "open" sphere was one like Latin America under the Good Neighbor Policy, wherein, it was argued, the United States did not meddle in the internal affairs or undermine the sovereignty of the individual nations but wherein United States security was essentially guaranteed and Washington cued the foreign policies of the Western Hemispheric countries. (It would have come as a surprise to many Latin Americans who were familiar with the history of the U.S. presence in Panama or who lived under the U.S.-backed dictator Fulgencio Batista in Cuba that they basked in the sun of an "open" sphere free from North American intrusion.) On the other hand, Americans found an "exclusive" sphere anathema. It suggested deep intervention in the internal affairs of sovereign states by the dominating power, the direct control of policy, the suppression of civil liberties, and the intrusive management of their foreign policies, denying them even the appearance of independent diplomatic and economic relations.[41]

Near the end of the Second World War some American officials seemed inclined to grant the Soviets an "open" sphere in Eastern Europe. They balked, however, at a sphere which might be used as a platform for expansionism, which excluded American influence, or which resembled a Soviet imposition of totalitarian methods. Harriman complained in early 1945 that "Soviet control over any foreign country did not mean merely influence on their foreign relations but the extension of the Soviet system," including the secret police and the extinction of freedom of speech.[42] At the same time Undersecretary of State Joseph C. Grew feared that the Soviets were establishing more than a sphere of influence and were in fact "taking complete charge in satellite countries."[43] A year earlier a State Department committee had distinguished between a "minimum" and "maximum" Soviet "pattern" in Eastern Europe. An American specialist on Soviet affairs, Charles E. Bohlen, commented during the committee's deliberations that a "minimum program," constituting an "assurance of friendly and independent governments in Eastern Europe for the purpose of guaranteeing Soviet security" but Soviet noninterference in internal affairs, would not constitute a threat to American interests. But should these states lose their independence through a "maximum" Soviet program, the United States would have to resist this apparent development of a "one-power aggregation" in Europe.[44] Under Truman the United States did.

Americans watched with growing dismay as Moscow took unilateral and often heavy-handed steps to secure some of the Eastern European states in the Soviet sphere of influence. Reacting to local circumstances, the Soviets followed different policies in different countries, and they did not have dominant power in Eastern Europe until at least 1948. In Poland, which "had become a symbol of our ability to work out problems with the Soviet Union," the Soviets brusquely installed the Communist Lublin Poles in office, arrested non-Communist officials, fixed voting lists to eliminate "fascists," postponed elections, suppressed civil liberties, imposed restrictions on travel, deported people, grabbed war booty, and annexed eastern portions of that much-abused country.[45] That same month Churchill complained privately that the Soviets were dropping an "iron screen" across Europe by setting up puppet governments.[46] In Rumania they abruptly forced King Michael to appoint Communist Petru Groza as prime minister and annexed Ruthenia and other districts from the former Axis satellite. The USSR completely absorbed the Baltic states of Estonia, Lithuania, and Latvia. In Bulgaria Communists formed an unrepresentative government. In Yugoslavia Josip Broz Tito practiced an independent brand of communism, but most Western observers wrongly considered him a stooge of Moscow. Finland was defeated by the Soviets in the war and had to sign postwar agreements which signaled subservience to Moscow in foreign policy questions but freedom in internal matters. In the fall of 1945 Hungary conducted elections in which the Communists won only 17 percent of the vote; in 1947 the Communists staged a coup and took power. In Czechoslovakia the non-Communist government of Eduard Beneš tried to develop both cordial relations with Moscow and ties with the West but fell in 1948 during a political crisis which brought the Communists to power. Soviet trade treaties and joint stock companies also demonstrated the Soviet penetration of Eastern Europe. Soviet Russia, noted one American official, was creating a "Soviet Monroe Doctrine" for the area.[47]

Despite the checkerboard pattern of Soviet behavior in Eastern Europe—permitting free elections in Hungary and Czechoslovakia but denying them in Poland, for example—the Truman administration came to see the Soviet sphere of influence as an impenetrable bloc, an "exclusive" sphere. Truman officials saw Soviet expansion and haughty unilateralism—"the old problem, really," remarked Bohlen, "of progressive aggression."[48] They attributed the evilest of intentions to the Soviets. Ambassador Harriman believed that the Soviet Union was becoming a "world bully."[49] Soviet decisions and actions, of course, were hardly reassuring, and the Soviets seemed to care little about the negative impressions they were creating abroad. Insensitive and inhumane, the Soviets proved uncooperative in repatriating American prisoners of war from Germany and Eastern Europe.[50] They also abominably treated returning Red Army soldiers who had been prisoners of war; apparently the Stalinist dictatorship thought that these men had been infected with Western ideas. Some Americans recalled the Nazi-Soviet Pact of 1939 and concluded that Moscow could not be trusted. Truman and many of his advisers believed by mid-1945 that the United States had been "too easy" with the Soviet Union and that firmness might roll back Soviet influence from Eastern Europe and halt further advances.[51] Another worry dogged them: Might the Soviets reach into other areas, not even respecting the traditional spheres of others? Where does a large nation draw the line for its sphere? "If the policy is accepted that the Soviet Union has a right to penetrate her immediate neighbors for security," Harriman reasoned, "penetration of the next immediate neighbors becomes at a certain time equally logical."[52] The Russians "have gone imperialistic and are out to extend their spheres of influence in all directions and wherever possible," thought Byrnes.[53] The deputy director of the Office of European Affairs believed that even "to concede a limited Soviet sphere of influence" in Eastern Europe "might be to invite its extension to other areas. . . ."[54] Because the Soviets were seeking influence in such places as Libya, Manchuria, the Dardanelles, and Iran, moreover, it appeared that the Soviet Union—even if acting out of a sincere desire for security—was probing and thrusting, taking advantage of the chaotic and fragile postwar international system. The trouble with a military frontier, noted Bohlen, is that one hundred miles farther is always better.[55]

Many analysts argued that the United States, the most powerful postwar nation, was also bent on building and expanding a sphere of influence. At times the British complained as much as did the Soviets. American critics protested, too; they feared that the U.S. empire, already controlling the Western Hemisphere, was being extended. They were right. Washington continued to watch over the members of its traditional sphere of influence in Latin America, drawing its hemispheric neighbors closer in March 1945 through a new defense pact—the Act of Chapultepec. Lend-Lease aid to Latin American countries during the war, U.S. naval bases, support for particular political leaders, and the training of Latin American military officers permitted the United States to hang on to its vaunted position in the Western Hemisphere, despite noncompliant states like Argentina. Strong trade ties and large investments also signaled U.S. hegemony. In 1946–1947 one-quarter of U.S. exports flowed to Latin America; in 1950 direct U.S. investments in the area equaled more than one-third of the world total of twelve billion dollars, and about 40 percent of U.S. imports were drawn from its neighbors to the south.[56] During the 1930s and 1940s the United States self-consciously nudged out German and British interests.[57]

"I think that it's not asking too much to have our little region over here which never has bothered anybody," Stimson said. The Soviet Union should not complain, because it "is going to take these steps . . . of building up friendly protectorates around her." His aide John J. McCloy agreed that "we ought to have our cake and eat it too; that we ought to be free to operate under this regional arrangement in South America, [and] at the same time intervene promptly in Europe . . . ," as the United States had been forced to do twice in this century in two world wars.[58] It was necessary for the United States to develop a "solid group in this hemisphere," Assistant Secretary of State Nelson Rockefeller believed, or Washington "could not do what we wanted to do on the world front."[59]

Elsewhere, too, the United States drove in stakes. In the Middle East the State Department backed American oil companies in their pursuit of lucrative and strategic concessions for exploiting the black riches. By war's end American interests controlled nearly half of the proved oil reserves of the region. In Saudi Arabia, where American petroleum interests were extensive, U.S. officials worked to move its leader, Ibn Saud, away from the influence of the British, sought to secure future oil supplies, and built and operated the Dhahran Airport, "a vital link in U.S. round-the-world airplane operation." Technical assistance flowed to that Arab nation, so that, concluded a State Department report in 1946, it "is in a fair way to becoming an American frontier. . . ."[60] Earlier Roosevelt had informed Churchill that the United States would respect traditional British interests in the Middle East. Churchill, always the realist about spheres of influence, replied: "Thank you very much for your assurances about no sheeps eyes at our oilfields in Iran and Iraq. Let me reciprocate by giving you fullest assurance that we have no thought of trying to horn in upon your interests or property in Saudi Arabia."[61] The United States actually began to "horn in upon" British interests throughout the region, including Iran and Palestine (Israel), and London protested.

In Asia the United States expanded its interests, too. As in the past, Asian markets and strategic raw materials beckoned. America's Western European allies held colonies, and as distasteful as it was to Americans, they agreed that these possessions should be restored to their allies' empires to ensure the flow of resources to Europe and to satisfy imperial egos. And with the new configuration of world power, "it is our turn to bat in Asia," an American official remarked to a Briton.[62] In the Pacific the United States boldly took control of the former Japanese-dominated islands of the Carolines, Marshalls, and Marianas. Truman sounded just like other international power brokers when he tried to justify American sphere building: "Though the United States wants no territory or profit or selfish advantage out of this war, we are going to maintain the military bases necessary for the complete protection of our interests and of world peace."[63] Was this any different from what the Soviets were trying to do? asked Moscow. The Americans were attempting to "get away with" the Pacific Islands, complained British Colonial Secretary Oliver Stanley, but were wrapping their case "in a rather diaphanous cover of the usual idealism."[64] The United States used the United Nations "trusteeship" system to "cloak" American imperial intentions.[65] Churchill always worried that the growing American sphere of influence would impinge upon his own. Let the Americans have their Pacific island outposts, he said, "But 'Hands Off the British Empire' is our maxim."[66]

In defeated Japan the United States claimed supreme

power for itself in order to reconstruct Japanese society along liberal, capitalist, and nonmilitarist lines and later to ensure its place in the American sphere as a vital anti-Communist partner. A Far Eastern Commission of several nations existed, but it could claim negligible authority. The Allied Council of Japan, wherein the United States ostensibly shared power with the Soviet Union, Britain, and China, also became moribund quite early, leaving decisions in the hands of the strong-willed General Douglas MacArthur, who, Harriman noted, had the "last word" in the reconstruction of Japan. Harriman informed the Soviets that the United States was "very firm on the matter of keeping the power in American hands," and Truman told his cabinet that the United States "would run this particular business."[67] Japan, concluded Edwin O. Reischauer, had the "sham facade of international control." Indeed, "the Russians are right in believing that we seek to make Japan an ideological ally," and "our position there is not very different from that of Russia in the smaller countries of Eastern Europe, however dissimilar our motives may be."[68] Stalin growled that the USSR was "treated like a piece of furniture" in Japan, but it seems clear that he was unwilling to challenge U.S. authority there, perhaps because he hoped that Washington, to mollify Moscow on this issue, would make some concession to Soviet authority in Eastern Europe.[69] Byrnes admitted that "we were placed in an embarrassing position" because of obvious analogies with the Soviet presence in Eastern Europe.[70] The United States also tried with much less success to draw civil war-wracked China into the burgeoning American sphere in Asia. "I personally wanted the United States," remembered State Department official Dean Rusk, "to control every wave in the Pacific. . . ."[71]

Americans did not want to appear to be like other great powers and recoiled from popular comparisons between postwar Eastern Europe and Latin America, Poland and Mexico, or Rumania and Japan. Harry Howard of the Department of State once compared the Dardanelles, where the Soviets were seeking authority, to the Panama Canal. His superior, Loy Henderson, "hit the ceiling" over the analogy and reminded Howard that he was "no mere academician now but an advocate" of American interests. Anyway, Henderson, concluded, the canal was built by the United States, but the strait was an act of God.[72] As for Eastern Europe and Latin America, Americans justified their influence in the latter by distinguishing between open and closed spheres. Byrnes recognized that large nations like the Soviet Union had special regional security interests and that geographic propinquity dictated such special interests, but "the good neighbor, unlike the institution of marriage, is not an exclusive arrangement. The best neighbors do not deny their neighbors the right to be friends with others." In a speech in October 1945 Byrnes stood emphatically against "spheres of exclusive influence."[73]

To the Soviets, however, the distinction between "open" and "exclusive" spheres made no sense. They considered the United States' alleged "open" Good Neighbor sphere in Latin America virtually closed—evidence of capitalist imperialism. They perceived blatant U.S. intrusions in the internal affairs of the countries of the Western Hemisphere and elsewhere. From the Soviet perspective, moreover, if an "open" sphere came into existence in Eastern Europe, anti-Soviet groups might come to power and invite outside powers into this area of prime importance to Soviet security. At a time of Soviet economic weakness, increased U.S. trade with Eastern Europe might lead to American economic, hence political, influence among the Soviet Union's neighbors.

The Soviets also charged the United States and Britain with following a double standard.[74] Accusations were flung back and forth. When Britain complained about Eastern Europe, the Soviet Union protested Anglo-American perfidy in Greece, Italy, and Japan. "The United Kingdom had India and her possessions in the Indian Ocean in her sphere of influence; the United States had China and Japan, but the Soviets had nothing," remarked Stalin. Bevin shot back that "the Russian sphere extended from Lubeck to Port Arthur."[75]

Surely, Stalin could not deny it; he played the spheres of influence game as much as any leader. At Yalta, for example, Churchill appealed for French great-power status through the granting of a zone in Germany to France. In making his case, he said that France was to Britain what Poland was to the Soviet Union. Stalin, who had been trying futilely to gain Anglo-American recognition of the Soviet-backed Lublin government in Poland, seized the moment: "Why was more to be demanded of Poland than of France?" Who had elected Charles de Gaulle? Yet his French government was recognized.[76] At the Potsdam Conference Stalin sparred with Truman. The president asked for recognition of the Italian government which the United States had helped bring to power—a conservative Christian Democratic regime.[77] The Soviet marshal complained that Rumania, Bulgaria, and Hungary were being treated like "leprous states." He would recognize Italy, where the "Russians had no rights," if Truman would recognize the governments of the Eastern European countries.[78] They were stalemated then and later, but eventually Stalin recognized the Italian government and Truman recognized the Eastern European regimes (including Poland).[79]

The Soviets also claimed that America's repeated call for the "open door" in the world economy was actually a cloak for expanding the United States' sphere of influence at the expense of others. When Moscow viewed the United States, it saw more than atomic bombs and foreign bases, more than superiority at the United Nations or a sphere in Latin America and Asia. It saw economic power.[80] Stalin apparently thought the "open door policy as dangerous to a nation as foreign military invasion."[81] The influx of American capital and trade into an economically weak area like Eastern Europe, as Molotov stated in 1946, might make the United States "master." The principle had to be applied "consistently." If the United States had preferential commercial arrangements with Cuba and the Philippines, why could not the Soviet Union make such exclusionist deals with its neighbor Rumania? As for the Anglo-American call for international control of the Black Sea straits: "Are the advocates of the principle of 'equal opportunity' willing to apply it to the Panama Canal as well?" And to the British Suez Canal?[82] After the Soviets at Potsdam had rejected Truman's plea for the internationalization of waterways, the president would not admit a double standard and drew an exaggerated conclusion: "The Russians were planning world conquest."[83]

In Iran, in early 1946, the United States and the Soviet Union clashed in a classic contest for spheres of influence. Both sought influence over Iranian political groups (the Soviets in the northern province of Azerbaijan and the Americans in the capital of Teheran). Both pursued oil concessions, which in themselves provided avenues to influence, as the British learned from their large holdings in the Anglo-Iranian Oil Company. Both maintained military personnel in the Middle Eastern nation. After the British and American forces left, however, the Soviets stayed, violating a treaty deadline for withdrawal in early March 1946. The United States supported a United Nations investigation, whereupon the Soviets walked out of that body. Washington charged that the Soviets were attempting to create a satellite in Iran, and Moscow countered that the Anglo-Americans were gaining control of a country which bordered the Soviet Union. Great Britain dominated Iranian oil, and advisers from an American military mission, under the leadership of Army Major General Robert W. Grow, tutored the Iranian Army. The

Soviets defused the crisis by signing an agreement with Iran in early April. The accord provided for Soviet military withdrawal and the establishment of a joint Iranian-Soviet petroleum company. But American influence in Iran increased after Ambassador George V. Allen "every day, in every way we can think of," urged the Iranian government to take a firm line against the Soviets throughout 1946.[84] The Iranian parliament never ratified the agreement. The Soviet Union fumed, the United States claimed a Cold War victory, and Iran entered the American sphere of influence.[85]

In early 1946, when the Iranian crisis began to smolder, Truman and other officials grew impatient with the Soviet Union, and the doctrine of containment found greater expression. The list of irritants swelled: no elections in Eastern Europe, unilateral decisions, bombastic Communist language, Soviet atomic spies in Canada, and Soviet vetoes in the first sessions of the United Nations. "I'm tired of babying the Russians," President Truman grumbled in January, after the meager results of the Moscow foreign ministers' meeting the previous month. They had to be faced with an "iron fist."[86] Stalin's speech of February 9 on the eve of voting for the Supreme Soviet seemed so dogmatically ideological in its denunciation of capitalism that American policy makers thought that "it will henceforth be the Communist and fellow-traveler Bible throughout the world."[87] Stalin charged that the Second World War stemmed from the capitalist nations' attempts to "re-divide the 'spheres of influence' in their own favor." Capitalism, he said, "contains in itself the seeds of a general crisis and of warlike clashes.[88] Americans overreacted to the speech, which was primarily directed at a domestic Soviet audience (especially Communist party members), whose themes were predominantly domestic (championing a new five-year plan, for example), and which spoke only briefly about international questions (and, at that, not about the present but about the past).[89] Secretary of Commerce Henry A. Wallace, on the other hand, argued that Stalin's speech amounted to a response to American military expansion; the United States, Wallace said, was "setting up bases all the way from Greenland, Iceland, northern Canada, and Alaska to Okinawa, with Russia in mind. . . . We were challenging him and his speech was taking up the challenge."[90] The British, it seems, paid far less attention to the speech, but they did note the "fluttering of the dovecotes" caused by Stalin's address in the United States.[91] A British diplomat observed in mid-February 1946 that American "opinion against Russia had hardened. . . ."[92] George F. Kennan's influential "long telegram" of February 22 from the American Embassy in Moscow represented and advanced that hardening: "We have here a political force committed fanatically to the belief that with the [United States] there can be no permanent modus vivendi."[93]

Less than a month later, on March 5, former British Prime Minister Winston Churchill stung the Soviets with his "iron curtain" speech in Fulton, Missouri. Truman sat on the platform with Churchill that day, and the president had encouraged and approved the speech's message before the renowned Briton spoke.[94] Stalin reacted angrily to Churchill's stern, critical words about the Soviet sphere of influence and his call for an Anglo-American partnership against the Soviet Union. "Russia was not attacking," cried Stalin; "she was being attacked." He told the British ambassador in Moscow that he "knew it was said that Mr. Churchill was not a member of the British Government, but he held an important position in England and his speech had not been repudiated."[95] Indeed, Stalin must have sensed that Britain, war-weakened and dependent upon foreign economic assistance, was entering the American sphere and that Truman embraced the hard-line Fulton message.

The question on American minds, Ambassador Walter Bedell Smith told Stalin in April, was "what does the Soviet Union want and how far is Russia going to go?"[96] By May 1946 Truman felt the need to "tell Russia where to get off. . . ."[97] It was time to "kick the Russians in the balls," a prominent lawyer blurted to a horrified Secretary Wallace.[98] The United States decided to deny the Soviet Union a large reconstruction loan but offered $3.75 billion to Britain. The Americans, observed a British diplomat in May, had become "far tougher" toward Moscow.[99] The abortive Baruch Plan for the gradual abolition of nuclear weapons also created rancor in the summer of 1946. American leaders suspected correctly that the Soviets would reject this proposal because its stages guaranteed that the U.S. atomic monopoly would remain in place until international controls were instituted.[100] The United States was not about to surrender its atomic supremacy when Soviet-American relations were deteriorating so ominously.

In April the battleship *Missouri* sailed to the Mediterranean, and in August the aircraft carrier *Franklin D. Roosevelt* cruised in those strategic waters. The Soviets grew worried, but Admiral William Halsey bellowed that "it is nobody's damn business where we go. We will go anywhere we please."[101] American warships visited Plymouth, Malta, Gibraltar, Piraeus, Suda Bay, and elsewhere in the area, and American planes landed at Athens, Algiers, Marseilles, Naples, and Rome.[102] The United States was in essence outlining its geographical sphere of influence and warning the Soviets not to cross the line.

In Germany in 1946 there was little movement toward economic unity because of both Soviet and French hesitancy to rebuild their former enemy. The Soviets began to tie their zone to the Soviet economy, while the Americans and British seized as much as ten billion dollars' worth of scientific, technical, and commercial information (patents, trade secrets, invention records, designs, and the like) from their zones.[103] In May, angry that neither the French nor the Soviets would cooperate to sustain a German economy that could stand on its own feet, Military Governor Lucius Clay ended reparations shipments from the American zone. "After one year of occupation," he observed, "zones represent airtight territories with almost no free exchange of commodities, persons and ideas."[104]

In April, at the Council of Foreign Ministers meeting in Paris, Secretary Byrnes formally launched what for him was a pet project and a test of Soviet intentions. He proposed to the Soviet Union that it join the United States in signing a twenty-five-year treaty on German disarmament and demilitarization—in short, a security guarantee against a revived Germany. The Soviets would not consider such a treaty, Molotov replied in July. They may have rejected the proposed treaty because they would not entrust their security to Americans or to a paper document, because they did not want an American presence in Europe, or because they believed that the treaty was a ruse to permit termination of reparations shipments to the Soviet Union. Byrnes concluded that the Soviets were more interested in expansionism than security.[105] By December 1946 the United States and Great Britain had merged their German zones, the first step toward a new West German state.

A dispute over Turkey in the summer of 1946 spotlighted the acrimonious quest for spheres. In August the Soviets presented their position on the Dardanelles to Ankara. They had long insisted on a share in the governance of the strait, which, they crossly pointed out, had been used by German armed vessels during the war to enter the Black Sea and ravage the Soviet Union. Only the Black Sea nations, argued Moscow, should have a postwar role in controlling that strategic artery. Washington, reiterating the open door thesis, sought an international governing body, with Britain and the United States as members, and rejected an apparent Soviet bid for a naval base in Turkey. When the Soviet Union made its case in August, Washington interpreted it as a set of demands prefacing a Soviet grab for Turkey. Exaggerated language filled Washington conference rooms. From Turkey, Ambassador Edwin Wilson added to the alarm when he cabled dire warnings of a Soviet thrust through Turkey into the Persian Gulf and Asia. On August 15 President Truman approved a memorandum which concluded that "the primary objective of the Soviet Union is to obtain control of Turkey." The United States would resist any Soviet "aggression," by "force of American arms" if necessary.[106] To Americans, Turkey had become a link in a global chain that must be not only denied to the Soviet sphere but secured in the American sphere. An infuriated Soviet Union once again licked its wounds, fearing that another one of its neighbors was inviting a foreign threat to sit at the Soviet border. Although, as in the earlier case of Iran, the Soviets made no military move against Turkey, and the rhetoric about Soviet intentions of world conquest lacked evidence, if not credibility, Americans again thought the worst and pulled Turkey toward the U.S. sphere of influence.[107]

As the United States "got tough" in the first half of 1946, so did the Soviets. In April a conspicuous anti-American bias, theretofore muted or nonexistent, marked Soviet editorials. Increasingly the United States, the practitioner of "atomic diplomacy," was highlighted as the leader of an Anglo-American coalition seeking world hegemony. They were "ganging up" against Russia, spoiling the once-flourishing wartime cooperation evident at Yalta. The heated rhetoric became hotter through 1946. An "Anglo-American bloc," concluded a Soviet editorial which reviewed the year, was attempting to substitute an "imperialist trust for a democratic peace."[108]

On September 27, 1946, the Soviet ambassador to the United States, Nikolai Novikov, sent the USSR Foreign Ministry a long cable in which he summarized his view of American foreign policy. Whether the document was intended for propagandistic use or for internal Kremlin consideration is not clear, but Novikov's assessment was blunt: U.S. foreign policy "reflects the imperialist tendencies of American monopolistic capital" and "is characterized . . . by a striving for world supremacy." With nations still economically hobbled, the United States was moving toward "world domination." He made the best case possible for Soviet power—troops in Germany and "friendly" regimes in Eastern Europe, all of which would serve to block U.S. machinations. The ambassador discussed the military power of the United States with some awe and disparaged U.S. expansionism (in collusion with Great Britain) in the Mediterranean, Middle East, and Asia. In Germany, he complained, the United States was not taking the stringent measures necessary to prevent the "revival of an imperialist Germany." Indeed, Germany and Japan were being rebuilt so that they could become American allies in a future war. Novikov predicted that the Anglo-American coalition could not last because the British would discover and resent their subordinate, dependent role. As for President Truman, he was "a politically unstable man" representing the "reactionary" wing of the Democratic party. Make no mistake about it, an alarmed Ambassador Novikov told his colleagues in Moscow, the United States was preparing for a future war—against the Soviet Union.[109]

By the fall of 1946, then, both major powers, glaring at each other from their respective spheres of influence and often using shrill language, had become convinced that the other was hell-bent on expansion that might spark war. Most Americans attributed international troubles to the Soviet Union. From France, for example, Ambassador Jefferson Caffery gloomily reported the growing appeal of the French Communist party, "the advance of the 'Soviet Trojan Horse.'"[110] Secretary Wallace did not agree with the tendency to blame all on the Soviets, and in a Madison Square Garden speech in September 1946 he publicly criticized his own government for its hard-line policy. Truman fired him from the cabinet. The next month renowned religious philosopher Reinhold Niebuhr captured in a few taut words in *Life* magazine what he and many other Americans were thinking: "Russian truculence cannot be mitigated by further concessions. Russia hopes to conquer the whole of Europe strategically and ideologically."[111]

To head off just such an eventuality, the United States had been employing its vast wealth through a variety of loans and relief programs to assist other nations to recover from the war's devastation and to draw them into its sphere of influence. Export-Import Bank loans, largely extended to Europe, totaled more than $2 billion by June 1946; billions of dollars' worth of military-related surplus property, including ships, were transferred to friendly nations; and United Nations Relief and Rehabilitation Administration aid of almost $4 billion (the United States provided three-quarters of this amount) flowed abroad. The United States contributed $3.175 billion to the World Bank and another $2.75 billion to the International Monetary Fund.[112] In September 1946 Byrnes recognized the relationship between foreign aid and spheres: "We must help our friends in every way and refrain from assisting those who either through helplessness or for other reasons are opposing the principles for which we stand."[113]

4

POLARIZATION
The Cold War, 1947–1950

THE SETTING was hardly friendly for a speech its drafters thought as important as any since Pearl Harbor. Most members of the Eightieth Congress wanted less, not more, spending, and many of them held little respect for Harry S. Truman, the Democratic president whose administration the American voters had repudiated in the fall 1946 elections by putting both houses of the Congress into the hands of the Republicans. On March 12, 1947, at a joint session of an unwelcoming Congress, Truman had a selling job to do, and he issued his Truman Doctrine with often alarmist language. He said it "must be the policy of the United States to support free peoples who are resisting attempted subjugation by armed minorities or by outside pressures." The world, he stated, was now divided between two "alternative ways of life." The legislators heard Truman's unvarnished case for a more activist U.S. foreign policy in an intensified Cold War.

The immediate impetus for this dramatic announcement of a global doctrine was the civil war in Greece, where Communist-led rebels battled the British-backed conservative government in Athens. The insurgents received sanctuary and aid from Yugoslavia. Because U.S. officials thought Yugoslavia's Communist government was merely Moscow's puppet, they assumed that the Soviet Union itself was directing the Greek rebellion. It was not. In fact, Stalin had pleaded with Tito to halt his assistance to the Greeks, and Moscow had given the Greek insurgents no Soviet help. But because American officials, gripped by a Cold War mentality that interpreted most trouble spots as Communist-inspired or at least Communist-exploited, ranked Greece as a strategic site, they decided to prevent this "ripe plum" from falling into "Soviet hands."[1] When the economically hobbled British could no longer maintain the Mediterranean nation in their sphere, the United States decided to intervene and to draw the fabled but now enfeebled birthplace of "democracy" into the expanding American sphere of influence. "If Greece should fall under the control of an armed minority," Truman concluded in this early version of the domino theory, "the effect upon its neighbor, Turkey, would be immediate and serious. Confusion and disorder might well spread throughout the entire Middle East." Western Europe might also succumb.[2] To halt this perceived Soviet probe of a "soft spot," and to interrupt a feared chain reaction, the president successfully requested in his Truman Doctrine address that Congress approve four hundred million dollars for aid to Greece and Turkey.[3] As for the United Nations, Truman bypassed it in this unilateral American aid program. Among chagrined diplomats in the New York-based organization the opinion was that the United States regarded the new international body as no more than "a lost child."[4]

"Containment" became the American byword, especially

after George F. Kennan, writing as "Mr. X," published an article in the July 1947 issue of *Foreign Affairs* that recommended a "policy of firm containment, designed to confront the Russians with unalterable counter-force at every point where they show signs of encroaching upon the interests of a peaceful and stable world."[5] As Acheson put it, the United States had to resist a Soviet "pincer movement" threatening Iran, Greece, Turkey, Germany, France, and Italy. The stakes seemed large. "You weren't going to have a strong Turkey if Greece went to pieces. And furthermore, each country to the west, which might be penetrated, would automatically bring about the collapse of countries to the east of that."[6]

Many critics at the time claimed that the Truman administration exaggerated the Communist/Soviet threat to the Mediterranean and to Europe and used a chain reaction theory that lacked evidence. Officials posited a Soviet threat but never demonstrated it. The Soviet threat to Greece and Turkey, for example, was known only to those who imagined it. Indeed, the Truman Doctrine actually did not fit the very first places toward which it was directed. The Soviets were not subverting Greece, and they were not moving against Turkey.[7] Some critics suspected that the United States was exploiting a domestic crisis in Greece to build an American military presence in the Mediterranean and to surround the Soviet Union. Walter Lippmann, moreover, judged the containment doctrine a "strategic monstrosity" because the United States would soon find itself aligned with an "array of satellites, clients, dependents and puppets" just because they were anti-Communist. He worried, too, that containment emphasized confrontation rather than diplomacy and that it did not distinguish between areas peripheral and vital to American security.[8] Alarmist, open-ended, vague, rigid doctrines— "rhetorical diplomacy"—seemed destined to draw the United States into danger.[9] Then, too, the ultimate logic of the containment doctrine was that the exercise of containment leads to American expansion abroad, expansion leads to empire building, and, in the end, a global empire leads not to U.S. security but to insecurity, hence to the need for more expansion.[10] As a Canadian diplomat explained, "by its very nature a desire on the part of a great power to expand its defence area is an illimitable process. The appetite for security grows with eating."[11]

In the years 1947 and 1948, invoking the containment doctrine, the United States sought to build an international economic and defensive network to confirm and protect American prosperity and security—American hegemony. For Western Europe, several American objectives became evident: economic reconstruction, prevention of leftist and Communist political victories, ouster of Communists from governments, European integration, incorporation of the western zones of Germany into a Western European economic system linked to the United States, settlement of colonial disputes that were draining the mother countries of scarce resources, blockage of "third force" or neutralist tendencies, and creation of a defensive alliance.

The Marshall Plan became the first American instrument designed to achieve these goals.[12] Although by 1947 the United States had spent some nine billion dollars since V-E Day to help Western Europe recover from the staggering impact of the war, that area still desperately needed outside aid. To Americans who believed that the Soviets were prowling about, looking for chaotic environments to exploit, there seemed to be an urgent need for a major American counteroffensive. Americans thought that political extremism flowed from economic instability and that the large Communist parties in France and Italy, in particular, would come to power unless the United States sponsored a new, massive, and coordinated American aid program. An interdepartmental committee report concluded that it was important "to maintain in friendly hands areas which contain or protect sources of metals, oil and other national [*sic*] resources, which contain strategic objectives, or areas strategically located, which contain a substantial industrial potential, which possess manpower and organized military forces in important quantities, or which for political or psychological reasons enable the U.S. to exert a greater influence for world stability, security and peace."[13]

U.S. leaders defined Western Europe as part of the growing American sphere of influence—the "keystone in the arch which supports the kind of a world which we have to have in order to conduct our lives . . . ," as Acheson later noted.[14] On June 5, 1947, Secretary of State George C. Marshall told a Harvard University commencement audience that the United States would help Europe rebuild itself. He did not specifically exclude Eastern Europe and the Soviet Union from his offer, but few American officials expected participation by members of the Soviet sphere. The European Recovery Program (ERP) was an American-directed project for "friends" of the United States, to recall Byrnes's 1946 comment. *"The United States must run this show,"* insisted Undersecretary of State Will L. Clayton.[15]

American diplomats not only saw the ERP as a means to shore up Western Europe but also hoped that success there would undermine the Soviet sphere. One of the tenets of the containment doctrine was that holding the line against the Soviets would eventually throw them on the defensive. "If we can get the grass to grow a little greener" in Western Europe, said Harriman, "that success will roll back behind the iron curtain. . . ."[16] Truman also envisioned a rollback of Soviet influence: "If that European recovery program works, we will raise the Iron Curtain by peaceable means" because people would be attracted to the higher standard of "personal welfare" in Western Europe.[17] Actually the Marshall Plan and the hostile Soviet reaction to it divided Europe even more sharply.

In July 1947 V. M. Molotov led a large Soviet delegation to Paris to discuss a Europe-wide program. He gruffly departed after a few days, charging that the United States was attempting to undermine the sovereignty of individual nations. It was a "clean break," concluded Bevin, with "no doors left open."[18] Both sides shoved aside the fledgling Economic Commission for Europe, a continent-wide agency. The Soviet Union did not join the ERP; Moscow's pressure on the Eastern European countries and East Germany also kept them out. The Department of State explained why: "If the USSR chose to participate in the recovery program, it would have been obliged to sacrifice the exclusive economic controls established in Eastern Europe since the war and to permit a western reorientation of satellite economies into the broader European economy envisaged by the program. Such a course, which would jeopardize Soviet hegemony in Eastern Europe, was unacceptable."[19] The United States reaped propaganda advantage by claiming that the Soviet Union had divided Europe by rejecting the Marshall Plan. Exaggerated Soviet rhetoric, spread through the Cominform, the Soviet propaganda agency created in September 1947, further aggravated the division. The Marshall Plan, which ultimately expended thirteen billion dollars, was, according to Communist bombast, an "American design to enslave Europe."[20] Thus the war of words continued, and the lines separating the spheres were cut more deeply. In short, it was a question of spheres of influence, and the Soviets chose not to have theirs diminished and America's enlarged at their expense.

American leaders knew that there was something to Molotov's charge that the United States would be intervening in the domestic affairs of other nations. "In the end," concluded Kennan, "we would not *ask* them, we would just *tell* them what they would get."[21] Senator Henry Cabot Lodge of Massachusetts exaggerated but nonetheless made a telling point when he said that "this Marshall plan is going to be the biggest damned interference in internal affairs that there has

ever been in history. We are being responsible for the people
who stay in power as a result of our efforts." Indeed, "it
doesn't do any good to say we are not going to interfere when
the people in power stay there because of us."[22]

Many Western Europeans themselves bristled under
American pressure at the same time that they welcomed
American aid. Indeed, before the new American economic
offensive, they regretted that their "powerlessness" left them
vulnerable to U.S. leverage, if not commands.[23] Despite rhetoric of an Anglo-American "special relationship," even
America's junior Cold War partner Great Britain resented
America's postwar power. The British, sour about their decline caused by the ravages of war, complained against American "arrogance" and the "ham-fisted" way Americans conducted international relations.[24] "England is so weak she
must follow our leadership," observed Harriman in 1946.
"She will do anything that we insist and she won't go out on a
limb alone."[25] The "Anglo-American alignment," as Ambassador Walter Bedell Smith called it in 1946, was always friction-ridden because Washington and London had competing
interests. They tangled over the American refusal, despite a
wartime agreement, to share in the development of atomic
energy and in the building of a British bomb. They feuded
over American movement into Asia and the Middle East, the
Palestine question (partitioning the territory to create a new
nation of Israel),[26] and the question of decolonization. Most
British diplomats, unlike their American counterparts, did
not see communism as monolithic. London recognized the
new Communist government of China; the United States did
not. The British balked at American insistence that they
open their sterling bloc trade system by accepting nondis-
criminatory trade principles. The American loan of $3.5 bil-
lion in 1946 particularly rankled the British. The chancellor
of the exchequer explained that "we retreated, slowly and
with a bad grace and with increasing irritation, from a free

gift to an interest-free loan, and from this again to a loan bearing interest. . . ."²⁷ Resentful that they had become dependent upon the United States, the British also thought they deserved better. "It is aggravating to find that our reward for losing a quarter of our national wealth in the common cause [during the war]," bitterly wrote the British magazine *The Economist*, "is to pay tribute for half a century to those who have been enriched by the war."²⁸

The French, too, came to resent their subordinate status, and Paris, jealously guarding national sovereignty, more than once unsettled the American sphere of influence in Western Europe. France insisted on returning to its Indochinese empire after the war, and although Americans acquiesced, they frequently criticized French rule as repressive and self-destructive. The status of Germany especially posed a sharp Franco-American difference of opinion. While Americans sought to rebuild Germany and to integrate it into the Western European economy, the French worked to keep its neighbor weak and divided, its industrial Ruhr area internationalized. But the French had to give way, Foreign Minister Georges Bidault understood, because if France obstructed U.S. plans for Germany, France had "not a ghost of a chance of benefitting from Marshall aid. . . . If we want to act single-handedly, we lose everything."²⁹ As General Bryan Robertson, the British commander in chief in Germany, knew, "he who pays the piper calls the tune."³⁰ France was becoming dependent upon American assistance: The United States extended a $550 million loan in late 1945, a $650 million loan the following spring, and $284 million in "interim aid" in fall 1947 before Marshall Plan funds began to flow; the American-dominated World Bank also loaned France $250 million in May 1947. U.S. officials drove hard bargains with the French not just on German questions: They required France to buy with these dollars particular American products (cigarettes and chewing gum seemed the most annoying) and to follow private enterprise and fiscal stabilization policies.[31] The publisher of *Le Monde* grumbled to Walter Lippmann that "France under the Marshall Plan and the Truman Doctrine was becoming a sort of Philippines."[32]

Some Europeans argued that they should organize a "Third Force" between the United States and the Soviet Union in order to preserve Western European independence. But such arguments receded in the face of Europe's dire need for outside assistance and the offer of Marshall Plan aid.[33] No such direct challenge to U.S. authority developed in the late 1940s, and the Marshall Plan participants cooperated more than they feuded. Unlike Eastern European nations, in which the Soviets often ran roughshod over opponents and imposed governments on resentful peoples, Western Europe countries maintained their sovereignty and a much higher degree of independence and shared decision making. Still, identifying this early Cold War friction within the American sphere of influence is necessary to explain the wrenching tensions that later weakened the U.S. position in Western Europe.[34]

While the United States and Western Europe groped toward economic cooperation through 1947 and 1948, the Soviet Union and the United States growled and snapped at each other. Each, it appeared to the other in mirror image, was intent upon world conquest. American officials thought that the Soviets were tactically flexible and would attempt to expand their sphere of influence not through military means but by measures short of war, by exploiting economic dislocations, by political subversion through "stooges," and by hostile propaganda designed to split Westerners.[35] The Soviet Union, concluded the National Security Council in March 1948, was engaging the United States in a "struggle for power, or 'cold war,' in which our national security is at stake and from which we cannot withdraw short of eventual national suicide." The United States, to meet this global threat, needed to undertake "a world-wide counteroffensive against Soviet-directed world communism."[36]

In Western Europe the United States worked to eliminate Communists from the governments of the region. The American Cold War assumption was simple: Communist parties anywhere owed their very beings to the Soviet Union. Communists everywhere were labeled stooges for the Soviets; the French Communist party, claimed American Ambassador Caffery, was the "Soviet Trojan horse."[37] Such thinking overlooked the indigenous and cautiously independent status of Western European Communist parties that were traveling different roads to socialism. The Soviets sought to subordinate such parties to Moscow's foreign policy goals, of course, but they did not always succeed. And the Soviets, right after the war, actually urged Communists abroad to forswear insurrection in favor of political participation. Beginning in late 1947, however, Soviet hegemony came down hard on them at the time of a hotter Cold War, the Marshall Plan's entry into Europe, and Titoist Yugoslavia's defection from the Soviet sphere.[38] But Americans were not seeing such complexities; they saw only creeping communism, especially in economically destabilized France and Italy, and they advocated the ouster of Communists from the governments of those two nations.

To blunt the popularity of the Communists in Italy, American officials tried at first to build a center-left government but eventually backed the Christian Democrats. In May 1947 the Communists were evicted from the Italian coalition government. Then, in April of the following year, the Christian Democrats won the national election, handing the Partito Comunista Italiano and the Social Democrats a stunning defeat. American officials applauded the government of Alcide de Gasperi, and well they should have, for U.S. intervention had helped produce the result. During 1947–1948 American appeals to the Vatican led to the muzzling of left-wing Catholic priests; Pope Pius XII criticized the Communists; American labor leaders urged their Italian cohorts to snub the Communists; Italian-Americans organized an anti-Communist letter-writing campaign to Italy. American foreign aid flowed to Italy with great fanfare. The United States also launched a propaganda effort to persuade Italians that without American foreign aid their war-torn nation would never enjoy prosperity—in short, a vote for Communists was a vote against Marshall Plan assistance. Perhaps most important, the United States used its newly formed Central Intelligence Agency to fund covertly political parties that took an anti-Communist stand.[39] In France, too, in May 1947 the Communists were booted out of the government.

In the Cold War environment of increased overseas activism, the United States streamlined its system for making and executing national security decisions. The Truman administration and Congress cooperated to pass the National Security Act in July 1947. This act created the Department of Defense to coordinate the three armed services, a National Security Council (NSC) of top-level officials to advise the president, and the Central Intelligence Agency (CIA). The CIA was authorized to coordinate intelligence gathering and to evaluate intelligence data for the NSC (and thus for the president). From September 1947 onward the CIA presented to the NSC a monthly review of the "world situation." Although the law did not specify covert actions as a CIA duty or empower the agency to intervene secretly in the affairs of other countries, a "catchall" clause left vague the definition of its future roles: The agency could perform "such other functions and duties related to intelligence" as directed by the NSC.[40] Beginning December 1947 the NSC issued secret directives to identify the CIA's covert missions, including "psychological operations," "economic warfare," "sabotage," "subversion against hostile states," and "political and paramilitary operations" aimed primarily against the Soviet threat and Moscow's agents in Western Europe. But the CIA was also asked to counter the radical Huks, who were rebelling against the U.S.-backed Philippine government, and to further the cause of the Nationalists in China. It became clear that the agency was misnamed, for its work had as much to do with political action as with the collection of information. The CIA dispatched spies, conducted sabotage, cooperated with British intelligence, built clandestine links with anti-Soviet dissidents in Rumania and other Eastern European nations, air-dropped Ukrainian nationalists into the Soviet Union, infiltrated East Germany's government, developed counterintelligence programs to undercut Soviet agents, secretly ran the Civil Air Transport in Asia, and funded anti-Communist political groups in Western Europe. Although the CIA became famous for some of its failures, the agency gradually evolved as a major and often successful instrument of American foreign policy—as demonstrated in Italy.[41] The United States also cranked up its propaganda apparatus with the Voice of America (founded in 1942), Radio Free Europe (1950), and the U.S. Information Agency (1953).

These agencies, like so many other U.S. institutions, worked to create an American-directed international order. In Asia the task proved formidable. There the United States struggled to calm the process of decolonization, win the favor of newborn nations, shore up allies, and restore Japan to economic health and friendship with the United States. The Truman administration tried to satisfy these goals by supporting the reestablishment of French rule in Indochina; by pressing the Dutch to recognize moderate Indonesian nationalists and grant the East Indies independence, so as to head off the Communist appeal there (Indonesia became independent in 1949); and by continuing aid to the faltering Jiang regime in China. In Latin America the United States in a September 1947 treaty further rallied its neighbors into an inter-American military alliance known as the Rio Pact. In April of the following year the Organization of American States brought further structure to the U.S. sphere in Latin America. Fourteen Latin American countries hosted U.S.

military missions, as did Greece, Turkey, Iran, the Philippines, China, and Saudi Arabia. The United States helped create the Brazilian War College, whose military students were taught the American view of worldwide Communist aggression. American occupation forces in Germany, Austria, Trieste, Japan, and (until 1949) Korea and "military understandings" with Brazil, Canada, and Mexico further revealed the extent of American military expansion. The United States also decided to support the British "strategic position" in the Middle East.[42]

American planners assumed that if the Soviet Union did the unlikely and risked war with the United States, the American monopoly of the atomic bomb would eventually turn back the Soviet thrust. In the summer of 1947 the American atomic bomb program accelerated to produce more bombs. The Bikini Island atomic tests of 1946 had demonstrated just what America's weapons could do to an enemy. Atomic bombs could nullify "any nation's military effort and demolish its social and economic structures," and "in conjunction with other mass destruction weapons it is possible to depopulate vast areas of the earth's surface, leaving only vestigial remnants of man's material works."[43] In a war the atomic destruction of Soviet industrial cities, it was believed by late 1947, would force Moscow's early capitulation. The atomic bomb gave the United States a "tremendous strategic advantage," for "it is a weapon which can be used to destroy both the will and the ability of the enemy to wage war."[44]

War scares marked early 1948. In February Communists took command of the Czech government. Kennan read the event as the Soviet defensive reaction to the American economic aid offensive in Western Europe and the rebuilding of West Germany, which Stalin had to interpret as threatening to the Soviet sphere.[45] Other Kremlin watchers saw simple Soviet aggression, and the Czech coup "scared the living bejesus out of everybody."[46] Acheson remembered that events in Czechoslovakia sent "a very considerable chill" through American diplomats, who worried about a "quick [Soviet] overrunning of Europe."[47] The suspicious death of Jan Masaryk, the Czech foreign minister, particularly unsettled and angered Americans. He had leaped from his apartment to the ground below, announced the Communist government. Others, doubting suicide, leaked word from Prague that the U.S.-educated Masaryk had been pushed out his window. Son of the very first Czech president, young Masaryk stood as the symbol of a proud, independent Czechoslovakia.

Rumors shot around Washington in March that war might be imminent. "We are faced with exactly the same situation with which Britain and France were faced in 1938–39 with Hitler," Truman told his daughter.[48] A leaked March 5 cable from General Clay in Germany suggested his feeling that the Soviet Union might initiate some abrupt military action. Truman went before a special joint session of Congress and denounced the Soviets for spoiling the postwar peace and subjugating Eastern Europe. He also called for congressional passage of Marshall Plan legislation, the restoration of Selective Service, and universal military training. The conclusions reached by a study group of prominent citizens at the Council on Foreign Relations in New York reflected the impact of the early 1948 "war scare:"

When the group first assembled [in October 1947], many of its members were inclined to believe that our major difficulties in dealing with the Soviet Union were caused by its suspicion and fear of the Western powers and that this suspicion might be removed by a reasonable policy on our part, a policy which other members of the group believed to border on appeasement. . . . At the present time [April 1948], almost no member of the group continues to feel that it is worth while to attempt to lessen Soviet suspicion by concessions on our part. . . . The emphasis is now definitely on firmness.[49]

In May, dismissing them as propaganda ploys, Washington reacted negatively to Soviet overtures for negotiations to discuss ways to ease international tensions. Were the Soviets conciliatory and serious? Would talks have quieted the Cold War? The answer is unknown because discussions never got under way.[50] Diplomacy itself had become a casualty of the Cold War.

Embittering disputes in Germany also demonstrated that the two major powers, basically abandoning diplomacy, were intent upon building spheres of influence. American officials believed that an economically healthy Germany was vital to a healthy Western European economy and the success of the ERP. The Soviets wanted a weak Germany. Deep in East Germany Berlin remained divided. The Berlin crisis of 1948–1949 starkly exposed the great postwar schism. In March 1948 the three Western occupying powers announced that they intended to join Germany with the economic reconstruction of Western Europe, that the next year the three Western zones would be united as Trizonia (Britain and the United States in December 1946 had fused their German zones as Bizonia), and that the coal and steel center of the Ruhr would be controlled by the three. Four months later they introduced a currency reform program for their zones and for West Berlin. The Soviets answered by sealing Berlin off and declaring that the Western zones of Berlin were being merged economically with the Soviet zone. The United States responded to the blockade with a heroic airlift of food and supplies to Berlin. The United States also deployed B-29s to England; they were not outfitted to carry atomic bombs, but the Soviets did not know that. Such steps reassured Western Europeans who might have been leaning to neutralism because they were doubtful that the United States would ever risk war to help them. The crisis was defused in May 1949, when the Soviets, who had initiated the blockade to prevent Western efforts to spur German economic revival but who

certainly feared American strategic power, lifted the blockade without having achieved their goal. After years of hesita-
tion because of their own fears of a reconstructed Germany,
the French merged their zone with the British and American
zones in September 1949 to form the Federal Republic of
Germany, or West Germany. The Soviets in turn erected the
German Democratic Republic, or East Germany. West Germany, with its valuable industries and resources, now sat
more firmly within the American-dominated sphere.[51]

The dramatic break between Josip Tito's Yugoslavia and
the Soviet Union in mid-1948 also illustrated the division into
spheres. Moscow tried unsuccessfully to discipline this independent-minded member of its sphere as Washington warily
watched. It took American diplomats several months to accept the reality that there was a rift in the "international
Communist movement," but the United States gradually
edged toward closer commercial relations with the Balkan
country, extending loans in 1949 and military aid two years
later.[52] Still, Tito would not leave one sphere to join another.
"We have never given anybody reason to hope that we would
join the Western bloc or any other bloc for that matter," he
noted.[53]

The two major powers also built their military spheres in
Europe. In February 1948, with American encouragement
and with the Czech crisis as a backdrop, Britain, France,
Belgium, Luxembourg, and the Netherlands formed the
Brussels Pact for collective defense. The Europeans knew
that the pact could be effective only if the United States became linked to it. In fact, they initiated the agreement in
order to demonstrate to Americans that the European unity
Washington required as a precondition for U.S. participation
and aid had come into place. In the crisis atmosphere of the
Berlin blockade and airlift, this alliance eventually blos-
somed in April 1949 into the North Atlantic Treaty Organization, wherein the United States, Canada, and European na-

tions created a formal security alliance. The United States became the pivotal NATO member, providing a security shield and the funds and military equipment to make the regional association ultimately viable. The first Mutual Defense Assistance Act (October 1949) authorized nearly two billion dollars in military aid to NATO members and to Greece, Turkey, Iran, Korea, the Philippines, and China. Containment was being militarized.[54]

Although NATO was designed to serve as a deterrent, with the atomic bomb as the conspicuous weapon, few leaders were anticipating a Soviet military thrust, and few anticipated the deployment of large numbers of American troops in Europe. George F. Kennan, opposing the militarization of containment, even thought that NATO was altogether unnecessary; he made the case for a unilateral American declaration on behalf of European defense but lost the debate within the Truman administration. Kennan worried that from the perspective of the Soviets, NATO left them only two conceivable possibilities for the future: "either the firm retention of their hold on eastern and central Europe, or a military conflict." NATO, in short, would cause the Soviets to clamp down more tightly in their sphere, reduce the chances that Germany could ever be reunited, and heighten militarism on both sides. In the final analysis, he and his fellow Soviet expert Charles E. Bohlen agreed that the United States was exaggerating the Soviet threat.[55]

As Bohlen came to understand, NATO at first was designed less as a huge military establishment than as a device to lift Western European spirits, to create a secure environment that would encourage capital investment for economic recovery, to thwart internal subversives or Communists, to rearm West Germany within a European institution so that the French and others would not be as alarmed about a resurgent Germany, and to tie the NATO countries more closely to the American sphere, lest they tilt toward neutralism or appeasement. A popular saying had it that the purpose of NATO was to keep the Soviets out, the Americans in, and the Germans down. "Appeasement psychology, like isolationism in the US, is not deeply buried," Harriman believed. Thus it was necessary to create a defensive network in Western Europe to prevent a "neutral third group" from forming.[56] Europeans had to be given a "will to resist," as Acheson phrased it, or a "general stiffening of morale," as John Hickerson remarked.[57] American leaders thought that the European Recovery Program would fail unless there was a "sense of security" to accompany it.[58] "If everyone believes that the next year or next month all his efforts may be wiped out," Acheson told a Senate committee, "they are not going to make that type of effort which is necessary for recovery. So there is this very close link between recovery and confidence."[59] NATO, then, would shore up the American sphere and draw a line which the Soviets were warned not to cross. "The Atlantic Pact," Senator Tom Connally reasoned, "is but the logical extension of the principle of the Monroe Doctrine."[60]

The Soviets reacted angrily to this strengthening of their adversaries and the much-hinted plans to rearm Germany, sensing "a new, sharper phase" of the postwar struggle and condemning the pact for "trying to kindle the flames of a new war. . . ."[61] Moscow eventually tried to match NATO with its own military scheme, the Warsaw Pact (founded in 1955), just as it had answered the Marshall Plan in 1949 by organizing the Eastern European nations into the Council of Mutual Economic Assistance—an organization that had little to do with aid but much to do with Soviet control.

In 1949, too, the contest for spheres also took a decisive turn in Asia. After years of ultimately futile American aid (more than three billion dollars), Jiang Jieshi's corrupt and unpopular regime collapsed; in October Mao Zedong's Communists proclaimed the People's Republic of China. The

United States had sought to contain Mao but found Jiang an ineffective instrument. Always fearing that the Chinese Communists were "willing to lend" themselves to "Soviet purposes," as Kennan wrote in his long telegram of 1946, American leaders played down Sino-Soviet differences and the intensity of Chinese nationalism and concluded by mid-1949 that Mao's emerging government served not Chinese interests but those of the Soviet Union.[62] China, many American analysts feared, might become a springboard for Soviet aggression in Asia, a tool for spreading communism throughout the region.[63] Stalwarts of the "China lobby," such as the publisher Henry Luce and Congressman Walter Judd of Minnesota, castigated the Truman administration for having "lost" China, for having "lost" a member of the American sphere, for blocking communism in Europe but failing to do so on the Asian front. Did not the president's own containment doctrine say that the United States would act globally? Truman and Acheson could agree that China was "lost," but they blamed Jiang, not themselves, and they recognized that American resources were simply inadequate to take on a prolonged land war in China. Acheson guessed that one million American troops would be needed to stop Mao's Chinese Revolution. Once in, "how to let go of the thing?" The financial costs would be immense, funds would have to be shifted away from the European front, and, "would we have ended up enemy foreigners?"[64]

Soviet-Chinese relations were anything but cordial, and some American diplomats were already remarking on the sources of a Sino-Soviet split and calling Mao an Asian Tito. The United States, nonetheless, snubbed opportunities to talk with the Chinese Communists. "We can't be in a position of making any deal with a Communist regime," Truman told his cabinet.[65] He instructed the State Department, after a May 1949 overture from Chinese Communist leader Zhou Enlai, that there should be no "softening toward the Communists.""⁶⁶ All the while Chinese leaders publicly denounced the United States and spoke of their socialist brotherhood with the Soviets. Even though China had not actually moved into the Soviet sphere, the appearance was otherwise, especially by February 1950, with the signing of the Sino-Soviet Treaty of Friendship and Alliance. Britain, Norway, India, and other nations extended diplomatic recognition to the People's Republic, but the United States would not. The sensible argument of the British and others was that the best way to contain the Soviet Union in Asia was to nurture proud, independent-minded Chinese nationalism and thus contribute to Sino-Soviet differences. In 1950 British Prime Minister Clement Attlee told Truman that the rigid American position was mistaken. Attlee disputed the view that the Chinese Communists were mere Soviet satellites. Sometimes "you scratch a communist and find a nationalist." Truman shot back that they were "complete satellites" and that the "only way to meet communism is to eliminate it."⁶⁷ The British were appalled by the lack of careful American analysis.

If the "fall" of China was not enough, more bad news for the United States came in September 1949. An American B-29 equipped with sensitive instruments, flying over the North Pacific, detected unusually high radioactivity in the atmosphere. A study of the data led to a startling conclusion: The Soviets had exploded an atomic bomb. American leaders had thought that the Soviets were years away from such an accomplishment. Their nuclear monopoly erased, American officials huddled, worried about the future. Would the Soviets use the weapon to blackmail Western Europe, to intimidate other nations that had not yet gravitated to one of the two poles of the Cold War? Perhaps Western European neutralist tendencies would be rekindled.

Stalin actually may not have interpreted the Soviet atomic test as an unqualified advance for the Soviet Union. He was certainly not pleased that his nation's atomic success persuaded the Truman administration to accelerate its production of atomic weapons and push ahead on a thermonuclear bomb—the H-bomb. He had to worry, too, that the United States might react to the Soviet triumph with a preemptive nuclear attack.[68] After all, some prominent Americans had been noisily advocating "preventive war" for years—that is, strike the Soviet Union's military assets from the air, eliminating them before they could ever be used.[69] And the United States possessed overwhelming nuclear supremacy. The Soviet Union lacked the capability to strike the United States (except by a one-way suicide bomber mission), but the latter, by June 1950, had almost 300 atomic bombs and more than 260 nuclear-modified airplanes that could drop them on Soviet targets.[70] Whether this nuclear hegemony would serve the purposes of deterrence or compellence, or both, had yet to be answered. But there could be no doubt about America's frightening superiority and ability to kill a nation.

In late 1949 and early 1950 the Kremlin called for "peaceful coexistence." For the Soviets, the failure of the Berlin blockade and decisions in the American sphere of influence—the Marshall Plan, the creation of NATO, the launching of the expensive Mutual Defense Assistance Program, the revitalization of Germany, and Western steps toward a united command in Europe—signaled an American thrust to roll back the Soviet sphere. Now, at mid-century, the Americans looked more menacing than ever before to Soviet security. The Soviets tightened their sphere, escalating political violence and purges in Eastern Europe to expunge independent or Titoist tendencies.[71] But they also urged a Soviet-American dialogue.

Officials of the Truman administration pondered the changed world of late 1949 and early 1950. Advice was not wanting. From Britain Winston Churchill recommended a summit conference. India's Jawaharlal Nehru urged great-power compromise. UN leaders also called for Soviet-American negotiations. Communist censors permitted journalist Harrison Salisbury to send dispatches from the Soviet Union which reported that Soviet diplomats were serious about bilateral talks. Wanting no part of "appeasement," President Truman and Secretary Acheson eschewed negotiations. They would not be taken in by the Soviet "Trojan dove," announced Acheson.[72] Nor, he said, would the United States "pull down the blinds and sit in the parlor with a loaded shotgun, waiting."[73] Indeed, recognizing the destabilizing impact of the Second World War on the international system, which had contributed to "breeding grounds of conflict," Acheson vowed publicly in early 1950 that America was "playing for keeps" in a global contest with the USSR and would go around the world creating "situations of strength."[74] More sphere building seemed in the offing.

While the major antagonists squabbled in public, momentous decisions were being made in Washington. In late January 1950 Truman tersely announced that the United States intended to develop the hydrogen bomb (the world's first "superbomb" was exploded on November 1, 1952). It was not a decision American leaders were eager to make, and they took it against much advice to the contrary from scientists like J. Robert Oppenheimer and diplomats like George F. Kennan, who argued for a diminution, not an expansion, of the arms race.[75] "What a depressing world it is," remarked Acheson when he heard that scientific wisdom indicated a hydrogen bomb could be built.[76] Truman was characteristically brief when his advisers urged development of a weapon a thousand times more powerful than that which had decimated Hiroshima. "Can the Russians do it?" Truman asked. "Yes" came the answer. "In that case we have no choice."[77]

In February 1950, following the advice set out in a National Security Council paper of the previous December that the United States should create "friendly and independent" Asian states to "contain and reduce the power of the

U.S.S.R.," the United States extended diplomatic recognition to the French puppet regime of Emperor Bao Dai in Vietnam—signaling a new and ultimately costly American commitment in Asia.[78] In May the United States extended military assistance to the French for use in Indochina. As the historian Robert J. McMahon has written, U.S. policy makers "saw the French effort there as part of the West's worldwide struggle to contain communist expansion. That Ho Chi Minh's forces had indigenous roots was incontestable but also largely irrelevant."[79] Communism was communism, and the American sphere, even those parts stretching into the colonial world of America's allies, had to be shored up against a perceived Soviet onslaught. The American objective of Japanese economic restoration also explains the American decisions on Vietnam. In 1948, after occupation policies had brought political, social, and economic reforms to the defeated enemy, the United States decided to rebuild Japan as an anti-Communist bulwark in Asia. Reindustrialization was the goal, and the key to this process was markets and raw materials in Southeast Asia (and Korea). If Ho Chi Minh beat the French in Vietnam, American policy makers believed, Japan would suffer economic distress and then political instability.[80] To save Vietnam from communism was to save Japan for the American sphere.

In late January 1950 Truman had directed the State and Defense departments to undertake a thorough review of American military and foreign policy. Three months later they delivered National Security Council Paper No. 68 (NSC-68), a blunt plea for a much-expanded American defense establishment and an activist containment doctrine. Describing "a shrinking world of polarized power," this long document advised the president that the United States had to "take new and fateful decisions" to develop "a successfully functioning system among the free nations." NSC-68 depicted an aggressive communism on a global march. Relief from this menace was not imminent; only when the Soviet system itself decayed would the Kremlin's "design" be frustrated and world peace be achieved. The United States had to follow two courses: first, the development of "a healthy international community" and second, the containment of the Soviet system. This combination of expansionism and containment could be realized only if the United States launched a costly program of military spending, necessitating higher defense budgets from Congress and increased taxes. A "consensus" in the American public, NSC-68 advised, would have to be cultivated to back this dramatic buildup. The report was superficial and exaggerated, but it captured the American Cold War mentality of the time.[81]

One question, of course, was how to "sell" the recommendations of NSC-68 to the American people. As an Acheson aide recalled, "we were sweating over it, and then—with regard to NSC 68—thank God Korea came along."[82] The Korean War, which broke out in June, when the Soviet-equipped forces of North Korea moved massively into American-backed South Korea, was a "we-told-you-so" event. It seemed to confirm all the worst assumptions about Soviet aggressive proclivities, even though the Soviet role in starting the war remains unclear and enough indigenous sources existed to have triggered conflict.[83] If Stalin did not originate or plan the invasion, he certainly responded favorably to North Korean leader Kim Il Sung's call for an invasion. Kim thought the invasion would spark a revolution that would sweep the south, end Syngman Rhee's rule, and produce a reunited Korea.[84] Why did Stalin not try to block Kim's ambitions? And just how much did the Soviets know about Kim's plans and the timing? We do not know, but we can speculate that Moscow saw little risk and possible advantage. Guessing that the Americans would not intervene, Stalin could foresee a Korea reunited under a pro-Soviet government that would serve to check Mao's China. Then, too,

Kim's success in Korea might stir debate in Japan, destabilize its politics, and thus derail the American drive for the long-delayed Japanese peace treaty. The Soviets feared a resurgent Japan almost as much as a revitalized Germany. Or perhaps the Soviets reasoned that dramatic events in Korea would divert American attention from Europe and permit the Soviet Union more time to reconstruct its ailing economy, expand its nuclear arsenal, and secure its foothold in Eastern Europe. Maybe Moscow believed that such a war would make the independent-minded Chinese lean more emphatically to the Soviet camp.[85]

Americans spent little effort puzzling over Soviet motives, and they summarily dismissed the local origins of the conflict. They simply assumed it was a Soviet probing of a "situation of weakness" that threatened the Pacific rimland and might spread elsewhere. The United States soon came to the aid of an embattled member of its sphere of influence, South Korea; made further commitments to the French in Indochina, to the Philippines, and to Jiang on Formosa; and, more generally, began to act upon the counsel of NSC-68. Determined since the Second World War to expand its influence worldwide while necessarily curbing that of others— allies, Communists, neutrals, leftists, and revolutionaries alike—the United States, even as its soldiers bled in a land war in Asia, was in 1950 near the peak of its postwar power in a much-splintered world. Observers who knew hegemony when they saw it spoke of a "Pax Americana." Some wondered how long it would last.

Why did the postwar leaders of the great powers not behave in such a way as to minimize the inherent and war-induced conflict of the international system? Why did they perceive each other as threatening aggressors with whom compromise seemed impossible? And why did they develop opposing spheres of influence? Foreign policy is devised by individuals who must react not only to the external stimuli of the international environment but also to their peculiar domestic stimuli—strategic needs, economic necessities, ideological tenets, political pressures, interest groups, or powerful individuals. To determine why the United States and the Soviet Union behaved as they did after the Second World War, this study turns next to the internal characteristics of the antagonists—those fundamental and tactical elements that establish their joint responsibility for the beginnings of the Cold War.

5

ACTIVISM
American Ideology,
Economic-Strategic
Needs, and Power

THE POSTWAR international system, lacking stability and rife with tension, provided its two most prominent members with numerous opportunities to clash as they built their spheres of influence. The United States and the Soviet Union, groping toward their different definitions of the new global order, etched bold lines across the postwar world and entered a Cold War of competing spheres and alliances. "Something new had to be created," recalled Dean Acheson. The role for the United States "was one of fashioning" a new system "after the destruction of the old world."[1]

Systemic conditions, as we have seen, drew the major powers into conflict. But the responses of the

United States and the Soviet Union to the profound problems bequeathed by the Second World War were shaped by their own particular national experiences. Nations do not simply react to the international environment or to the foreign policies of other countries. They also act purposefully to expand and protect what in general they consider their national wellbeing or, in the case of the United States, to shape an "environment in which the American experiment of life can prosper."[2] Internal stimuli, then, also prompted the American and Soviet governments to "fashion" a new postwar international system of spheres of influence.

This chapter discusses the internal factors that propelled the United States to center stage in the early Cold War and launched it toward an activist, expansionist, and globalist foreign policy. Americans' ideas about themselves and the world, economic and strategic needs, and power help explain why the United States wanted to and had to become a central participant in the making of the postwar world. These fundamental factors transcended personalities or changes in administration; both Franklin D. Roosevelt and Harry S. Truman were guided by them. Foreign policy, diplomat Charles Bohlen reminded Americans, was rooted not in particular leaders but "in our American traditions and in the requirements of the national interest."[3] The *fundamentals* or *whys* of American foreign relations, therefore, were distinct from the *tactics* or *hows* of diplomacy. Policy makers, as chapters 6 and 7 demonstrate, determined not the fundamental factors themselves but how they were to be satisfied and exercised.

American ideology encompassed dreams about the new world order—what Americans wanted to avoid, sought to create, and hoped to enjoy. American "core values"—the economic and political principles Americans deemed essential to U.S. prosperity and security and hence worth fighting for—were deeply rooted in the past.[4] The list was long, and the parts were closely related: an "open door" world of equal

trade and investment opportunity; private or capitalist enterprise, as opposed to government ownership of the means of
production; self-help; labor-business cooperation to avoid
class antagonisms and to ensure higher productivity, the
guarantor of abundance; multilateralism or cooperation in
foreign commerce; freedom of the seas; the right of self-determination and self-government; democratic, constitutional
procedures; the limitation of force in international relations;
"good neighborism"; and freedom of religion and speech.
Woodrow Wilson immortalized many of these ideas in his
famous Fourteen Points, Roosevelt implanted some of them
in the Atlantic Charter, and Truman listed many of them as
the "fundamentals" of American foreign policy in his Navy
Day speech of October 1945.[5] All in all, Americans championed an "open world"—a world receptive to political democracy and capitalist enterprise.

Americans in the postwar years, remembering the trage-
dies wrought by economic depression, aggression, and war in
the 1930s, frequently spoke of the interlocking connection
between peace and prosperity. Just before his death President Roosevelt told Congress that "we cannot succeed in
building a peaceful world unless we build an economically
healthy world."[6] Indeed, "hungry people are not reasonable
people," concluded a State Department official.[7] Americans
believed that economic instability and poverty bred political
chaos, revolutionary behavior, totalitarianism, violence, aggression, and war. They assumed that deteriorating economic
conditions attracted political extremists (like Communists),
who always preyed on weaknesses and dislocations. George F.
Kennan expressed the prevailing sentiment starkly: "World
communism is like a malignant parasite which feeds only on
diseased tissue."[8] Economic reconstruction and the revival of
free-flowing world trade and finance offered one route to prosperity and, in turn, peace. "Nations which act as enemies in
the marketplace," Undersecretary of State Will Clayton

mused, "cannot long be friends at the council table."[9] President Truman stated that "in fact the three—peace, freedom, and world trade—are inseparable."[10]

Because the postwar world economy was interdependent, Americans understood that economic catastrophes did not respect national boundaries. Secretary of the Interior Julius Krug remarked that "depressions are as catching as the common cold," and W. Averell Harriman, describing the United States as the "financial and economic pivot of the world," feared that "economic stagnation in the United States would drag the rest of the world down with us."[11] To prevent contagious depressions, to ensure that the world did not plummet again into the depths of depression, the United States had to restore and maintain its primacy in the international economy. Secretary of State George C. Marshall told a Harvard University audience, in advocating the plan for economic recovery that eventually bore his name, that "it is logical that the United States should do whatever it is able to do to assist in the return of normal economic health in the world, without which there can be no political stability and no assured peace."[12] Acheson summarized the question earlier when he explained that the "great difference in our second attempt to establish a peaceful world is the wide recognition that peace is possible only if countries work together and prosper together. That is why the economic aspects are no less important than the political aspects of peace."[13] Loans, grants, the World Bank, relief aid, the Marshall Plan, the Point Four program of technical assistance to developing nations—all were designed to build an economically secure world in which hungry people did not gravitate toward "false doctrines."[14]

Americans scorned revolution, radicalism, and violent political change. Indeed, despite their rhetoric about 1776, they embraced a strong antirevolutionary ideology that explains why the United States opposed most modern revolutions.[15] The Mexican, Russian, and Chinese revolutions, for example,

represented challenges both to America's core values of liberal capitalism and political democracy and to American
overseas material interests. As a counter to revolutionary
upheaval and political chaos, Americans pointed with pride
to their Bill of Rights, their enduring Constitution, and their
stable, representative form of government. What is more,
they assumed that other peoples would want the same and
should be shown the way to such political order. Roosevelt's
special aide Harry Hopkins expressed this universalist attitude in 1945:

> I have often been asked what interests we have in Poland,
> Greece, Iran, or Korea. Well I think we have the most important
> business in the world—and indeed, the only business worthy of
> our traditions. And that is this—to do everything within our
> diplomatic power to foster and encourage democratic govern-
> ment throughout the world. We should not be timid about bla-
> zoning to the world our desire for the right of all peoples to have
> a genuine civil liberty. We believe our dynamic democracy is the
> best in the world. . . .[16]

As Hopkins's impassioned words attest, embedded in the
American ideology was the belief that the United States was
blessed with superior principles and institutions which others
should adopt. Call it missionary zeal, a sense of manifest
destiny, conceit, arrogance, or chauvinism, Americans had it:
a self-satisfaction that they were an exceptional people. This
self-image, of course, obscured blatant violations of American ideals, evident, for example, in racial segregation at
home. In fact, the notion of American exceptionalism was
laced with racism—with assumptions about a "hierarchy of
race" that placed white Americans of Anglo-Saxon stock at
the top.[17]

The Puritan fathers expressed the self-flattering American
view when they delivered their lofty sermons against the per-

fidies of the Old World; American rebels in 1776 echoed the belief in exceptionalism when they cast off the British yoke; President James Monroe espoused his "doctrine" in 1823 to emphasize the uniqueness of the Western Hemisphere; Woodrow Wilson insisted in the era of the First World War that America was a beacon of sanity for mankind; and during the Second World War the United States became the "arsenal of democracy." "All nations succumb to fantasies of innate superiority," the historian Arthur M. Schlesinger, Jr., has written. "When they act on these fantasies, as the Spanish did in the sixteenth century, the French in the seventeenth, the English in the eighteenth, the Germans and Japanese and Russians and Americans in the twentieth, they tend to become international menaces."[18] Certainly postwar Americans never classified themselves as menaces. Rather, they saw themselves as benefactors, celebrants of the American success story, spreading their economic and political riches to the less fortunate through world leadership.[19] "The missionary strain in the character of Americans," a scoffing British Embassy in Washington reported, "leads many of them to feel that they have now received a call to extend to other countries the blessings with which the Almighty has endowed their own."[20]

Lessons from the immediate past also held a place in the constellation of American ideas. Dean Acheson believed that "only the United States had the power to grab hold of history and make it conform."[21] What history? The history of depression, political extremism, aggression, and war in the twentieth century. Americans recalled that they had jilted the League of Nations and had courted isolationism and an appeasement policy in the dreadful 1930s. Many Americans blamed themselves for permitting Japanese militarists, German storm troopers, and Italian Fascists to march and plunder. "History has bestowed on us a solemn responsibility," Truman remarked in 1944. "We shall, we must, be a mighty force at the peace conference. We failed before to give a genuine peace—we dare not fail this time.''[22] It was America's second chance—the opportunity to throw off the mistakes of the past and claim its rightful first ranking among nations. The United States would permit no more Munichs, no more appeasement, no more compromise with totalitarianism, no more depression, and no more Pearl Harbors.[23]

Leadership and preparedness became the new bywords. "We must continue to be a military nation if we are to maintain leadership among other nations," Truman told his cabinet in his worry about the dangers of demobilizing too rapidly. Secretary Byrnes added that "we must not make the mistake made after the last war."[24] As early as 1944 disapproving British diplomats observed that "Americans are slowly swinging towards the belief that since the British 'have made such a mess of the world' it is America's painful duty to take charge of everything."[25]

As an avid reader of historical works President Truman believed that history "has some extremely valuable lessons to teach."[26] The lessons he drew from history often reached as far back as the days of ancient Greece, but his immediate instruction came from the tumultuous events of the decade of the Great Depression. He and other Americans feared that the 1940s would be an ugly replay of the 1930s, and they came to believe that the Soviets were seizing the staff of aggressive totalitarianism wrested from the Nazis in World War II. NBC news analyst Clifton Utley expressed a popular postwar assumption: "If we run out again we will create a vacuum."[27] The experience of pre-1945 American-Russian relations helped conjure up the image of a self-interested, recalcitrant, revolutionary, untrustworthy nation bent on destroying Western capitalism—a burly, bewhiskered Bolshevik whacking away at the foundations of world order. The iconoclastic Bolshevik Revolution, the seizure of foreign-owned property, the refusal to honor czarist debt obligations, antagonism between Americans and Communists during the Allied intervention in the Russian civil war, anticapitalist propaganda, the ineffectiveness of American diplomatic recognition in 1933 in smoothing relations, and the gruesome Stalinist purges all served to sear this image on the American mind. The Nazi-Soviet Pact of 1939, furthermore, convinced Americans that Nazi Germany and Soviet Russia were really two of a kind, that as the *Wall Street Journal* put it, "the principal difference between Mr. Hitler and Mr. Stalin is the size of their respective mustaches."[28]

FBI Director J. Edgar Hoover, among others, coined a phrase for this simple Communist/Nazi analogy: "Red Fascism."[29] "There isn't any difference in totalitarian states," asserted Truman. "I don't care what you call them, Nazi, Communist or Fascist. . . ."[30] As Moscow spread its influence over Eastern Europe after the war, Americans warned against another system of "satellite" nations. "It looks like the same pattern that Hitler adopted in 1936 when he began to take over the small countries around him," brooded one congressman.[31] General John R. Deane, head of the American military mission to the Soviet Union during the war, wrote in his 1947 memoir that even the marching style of Soviet soldiers "closely resembled the [German] goose-step, with arms rigid and legs kicked stiffly to the front. . . ."[32] Thus, explained Americans, aggressive communism was succeeding aggressive nazism; in this way the 1930s and 1940s became linked in the American mind. Totalitarianism was once again thought to be roaming—this time as a Russian bear—far beyond its own habitat. "The image of a Stalinist Russia," Kennan argued a decade after popularization of the analogy, "poised and yearning to attack the West, and deterred only by our possession of atomic weapons, was largely a creation of the Western imagination."[33] Imagination or not, distortion or not, Americans imbibed and nourished this component of their postwar ideology, one of the fundamental forces making

an activist American foreign policy seem imperative in order
to prevent World War III.

Another wellspring of American foreign policy was the
fundamental factor of economic-strategic needs—those requirements of the domestic economy and national security
which had to be met in order to maintain American well-
being. Throughout their history Americans had been a
proud, successful trading people. Foreign commerce had always constituted a profitable segment of their economy, and
in the War of 1812 and again in World War I the United
States had been willing to fight to uphold the principle of
freedom of the seas for its merchants. In the 1930s Secretary
of State Cordell Hull, through the Reciprocal Trade Agreements Program and the Export-Import Bank, had attempted
to maintain America's prominent position in the global economy. Foreign trade was more than a pocketbook issue; from
the American perspective foreign trade contributed to economic health, which permitted them, and other countries as
well, to enjoy stable, democratic government. As the historian David Potter explained in his book *People of Plenty,*
Americans had long considered themselves democratic because they were prosperous and prosperous because they
were democratic.[34] Foreign trade held strategic importance,
too, helping the United States acquire vital raw materials
essential to the production of defense goods. Americans assumed in the peace and prosperity idiom, moreover, that
foreign trade created bonds of understanding among nations,
reducing chances for breaches of peace.

In the postwar era the United States was the largest sup-
plier of goods to world markets, with exports valued at ten
billion dollars in both 1945 and 1946 and fourteen billion
dollars a year later.[35] By 1947 the United States accounted for
one-third of the world's total exports and about half of the
world's industrial output. "Any serious failure to maintain
this flow," declared an assistant secretary of state, "would

put millions of American businessmen, farmers, and workers out of business."[36] American leaders, fearing a postwar recession, believed that successful and expanding foreign trade spelled the difference between depression and prosperity. Statistics buttressed such thinking. Although the value of exports seldom climbed above 10 percent of the gross national product, that seemingly low figure could be misleading. Key industries, such as automobiles, trucks, coal, machine tools, and steel, relied upon foreign outlets for their economic health. One-eighth of Monsanto Chemical's sales were to customers abroad, and General Motors shipped about 10 percent of its products overseas. Nearly 20 percent of American steelworkers owed their jobs to steel exports; the figure for coal miners was 18 percent. In 1947 about half of America's wheat was shipped abroad, and surpluses of citrus fruits, eggs, cotton, rice, and tobacco also needed foreign markets. Secretary of the Treasury John Snyder persuasively pointed up the significance of foreign trade: "The importance of U.S. exports to the American economy is evidenced by the fact that they exceed in volume such important single elements of the national product as expenditures on producers' durable equipment, consumers' expenditures on durable goods, the net changes in business inventories, the total expenditures by State and local governments or even private construction."[37]

Analysts predicted dire consequences should economic dislocations abroad, especially in Europe, inhibit foreign buyers from purchasing American products. The Committee for Economic Development, a group of businessmen heading America's largest corporations, anticipated "great readjustment, much inefficient production and a lower standard of living," and the president of the Chamber of Commerce, Eric Johnston, warned that a sharp drop in foreign trade "would mean vast population shifts, and . . . new ways of subsistence would have to be found for entire geographic regions."[38] Truman himself joined the "peace and prosperity" ideology with economic-strategic needs in a 1946 statement: "A large volume of soundly based international trade is essential if we are to achieve prosperity in the United States, build a durable structure of world economy and attain our goal of world peace and prosperity."[39]

American leaders also emphasized that exports paid for imports that were vital to American industry and to the military establishment. In many categories of raw materials the United States was a "have-not" nation. The director of the Bureau of Mines reported domestic deficiencies in zinc, tin, mercury, manganese, lead, cobalt, tungsten, chromite, industrial diamonds, nickel, bauxite, and copper—or a total of more than fifty materials.[40] Imported materials from fifty-seven different countries were necessary to American steel production. Truman noted that strategic raw materials from abroad contributed to a major new weapon in the American arsenal: "Without foreign trade . . . it would be difficult, if not impossible, for us to develop atomic energy."[41] Oil also held both economic and strategic importance. A Senate committee concluded that "the United States, accounting for about two-thirds of the entire world's petroleum consumption, is compelled to control an adequate share of foreign oil production and reserves to insure high living standards in its domestic economy," and Petroleum Administrator for War Harold Ickes worried whether the United States would be able to "oil another war in the future."[42] Petroleum, as World Wars I and II demonstrated and as the Japanese knew before Pearl Harbor, moved tanks, ships, and airplanes alike. Many American leaders feared that the Second World War, in its insatiable thirst for oil, had depleted American resources and that postwar consumption would outstrip supply. "Oil, enough oil, within our certain grasp seemed ardently necessary to greatness and independence in the twentieth century" was Herbert Feis's summary of American thinking, although he considered the fears exaggerated.[43]

America's security needs demanded not only economic expansion in order to satisfy raw materials requirements but also a global military watch. With the two vast oceans no longer providing natural defensive barriers, with the advent of atomic weapons, the air age, and wide-ranging naval fleets, Americans embraced a "preparedness ideology."[44] They believed it necessary to secure outlying bases to protect approaches to the United States and to permit the American military to police or deter disorders far from home. The shrinkage of the globe altered American strategic thinking. In a world contracted by science, events in distant lands once considered remote or tangential to American interests held greater significance than ever before for U.S. security. Americans worried about many more Pearl Harbors—surprise attacks from the air. "If you imagine two or three hundred Pearl Harbors occurring all over the United States," prophesied Assistant Secretary of State A. A. Berle, "you will have a rough picture of what the next war might look like. . . ."[45]

Because frontiers had been extended, because nations were brought nearer one another, and because the world had shrunk, the major powers coveted bases far from home, much as the United States had sought and acquired bases in the Caribbean in the early twentieth century to protect the Panama Canal. A 1946 Joint Chiefs of Staff (JCS) report emphasized that atomic bombings could be prevented only by intercepting the "carrying vehicles." Thus defense "must begin beyond" a nation's borders. In military parlance, "forward bases" far from the United States had to be acquired.[46] The JCS approved a list of twenty foreign locations where American military air transit rights were desired. Sites as far-flung as Algiers (Algeria), Cairo (Egypt), Dhahran (Saudi Arabia), Karachi (India), Saigon (French Indochina), Acapulco (Mexico), San José (Guatemala), and the Cook Islands (New Zealand) came within the JCS's definition of needs.[47]

The State Department itself formulated an extensive list of foreign bases considered "essential" or "required" for national security. Burma, Canada, the Fiji Islands, New Zealand, Cuba, Greenland, Ecuador, French Morocco, Senegal, Iceland, Liberia, Panama, Peru, and the Azores, among others, earned spots in this impressive example of the postwar American global perspective.[48] Many of these areas, in fact, became sites for the American military. Admiral Chester W. Nimitz reasoned that "the ultimate security of the United States depends in major part on our ability to control the Pacific Ocean," and he joined Truman administration officials in a policy of retaining under American control the Pacific islands (Carolines, Marshalls, and Marianas) captured from the Japanese.[49] "You mean to put them [American naval forces] everywhere?" Senator Claude Pepper of Florida asked Navy Secretary James Forrestal on the telephone. "Wherever there is a sea," Forrestal crisply replied.[50]

Nations seek to fulfill their ideological preferences and to realize their economic-strategic needs. Americans knew that principles could not be defended and extended, and that needs could not be satisfied, unless the United States possessed sufficient power. Another fundamental of American foreign policy was power. "International politics, like all politics," Hans J. Morgenthau has written, "is a struggle for power."[51] Power is the facilitator, the enforcer, the symbol of greatness, and the ability to modify the conduct of other states or to prevent them from influencing you. Power, of course, is not absolute, and it never reaches as far as the nation possessing it would like it to reach because of obstacles thrown up by the international system and the hostility of other nations. Priorities have to be set, but no nation possessing power is willing to give it up. The very existence of power thrusts a nation into the maelstrom of world politics. "Power like wealth must be either used or lost," claimed James Forrestal.[52] "Evasion of major international issues is a real possibility for Costa Rica," concluded a National Security Council paper. "For the U.S. it is an illusion. Our silence is as loud as our words."[53]

Foreign commentators sensed America's flush of power, wondered how it would be used, and often compared it to imposing members of the animal kingdom. *The Economist* (London) editorialized in 1947 that World War II "has enormously increased the scale upon which the United States now towers above its fellows. Like mice in the cage of an elephant, they follow with apprehension the movements of the mammoth. What chance would they stand if it were to begin to throw its weight about, they who are in danger even if it only decides to sit down?"[54] From the perspective of official London, the historian Christopher Thorne has written, the United States' quest for strategic predominance "began to take on some of the less endearing characteristics of a runaway rhinoceros."[55] Indeed, the British ambassador to Washington drew London's attention to "America's consciousness of superior power, or as one columnist puts it, 'her capacity for Promethean rule,' " and remarked, with a touch of ridicule, that Americans were "accustomed enough at home to the idea of bigger and better elephants. . . ."[56] Predominant power, not a balance of power, is what the United States sought.

Churchill grew annoyed with American protestations against the "power politics" of other nations while the United States flexed its own international muscle: "Is having a Navy twice as strong as any other 'power politics'? Is having an overwhelming Air Force, with bases all over the world, 'power politics'? Is having all the gold in the world buried in a cavern 'power politics'?"[57] Actually Americans had always known how to exercise power, their self-effacing lamentations to the contrary notwithstanding, and their expansionist record in the nineteenth and twentieth centuries stood as salient testimony. In the postwar world the foundations of their national power ensured that they would want to and had to advance that record.

Economic power, political power, and military power constituted the elements of national strength for Americans. Their vast economic power gave them a heady place in the world economy and influence over war-torn nations eager for relief and reconstruction funds. Harriman assumed in 1944 that "economic assistance is one of the most effective weapons" with which the United States could affect events in Russia's developing sphere in Eastern Europe.[58] Prime Minister Attlee recognized the impact of this economic power when his government asked Washington for a postwar loan. "We weren't in a position to bargain," he said. "We had to have the loan."[59] Soviet official Andrei Zhdanov summarized an assumption common to both Communists and non-Communists: "Of all the capitalist powers, only one—the United States—emerged from the war not only unweakened, but even considerably stronger economically and militarily."[60] America was the "workshop of the world."[61] This prominent economic status carried responsibility. "The United States is the only country in the world today," Secretary Marshall announced in 1948, "which has the economic power and productivity to furnish the needed assistance."[62] President Truman minced no words: "We are the giant of the economic world."[63]

Americans were proud that they had more airplanes, more automobiles, more refrigerators, and more bathtubs than anybody else. They produced and used more coal and steel than any other people. Their corporations controlled 42 percent of the proved oil reserves in the Middle East. By 1948 Americans produced about 41 percent of the world's goods and services. Their abundant fields yielded an agricultural surplus to feed a hungry world. The president boasted that the United States had "fifty percent of the world's industrial machine and produces two-thirds of the world's combined

industrial output. We are richly endowed with natural resources. We possess the mobility, the friends, and the goodwill . . . that enable us to supplement our supply of raw
materials with purchases throughout the world." In short,
Truman asserted in 1947, "we have it in our power today
either to make the world economy work or, simply by failing
to take the proper action, to allow it to collapse."[64]

The United States also enjoyed enviable international political power. As Truman said, America possessed "friends."
The members of the American sphere of influence, in Asia,
Latin America, the Middle East, and Europe, voted with the
United States within international organizations. In the Security Council of the United Nations the United States did not
have to exercise its veto power until 1970. Its friends and
clients in the council supported American positions with majority votes, therein bestowing a "hidden veto" power upon
the United States. The Soviet Union, in contrast, could rally
many fewer votes from its smaller sphere and had to resort
conspicuously to the veto—105 times between 1946 and
1969. As it was, a large percentage of the Soviet vetoes were
rendered impotent by American political power exerted
somewhere else in the United Nations.[65] For example, with
the help of the usually loyal votes of some twenty Latin
American governments, the United States commanded results in the General Assembly. In the period 1945–1966, the
United States repeatedly received a two-thirds majority vote
for its positions on Cold War issues.[66]

The United States also occupied a prominent position in
the United Nations Relief and Rehabilitation Administration, the agency launched by forty-four nations in 1943 to
help feed, clothe, and dispense medicine to the hundreds of
thousands of people uprooted by the war in Europe and Asia.
The United States provided three-quarters of UNRRA's four-
billion-dollar expenditure before the organization was dis-
banded in 1947. Yet although the United States carried

weight in high echelons, it did not control distribution in the field. UNRRA existed only so long as the United States was willing to fund the body. The Truman administration killed UNRRA because it decided that the United States should unilaterally distribute the benefits of its economic power to maximize political influence, rather than suffer the dissipation of that power in an international association. Acheson explained in 1947 that henceforth the United States would extend relief aid "in accordance with our judgment and supervised with American personnel."[67]

In both the International Bank for Reconstruction and Development (World Bank) and the International Monetary Fund, the United States enjoyed predominant power. Created in 1944 at the Bretton Woods Conference, these institutions were only nominally "international." They became instruments of American diplomacy because the bank and the fund were located in Washington, D.C., Americans sat as key officers (the president of the World Bank has always been an American), and the dollar was in great demand (all dollar loans from these organizations had to be approved by U.S. officials). Because the United States was the largest subscriber, moreover, it held one-third of the votes. In the early years of the World Bank, loans went to American friends like France and Denmark and were denied to countries closely linked to the Soviet Union, such as Poland and Czechoslovakia. A Bretton Woods negotiator recognized that the bank and the fund came to resemble "the operation of power politics rather than of international cooperation—except that the power employed is financial instead of military and political."[68]

"The surest guaranty that no nation will dare again to attack us," Truman stated shortly after World War II, "is to remain strong in the only kind of strength an aggressor can understand—military power." Military power, he knew, meant more than soldiers and armaments. He pointed to the productive power of American farms, mines, and factories and the abundance of natural resources as important parts of the totality of American military power. Indeed, the "United States now has a fighting strength greater than at any time in our history. It is greater than that of any other nation in the world."[69] The administration endured public pressure to "bring the boys home" hurriedly after the war, but despite demobilization, the United States still maintained the world's largest navy, an unmatched air force of long-range capabilities, a peacetime army far larger than ever before, and a monopoly of the deadliest weapon of all, the atomic bomb.[70] National security was ensured, and America's adversaries were at bay.

With its two-ocean navy, America was the postwar mistress of the seas. "The United States Navy faced no challenge in any class of vessel by any power in any ocean or sea," the historian Kenneth J. Hagan has written.[71] The president waxed proud in October 1945, when he detailed American naval superiority at the end of the war: "The fleet, on V-J Day, consisted of twelve hundred warships, more than fifty thousand supporting and landing craft, and over forty thousand navy planes. By that day, ours was a sea power never before equalled in the history of the world." Even after demobilization, he went on, "the United States will still be the greatest naval power on earth."[72]

Truman also applauded America's air force. In the "air age," Americans flew supreme, able to defend American skies, to deliver destruction to others, and to frighten would-be aggressors. In 1943 Hollywood producer Walt Disney released a film, *Victory Through Air Power,* which helped herald the new era and popularize the crippling capabilities of air power. According to one film critic, Disney impressed the "lay mind with the seemingly limitless potential of the airplane as an offensive instrument of war." Viewers of the dramatic film—including Roosevelt and Churchill, who viewed it one evening at the 1944 Quebec Conference—saw in "a roaring blaze of [T]echnicolor" the leveling of Japan by tons of air-delivered bombs.[73] Aware of their air superiority, American officials could agree with Harriman's statement in 1947 that American air power served to deter the Soviet military because "there is only one thing which the leaders of the Soviet Union fear, and that is the American air force."[74]

American armed forces joined naval and air power to enhance the impressive military standing of the United States. Total American military personnel numbered 3 million in 1946 (down from the wartime peak of 12 million), 1.6 million in 1947, 1.4 million in 1948, and 1.6 million in 1949. The army, which had major occupation responsibilities in Germany and Japan, accounted for much of this total.[75] Civilian and military officials often complained that the army was undersize and unready for combat, but an annoyed president trimmed the budget requests of all three armed services and lectured them that they exaggerated their needs.[76] He believed that the American military was adequate to meet security needs. Even so, the federal budget reflected the new sense of military preparedness. In fiscal year 1947 defense expenditures represented one-third of the budget, "fabulously large compared to the prewar defense budgets."[77] Secretary Forrestal was one who repeatedly complained about military inadequacies, but at the same time he boasted about U.S. supremacy. Like Truman, he knew that America's industrial strength also counted in judgments of military power, and he believed that large foreign aid programs— even though they might divert funds from the military— should receive priority. "As long as we can outproduce the world, can control the sea and can strike inland with the atomic bomb," Forrestal reasoned, "we can assume certain risks [spending less than the desired military appropriations so that funds could be spent instead in foreign aid programs] otherwise unacceptable in an effort to restore world trade, to

restore the balance of power—military power—and to eliminate some of the conditions which breed war."[78] Military
strength, then, lay not just in arms and men but in an
economically healthy, politically stable world.

The atomic bomb: Everyone mentioned it and stood in
awe of it. This novel weapon had proved its deadly power at
Hiroshima and Nagasaki, but it appears that in the postwar
era its power became more symbolic than real, more diplomatic than military. Truman was not sure that "it can ever be
used," and of course, it never was used again in battle.[79] Still,
American leaders thought their monopoly of the atomic device, which prevailed until the Soviets exploded their own in
1949, bestowed advantages on the United States. The bomb,
they hoped, would serve to restrain the Soviets and might
prompt them to make diplomatic concessions, especially over
Eastern Europe. The Joint Chiefs of Staff and General
Dwight D. Eisenhower agreed that the "existence of the
atomic bomb in our hands is a deterrent, in fact, to aggression in the world."[80] Harriman reported from Moscow in the
fall of 1945 that the Soviets themselves "recognized it was an
offset to the power of the Red Army. This must have revived
their old feeling of insecurity."[81]

Secretary Byrnes articulated more fully than most the potential diplomatic power of the atomic bomb. He "looks to
having the presence of the bomb in his pocket" as an "im-
plied threat" at the London Foreign Ministers Conference
(1945), Secretary of War Henry L. Stimson grimly recorded
in his diary.[82] At that stormy conference itself V. M. Molotov,
as if he had been reading Stimson's private diary, asked
Byrnes if he had an atomic bomb in his side pocket. Byrnes
quipped that southerners "carry our artillery in our hip
pocket. If you don't cut out all this stalling and let us get
down to work, I am going to pull an atomic bomb out of my
hip pocket and let you have it."[83] This apparently light moment carried heavy meaning: The United States was thinking

about the marvels of its atomic power, a point that put other nations on edge.

The United States did not have many atomic bombs at the beginning—probably seven in 1946, thirteen in 1947, and fifty in 1948. The numbers grew to nearly three hundred in 1950 and one thousand in 1953.[84] But the United States did not need many atomic bombs during the period of its monopoly, nor did it require many delivery aircraft (it had about twenty-five nuclear-modified B-29s in 1946). As Truman said, the U.S. atomic stockpile in 1946 "was enough to win a war."[85] This arsenal, it was believed, would also serve to deter the Soviets from starting a war. "American initiatives in 1947, 1948, and 1949, especially regarding Germany," the historian Melvyn P. Leffler has noted, "were premised on the belief that Soviet leaders were not likely to opt for a war they knew they could not win."[86] In the first Cold War years, moreover, had American leaders insisted that greater numbers of nuclear weapons were essential to meet their objectives, they most likely could have been produced faster, as the jump from the 1947 to the 1948 figures suggests.

The atomic bomb may have deterred war between the United States and the Soviet Union, but it also seems that the atomic monopoly impeded rather than advanced American diplomatic goals. Byrnes, for example, in the spring of 1946, complained that the weapon interfered with his efforts to negotiate peace treaties with Hitler's defeated satellites in Eastern Europe. At the March 22, 1946, cabinet meeting, Byrnes said he believed that the forthcoming Bikini atomic test was "ill-advised" and should be postponed—or abandoned altogether. The reason: The dramatic explosion in the South Pacific would disrupt the Paris Peace Conference. He remarked further that the operation had "developed into a big show on the strength of the atomic dictator"—the United States.[87] Holstered or unholstered, the atomic bomb had become a spectacular symbol of American technological ingenuity and supremacy—of American power. The United States would not turn the weapon over to an international control authority. "When we get down to cases," Truman remarked, "is any one of the Big Powers—are we?—going to give up these locks and bolts which are necessary to protect our house . . . against possible outlaw attack . . . until the community is sufficiently stable? Clearly we are not. Nor are the Soviets."[88]

Americans celebrated the supremacy of their national power and the superiority of their ideology. They were cognizant of the weight they carried in international affairs but not necessarily of the reactions that power might trigger.[89] They believed themselves to be exceptional, and foreign observers frequently reminded them of their rare status. American diplomats knew, too, that the prominent and activist international position of the United States spawned the envy and resentment of others. Byrnes mentioned that Americans appeared to others to "hog leadership," and John Foster Dulles came back from Europe in mid-1947 to report that "even in countries like Britain and France there is rising apprehension at our alleged 'aggressive imperialism.' "[90] Americans seemed surprised that their power and intentions evoked hostility and suspicion in others.

In the fall of 1945 Truman's cabinet discussed the question of universal military training. One of the participants questioned why the United States had to "police the world." The president, a former county official in Missouri, declared emphatically that America must shoulder this responsibility, for "in order to carry out a just decision the courts must have marshals" and "in order to collect monies for county governments it has been found necessary to employ a sheriff."[91] Joseph Jones, who helped write the momentous Truman Doctrine speech, captured the popular postwar American mood: "The moment is ours."[92] Exuberant, self-confident, proud of their heritage and ideals, instructed by lessons from the past, needing foreign trade, developing a global strategic outlook, and flushed with power, Americans wanted to and felt they had to seize the moment—"to grab hold of history and make it conform." They ultimately failed to do so because their power was not omnipotent but relative—with its effectiveness dependent upon local and international conditions—and because a bold and hostile Soviet Union, with another vision of history, arose as a challenger.

6

TOUGHNESS
Truman's Style of Diplomacy

WHEN the Soviet commissar for foreign affairs heard about the death of Franklin D. Roosevelt, he rushed in the dark of the early-morning hours to Spaso House, the American ambassador's residence in Moscow. V. M. Molotov was visibly shaken and pensive, wondering about the new man in the White House to whom the powers of government now belonged.[1] The British ambassador to the Soviet Union also worried. Archibald Clark-Kerr told Ambassador Harriman on April 13, 1945, the day after the president's death, that he was deeply troubled about the future of world affairs, because "so much that matters was gathered in the hands and heart of that man."[2]

The president of the United States in the 1940s, and after, was correctly recognized as the supreme decision maker and chief diplomat in the creation and conduct of American foreign policy. Roosevelt's successor, Truman, put it bluntly: "I make American foreign policy."[3] His assistant Clark M. Clifford once observed that the American government is a chameleon which takes its color from the character and personality of the president.[4] As the political scientist Franz Schurmann has written, the president transforms "ideological beliefs into structures of organizational power."[5] The principal diplomat, commander in chief of the military establishment, head of the National Security Council, primary authority over the Central Intelligence Agency, leader of his political party, chief executive of a huge bureaucracy, and initiator or vetoer of legislation, the president sits at the pinnacle of authority and influence, not only in the nation but in the world as well. By negotiating executive agreements instead of treaties (the latter require the Senate's approval), the president, moreover, enjoys discretionary authority and an aggrandizement of his powers in the making of foreign policy. Whether he exercises all the powers at his command and whether he is able to persuade others to follow his preferences depend upon the particular individual and the prevailing milieu. Most postwar presidents have enjoyed preponderate power in the American checks and balances system.

To emphasize presidential mastery of the American foreign policy process is to beg significant questions. Does it really matter who is president—a Roosevelt or a Truman? This question springs from one that humanists and social scientists have been grappling with for centuries: In the great scheme of things, do individuals count? If we accept the proposition, which was spelled out in the last chapter, that certain fundamentals stand at the heart of American foreign policy, we could argue that those basic beliefs and needs bind any president and even dictate his decisions. In other words, he has little freedom to make choices whereby his distinctive style, personality, experience, and intellect shape America's role and position in international relations in a way that is

uniquely his. It has often been said that a government official's behavior is a function not of his or her individual traits
but rather of the office that he or she holds and that the office
is circumscribed by the larger demands of the national interest, rendering individuality inconsequential. It has been argued, moreover, that to attribute importance to particular
individuals in international diplomacy, the scholar must
prove that other officials in similar posts would have acted
differently. These are compelling points, and they deserve
consideration.

By whom and how diplomacy is made and conducted
count in any comprehensive view of the Cold War. Conduct
or style (tactics) directly influence foreign leaders and hence
help shape the chances for success or failure in negotiations.
Harriman believed that "personal relationships could influence—even if they could not determine—the affairs of nations. . . ." In the last days of the 1944 presidential campaign
Harriman, as a Democrat and ambassador to the Soviet
Union, blended his political and diplomatic preferences when
he publicly told the American people that Roosevelt had
earned the confidence of foreign leaders, "an invaluable asset
in obtaining decisions which will further our interests and
build the kind of world in which we want to live. This confidence we can ill afford to lose at this critical and formative
time."[6] No doubt Harriman had in mind the working relationship between Roosevelt and Stalin and Stalin's own ear-
nest hope that the president would be reelected.[7]

Harriman's essential point—and the premise of this chapter—is that how people behave affects how others react to
them. How people behave influences the outcome of negotiations. If we shout or lecture, we may not be listened to. If we
are rude, others may take offense. If we do not explain ourselves well, we may be misunderstood. If we mislead, we may
never be trusted. If we take off a shoe and pound it on the
table, we may be considered emotionally unstable and unreli-

able. If we stalk out of a meeting in protest, we may be thought intemperate or uninterested in serious talks. If we strut in a haughty manner, others may be put off. If we are self-righteously rigid, others may decide not to talk with us. The opposites of these negatives, on the other hand, may facilitate communication and spur agreement. How we express ourselves—the words we use—may determine how persuasive we are. For example, when a government report on U.S. relations with nations rich in raw materials used the word "exploit" rather than "develop" to describe American purposes, a State Department official objected, for "the flavor of a word can make a great deal of difference in the effect of the document on sensitive readers in other countries."[8] George F. Kennan, who probably exaggerated the significance of diplomatic style but who nevertheless knew it held an prominent place, has written that "it is axiomatic in the world of diplomacy that methodology and tactics assume an importance by no means inferior to concept and strategy."[9] How something is done and who does it matter.

Throughout the Cold War American and Soviet leaders have frequently disparaged the style and personnel of the other, bemoaning the apparent negative impact upon negotiations. "If Roosevelt lived," Molotov mused in late April 1945, there would be much less chance of "complications" arising in Soviet-American relations.[10] Several months later he complained that Truman, unlike Roosevelt, did not hold a "friendly" attitude toward the Soviet Union.[11] In May, to allay such Soviet wariness about his administration, Truman sent the ailing Harry Hopkins—Roosevelt's trusted adviser and close friend—to meet with Premier Joseph Stalin. Stalin held Hopkins in high esteem because the American had made an exhausting trip to Russia in 1941 to demonstrate U.S. support for the Soviet Union after Germany's military attack of that June. The Soviet leader remembered that gesture, and as a result, the Hopkins-Stalin talks of 1945 proceeded in an amiable and constructive manner, providing one of the few positive moments in the emerging Cold War.[12] The American assumption had been that the outcome of this special assignment might be affected by whom the president chose to be his emissary.

Two years later Dean Acheson revealed how much he himself was affected by style. This polished, aristocratic public servant found the Soviets insulting, coarse, and offensive. "Senator," he remarked at a congressional hearing, "I think it is a mistake to believe that you can, at any time, sit down with the Russians and solve questions." He pressed the point: "You cannot sit down with them."[13] Out of office he was more outspoken: "I got along with everybody who was housebroken. But I was never very close to the Russians. They were abusive; they were rude. I just didn't like them."[14] It is not surprising, then, that Acheson was one among a growing number of top American officials who presided over a gradual abandonment of diplomacy itself in the Cold War.

Acheson's contemporaries thought that tactics were important, and they spent considerable energy in scrutinizing the personalities, methods, and styles of their adversaries and commenting at length about personal preferences. The international system was inherently conflict-ridden, and the fundamental characteristics of the United States and the Soviet Union determined basic interests and policies, but individuals and their styles exacerbated tensions and failed to blunt the sharper edges of the Soviet-American confrontation. At least we know that both Americans and Soviets thought so. Systemic disorders and fundamental needs and beliefs foment profound diplomatic crises, but key individuals, operating with their particular traits, interpret the crises and make choices that determine whether they are kept manageable and defused quickly or are prolonged and escalated to the brink of war. Top diplomats decide whether to talk or not. To understand the sources of Cold War conflict, then, we must fathom not only the international system and national needs, ideology, and power but also the personalities and styles of important decision makers.

Decision making in the Roosevelt and Truman administrations was concentrated in the hands of the president and a small circle of advisers. Roosevelt was a devoted practitioner of personal diplomacy, often neglecting to inform the Department of State about his plans and decisions. Roosevelt believed that through his magnetic personality and contagious charm he could establish, as Harriman recalled, "a close personal relationship with Stalin in wartime, to build confidence among the Kremlin leaders that Russia, now an acknowledged major power, could trust the West."[15] As Roosevelt told Churchill, "I think I can personally handle Stalin better than either your Foreign Office or my State Department."[16] Roosevelt may not have been wrong. Stalin often deferred to Roosevelt but did not hesitate to "stick a knife into Churchill whenever he had the chance."[17] Roosevelt's death in 1945 denies us a true testing of the credibility of his personalized diplomacy, but we do know that the Soviets sensed a serious change in style and attitude with the entrance of Harry S. Truman into the White House.[18]

Molotov witnessed the difference between the two presidents firsthand and early. On April 23, 1945, little more than a week after FDR's death, Truman met with the Soviet commissar. The new president sharply scolded the Soviet diplomat and demanded compliance with the Yalta agreement providing for the reorganization of the Polish government. Molotov insisted that the Soviets were working toward that goal. Truman pressed again, charging Moscow with failing to honor its side of the bargain. The usually blunt and irascible Molotov turned "a little ashy."[19] According to Truman, the Soviet diplomat said, "I have never been talked to like that in my life." Truman shot back in Dutch uncle style: "Carry out your agreements and you won't get talked to like that."[20]

Molotov stormed out of the White House. Harriman regretted that the president had gone "at it so hard," and Stimson
commented on Truman's "rather brutal frankness," but Truman himself gloated over what he called his "tough method":
"I gave it to him straight 'one-two to the jaw.' I let him have it
straight."[21] Truman's dressing down of the Soviet foreign
secretary suggested to officials in both Washington and Moscow that the new president was his own man, with his own
ideas and ways of conducting diplomacy—certainly not a replica of Franklin D. Roosevelt. A British diplomat at the Potsdam Conference noted a difference. "Roosevelt's death
changed everything," Lord Moran recorded in his diary.
"Truman is very blunt; he means business" and "can hand
out the rough stuff."[22]

Truman was, of course, strikingly different from Roosevelt
in background, personality, and style. Whereas the latter was
a compromiser, the former usually made up his mind
quickly, or at least gave this impression, and stuck stead-
fastly to his convictions. Blacks and whites, with few gray
areas, characterized Truman's thinking. Whereas Roosevelt
was ingratiating, patient, and evasive, using a variety of techniques from jokes to rambling storytelling to "discursive
flashes" to hard-nosed politicking to win his point, Truman
was brash, abrupt, decisive, impatient, and quick-tem-
pered—characterized by "promptness and snappiness," said
Stimson.[23] Truman prided himself on blunt, tart, unadorned
language; Roosevelt was a master of dissembling and used
disarming, vague phrases. THE BUCK STOPS HERE, read a sign
on Truman's desk. "Give 'em hell, Harry," his political aides
recommended, and the president usually did. Truman was
"best when he's been mad," noted one of his assistants.[24]
Privately the president exploded against the French over
German and Lebanese questions: "Those French ought to be
taken out and castrated." As for Charles de Gaulle: "I don't
like the son of a bitch."[25] In private his anti-Semitism was

expressed against "kikes" and his racism against "niggers."[26]

Churchill, long an unabashed commentator on human behavior, remarked favorably after meeting Truman at Potsdam that the Missourian was "a man of exceptional character and ability . . . , simple and direct methods of speech, and a great deal of self-confidence and resolution." Indeed, he "takes no notice of delicate ground, he just plants his foot down firmly on it."[27] Truman himself wrote to his mother about his chairmanship at Potsdam: "They all say I took 'em for a ride when I got down to presiding."[28] Indeed, he often demonstrated simplicity, bravado, and verbal sparring. Apparently preferring to "give them an earful," he displayed little of the traits of quiet deliberation, careful weighing of alternatives, low-key patience, or analysis and understanding of subtleties that are usually essential to constructive diplomatic talks.[29] A self-conscious, bumptious style of toughness came to stand as a trademark of the Truman administration and ultimately became an impediment to diplomacy. A Canadian diplomat watching the Cold War take shape in the fall of 1945 argued that the United States could allay Soviet mistrust "by abandoning the philosophy of the tough method and resorting once more to the Roosevelt touch. . . ."[30]

Secretary of Commerce Henry A. Wallace, who broke with the president over the emerging posture of toughness, noted in his diary that Truman "seemed as though he was eager to decide in advance of thinking."[31] Supreme Court Justice Felix Frankfurter thought Truman an "improvising man, who reminds me by contrast of [Louis] Brandeis. In regard to almost every problem Brandeis was impressed with the 'difficulties.' . . . Truman hardly realizes the difficulty of any problem sufficiently."[32] Not all agree.[33] Truman himself took enormous pride in his decisiveness. Dean Rusk, a State Department official, lauded Truman's ability to cut to the heart of an issue, and Clifford recalled the president's "preference for rapid, intuitive decision-making rather than careful, analytical staff work."[34] Truman once admitted that "he was not a deep thinker" and "I don't like to read long papers."[35] He said he was "not up on all details" and had "to catch the intricacies of our foreign affairs."[36] On April 21, 1945, just two days before his confrontation with Molotov, Truman told Secretary of State Edward R. Stettinius, Jr., that he, the president, "was very hazy about the Yalta matters" and was "amazed" that the agreement on Poland, the American interpretation of which he insisted Molotov accept, "wasn't more clear cut."[37]

Although an apt pupil, the new president had much to learn, for as vice president he had not been included in high-level foreign policy discussions. FDR guarded "his" diplomacy, permitting only a handful of chosen advisers to become privy to "his" foreign policy. During the entire 1944 presidential campaign Truman met personally with Roosevelt only five times; he met with the chief executive only three times between the inauguration and FDR's death. Roosevelt, Truman remarked with chagrin, "never did talk to me confidentially about the war, or about foreign affairs or what he had in mind for the peace after the war."[38] As a senator from 1935 to 1944 Truman had not paid particular attention to foreign affairs; he did not sit, for example, on the Foreign Relations Committee. This distance from important decisions meant that Truman probably did not understand, and certainly did not respect, Roosevelt's personally crafted wartime agreements with the Soviet Union.[39] Thus the new president was not sensitive to Stalin's protests that he, Truman, was not fulfilling the intent of those accords or continuing Roosevelt's policies. Then, too, because Roosevelt conducted a personal diplomacy that deliberately bypassed the foreign affairs bureaucracy—especially the State Department—his death gave long-ignored, disaffected officials an opportunity to reassert their policy-making roles and to gain the new president's ear and support for their counsel. Many of them were not saying the same things that Roosevelt had said, nor were they saying them the way he did.

Wallace wondered whether Truman "has enough information behind his decisiveness to enable his decisions to stand up."[40] The question was not just whether Truman had a fount of information but the kinds and sources of his information. First, the president used stored information or memory; he read history and recalled the past frequently, drawing lessons which served as guides for policy making.[41] Truman and many other Americans, as we have already noted, saw the 1940s as a potential replay of the 1930s—with depression, totalitarianism, aggression, and war.

Truman also used intelligence gathered by his advisers at home and by American diplomats and CIA agents abroad. As a novice president who had had little contact with high-level diplomacy or the major decisions of World War II, he looked in particular to his immediate circle of advisers for information and guidance. They reinforced and encouraged his propensity to read simple lessons from history, to see the Soviets as Nazis reincarnate, to distrust negotiations with unregenerate Moscow, and to put his tough, decisive style to work in diplomacy. Secretary of State Edward R. Stettinius, Jr., Admiral William Leahy, Undersecretary of State Joseph Grew, Ambassador W. Averell Harriman, Secretary of the Navy James V. Forrestal, White House assistant Clark M. Clifford, and Secretary of State James F. Byrnes, among others, were listened to by the president not simply because they held positions of authority but because they tended to share Truman's ideas and his diplomatic style. In other words, not only did they go to him, but he sought advice from them and drew comfort from the fact that the elite of the foreign affairs establishment thought and wanted to act much like him. Officials who disagreed with him, who regretted his "get tough" foreign policy, found themselves increasingly isolated. Secretary of War Henry L. Stimson, Secretary of Commerce Henry A. Wallace, and Secretary of the Treasury Henry Morgenthau, Jr., for example, all tried to persuade the president to be more tolerant of the Soviet Union; they resigned or were forced out in 1945 and 1946. The president preferred to surround himself with like-minded people.

Secretary Byrnes's view was that "the only way to negotiate with the Russians is to hit them hard, and then negotiate."[42] Stalin once quipped that Byrnes was the "most honest horse thief he had ever met."[43] Harriman, who was one of the first diplomats to discuss Soviet-American relations with the new president after Roosevelt's death, also suspected aggressive Soviet intentions and believed in pressing Moscow to adopt American guidelines for the postwar world. "When it comes to matters of greater importance," Harriman believed as early as September 1944, "we should make it plain that their failure to *conform to our concepts* will affect our willingness to cooperate with them. . . ." Moreover, on "vital" questions, the United States should inform Moscow that Washington would stand firm, and, he maintained, "I am satisfied that in the last analysis Stalin will back down."[44] The deputy administrator of the Foreign Economic Administration, Oscar Cox, spoke with Harriman in April 1945 and "was disturbed by the undertones of what he said. He seems to be trending towards an anti-Soviet position."[45] Truman told Harriman, surely knowing that the ambassador shared his opinion, that the president was not afraid of the Soviets because "they needed us more than we needed them." He did not expect to win 100 percent of the American case, the president added, but "we should be able to get 85 percent."[46] Truman and his advisers agreed that "plain talk" would help achieve this high percentage of victories.[47] The former ambassador to the Soviet Union, Joseph Davies, traveled with Truman to the Potsdam Conference and concluded that the president "was surrounded by powerful elements, many of whom were hostile to the Soviets, and did not wish to further good relations with them."[48]

From abroad also came encouragement for a frank expression of American determination in the face of perceived Soviet expansionism. Ambassador to Greece Lincoln MacVeagh exaggerated a Soviet threat and distorted the realities of the civil war, depicting it as the handiwork of Moscow; Ambassador Laurence A. Steinhardt misread Czech politics and undermined non-Communists by successfully urging upon Byrnes an abrupt severance of American aid to Prague; and Ambassador Arthur Bliss Lane repeatedly reported with embellishment Soviet machinations and brutalities in Poland, helping to set in the American mind the belief that what happened in Poland would happen elsewhere in the world.[49] Burton Y. Berry and Maynard B. Barnes, the American ambassadors to Rumania and Bulgaria respectively, reported that it was impossible to deal with the Russians, for as Barnes put it, they had a "record for double dealing."[50] Kennan, usually given to a different diplomatic style, advised in 1946 that a "Russian is never more agreeable than after his knuckles have been sharply rapped. He takes well to rough play and rarely holds grudges over it."[51] Right or wrong, this sort of suggestion accorded with Truman's instinctive toughness. The foreign affairs bureaucrats, one historian has written, usually sketched for Truman a picture of a ruthless Soviet Union. "Some of them used black and white to portray issues that might have been sketched more faithfully in grays."[52] The diplomats in the field witnessed at first hand ugly events stemming from Soviet or Communist activities. What they saw hardened their already tough cynicism toward the Soviet Union and their preference for a flexing of the American diplomatic muscle.

Whether their reports and advice were hyperbolic or not, Truman was receptive to such reporting and shared its tone and message. In September 1946, when the United States was engaged at the Paris Peace Conference in friction-ridden attempts to write treaties for Hitler's former Eastern European satellites of Rumania and Hungary, President Truman cabled Byrnes to "do everything you can to continue but in the final analysis do whatever you think is right and tell [the Soviets] to go to hell if you have to."[53] Although Byrnes and the American delegation were more polite than this, the thrust of the president's message was something that they already understood and endorsed because they had helped shape it. In 1947 former Secretary of State Cordell Hull questioned the American penchant for toughness. "It isn't any use kicking a tough hound around," he complained to Acheson, "because a tough hound will kick back."[54]

Unanimity of opinion, of course, was not always present in the foreign affairs establishment, although the president usually demanded and received compliance with his desires. When, in late 1945, Byrnes made compromises with the Soviet Union at the Moscow Foreign Ministers Conference on Eastern European issues, Truman upbraided his secretary of state. Byrnes had always been a political rival of Truman's (Byrnes had wanted to be the Democratic vice presidential candidate in 1944), and that may have exacerbated the matter. Also, Truman thought that Byrnes had failed to keep the president adequately informed about decisions made during the conference. "I'm tired of babying the Soviets," read a memorandum that Truman prepared for a meeting with Byrnes.[55] Three years later he recalled that "Byrnes lost his nerve in Moscow." Indeed, Truman lectured Byrnes that "his appeasement policy was not mine."[56] Byrnes, who continued through 1946 to negotiate with the Soviets in search of peace treaties, soon fell into line behind the president, moved in part by this display of presidential prerogative and power in the making of American foreign policy.[57]

Although Byrnes was willing to accommodate Truman, his colleague in the cabinet, Commerce Secretary Wallace, would not bow to presidential dictate. In 1945 and 1946 he urged Truman, to no avail, to chart a more conciliatory course toward the Soviets. Then, in September 1946, the independent-minded Wallace told an audience at Madison Square Garden that " 'getting tough' never brought anything real and lasting—whether for schoolyard bullies or businessmen or world powers. The tougher we get, the tougher the Russians will get."[58] For his renegade views Wallace was fired. Truman privately recorded his rather simplistic thoughts: "The Reds, phonies and the 'parlor pinks' seem to be banded together and are becoming a national danger. I am afraid they are a sabotage front for Uncle Joe Stalin."[59] At the press conference announcing Wallace's departure, Truman stated that "the government of the United States *must stand as a unit* in its relations with the rest of the world."[60]

Another example of division within the administration and the ultimate presidential mastery of the foreign affairs bureaucracy came in early 1948, when the White House staff was drafting a major address to Congress for March 17. Although some advisers thought that Truman should "scare" the country about the foreign danger, Secretary of State George C. Marshall, who had replaced Byrnes in January 1947 and in March of that year had expressed mild criticism of the president's strong rhetoric in the Truman Doctrine speech, opposed an alarmist message. Marshall was "nervous," according to a Truman aide, because the world was a "keg of dynamite" which the president should not ignite. Assistants Clark Clifford and George Elsey, on the other hand, thought that the President *"must,* for his prestige, come up with [a] strong foreign speech—to demonstrate his *leadership."* They were annoyed that Marshall and Senator Arthur Vandenberg, Republican chairman of the Foreign Relations Committee, were getting credit for foreign policy triumphs like the Marshall Plan, whereas the president's prestige had slumped because of his troubles with Palestine and China. Marshall thought that the final text of another speech, Truman's St. Patrick's Day speech of March 17, to be delivered later that day, was also "too tough." In this speech Truman depicted the postwar international conflict as a simple morality play of "tyranny against freedom."[61] For the message to Congress Marshall favored temperate, nondenunciatory language, whereas Clifford urged a "blunt" style, finding Marshall's approach too "timid." The president agreed with Clifford and said that Marshall's draft "stank."[62] Rejecting his secretary of state's advice, Truman sounded a bell of alarm in a message which helped produce a war scare.[63]

The president commanded the results of another squabble with the State Department in mid-1948—this time over the Arab-Jewish fight in Palestine and the establishment of the new state of Israel. The State Department, concerned about maintaining Arab states as economic and political friends, sought mediation and a trusteeship plan—anything that would forestall Arab hatred for the United States—but President Truman, sensitive to the large Jewish vote in the forthcoming presidential election and aware of Israel's strategic position in the Middle East, a potential U.S. asset in the Cold War, backed the creation of the new nation. Zionist appeals to Truman would never have worked, however, if Israeli forces had not won on the battlefield.[64] Marshall bluntly told Truman that he would vote against him in the election if the president recognized Israel for "domestic political considerations," but even he eventually had to agree that Israel could become a Middle East ally in an expanding American sphere of influence.[65] The American delegation to the United Nations almost resigned en masse after the president abruptly recognized Israel on May 14. Clark Clifford informed American diplomats that the president demanded their conformity. Truman, in fact, instructed State Department officials to avoid commenting on the issue "until after [the] elections."[66]

Once the president had announced his policy toward Israel, the foreign affairs bureaucracy knew that it could no longer debate it—at least not in public. As Clifford told Undersecretary of State Robert A. Lovett after the president named his first ambassador to the new Middle Eastern nation, Truman "had made up his mind," and "there was obviously no room for argument."[67]

Bureaucracies and their members can sometimes moderate the president's orders; they can both impede and facilitate the execution of policy, even though the White House holds the power of formulation.[68] The Point Four Program provides a case in point. In late 1948, after Truman's stunning victory over Governor Thomas Dewey in the presidential election, White House aides were looking for a "dramatic topic" to use in the inaugural address.[69] Ben Hardy, a lower-echelon officer of the State Department, had an idea: the use of technical assistance as a means of uplifting developing nations and drawing them into the American sphere. He timidly carried his scheme to the White House, knowing that his departmental superiors had no enthusiasm for such a program. Truman advisers Clifford and Elsey warmly received Hardy's pet project and gave it standing as "point four" in the president's January 1949 speech. Department of State officers balked at Truman's call for a "bold new program," for they were surprised by the announcement and had no plans whatsoever for such a venture.[70] Asked by the White House to come up with a program, they procrastinated; moreover, they only made lukewarm attempts to marshal public opinion and congressional support. The State Department, complained a Truman aide, was "deferring it as a major effort."[71] Finally, in May 1950, the authorization for Point Four emerged from a Congress that matched the hesitancy of the State Department. Having to compete with many other foreign policy demands, the program was launched with only meager appropriations.[72]

Usually, however, the president can make bureaucrats responsive and submissive to his wishes. "Presidential *power* is the power to persuade," the political scientist Richard Neustadt has written.[73] As chief executive the president can hire and dismiss—a telling power. As one observer has put it, "no man can *argue* on his knees."[74] The president chooses his key advisers, who in turn select bureaucrats who are expected to share the president's basic predilections. Thus the president determines who will whisper in his ear, a Harriman, Clifford, Wallace, or Marshall. Several months after entering the White House, Truman remarked that he, like Roosevelt, was surrounded by "prima donnas." He did not humor them, he said, as Roosevelt had: "I fire one occasionally and it has a salutary effect."[75] When Truman dramatically fired General Douglas MacArthur from his command in Korea in 1951, he demonstrated that power. "I could no longer tolerate his insubordination," Truman later wrote.[76]

Because of the prestige of his office, the president can also command publicity for his policies and arouse public support in the form of pressure on the bureaucracy. At his call, reporters, radio microphones, and television cameras will be in place for public announcements. His speeches gain national media coverage. The president largely decides which issues are worth the bureaucracy's attention and which are worth fighting over. If he feels intensely about an issue, that feeling of commitment is conveyed to his subordinates. He can also decide not to do something—not to recognize a new government, not to negotiate, not to intervene, not to send foreign aid. Furthermore, the president's ideology, his fundamental beliefs and ideals permeate the consensus-prone bureaucracy. An official in the foreign affairs establishment soon learns that he enjoys influence only so long as he has the president's encouragement and backing. "The State Department doesn't have a policy unless I support it," snapped Truman during a press conference.[77]

The "national security managers" fall in line with presidential preferences or leave government.[78] Bureaucrats tend to tell the president what he wants to hear. Sometimes they are reluctant to express opinions which might be looked upon with disfavor by superiors. Many Foreign Service Officers who watched the "China hands" fall victim to ill-placed right-wing charges that they had undermined Jiang Jieshi in order to help Mao Zedong, and who watched the State Department's loyalty board harass and dismiss talented diplomats, were intimidated into silence or learned to "play it safe."[79] Large bureaucracies tend by nature to become lethargic and unimaginative, thereby leaving the initiative to the president and his close advisers.[80] "Groupthink" is also at work. That is, members of a policy-making group tend to fall victim to group pressures for unanimity or consensus and to suppress their desires to express alternative policies which might disrupt or divide the group. The dynamics of working for concurrence, for consensus, for like-mindedness can thus reduce disagreement and the consideration of policy options.[81]

Even when dissent or irreconcilable conflict arises within the bureaucratic network, a governmental tradition usually asserts itself: An official who wants to stay at his post or who decides to leave government must not speak out, must not air his differences or grievances publicly.[82] Two illustrations: In early 1946 Chester Bowles, at the time the head of the Office of Price Administration, privately applauded Joseph Davies for his critique of the "get tough" policy. Then Bowles added: "As a member of the Administration I do not want to be in the position of criticizing the Administration even by remote implication and for that reason I am writing you this personal letter rather than endorsing your statement in public as I would prefer to do."[83] "I was always quite happy to do what the Under Secretary or Secretary [of State] decided should be done—even if I lost," recalled veteran diplomat

George McGhee. "Issues worth resigning over are few and far between," he concluded.[84] Henry Wallace, then, was a conspicuous exception. He took his case against the "get tough" policy to the electorate in the form of an unsuccessful 1948 presidential candidacy under the banner of the Progressive party.

The president, in short, was and is the master of American foreign policy. When the Soviets insisted that they would not be "intimidated" by American and British "methods"— which they thought were designed to "impose their will upon other countries, and on the Soviet Union particularly"—they meant the activities of Truman and his subordinates, who, the Soviets believed, had deviated from both the style and the policy of the Roosevelt administration.[85] Roosevelt had been "a farsighted statesman of the first rank," and his death "was a veritable gift to the gods" of American reaction and expansion, concluded one Soviet analyst.[86] Whereas Roosevelt and Stalin had "clicked," Truman and the Russian leader never warmed to each other.[87] Stalin was "an S.O.B.," concluded Truman after Potsdam. "I guess he thinks I'm one too."[88]

Stalin may have privately commented on Truman's parentage, but we do not know. In any case, it seems reasonable to suggest that the Soviet leader exaggerated the difference between Truman and Roosevelt by contrasting the two presidents' starkly different styles and personalities. As different as Roosevelt and Truman were as individuals, it does not appear that their basic policies clashed to the extreme extent that Wallace and the Soviets thought. FDR had to deal with the problems of war, of course, whereas Truman grappled with the issues of peace, so the question cannot be dealt with conclusively. Both presidents, nevertheless, saw diplomatic bargaining power in the American monopoly of the atomic bomb; both sought to use America's economic power as leverage in diplomacy; both held to the essential tenets of the American ideology, with its emphasis on the open world;

both wanted a United Nations Organization that would be dominated by the big powers, especially the United States; both envisioned a strong United States as the major actor in the postwar world. John D. Hickerson, director of the Office of European Affairs, recalled that FDR's death did not alter ongoing negotiations and programs conducted by the State Department: "We went right ahead; really we weren't conscious of any change."[89]

Still, the two presidents went about the business of diplomacy differently. Truman surrounded himself with advisers who thought the way he did; the more confident Roosevelt staffed his administration with both yes-men and naysayers. Roosevelt was more patient with the Soviets, more willing to settle issues at the conference table, more tame and less abusive in his language, less abrupt in his decisions, and more solicitous of Soviet opinion and fears than was Truman. Roosevelt accepted the reality of the Soviet sphere that Truman would not abide. Postwar conflict would have been present no matter which man was president. The characteristics of the international system and the clashing fundamental needs and ideas of the United States and the Soviet Union ensured tension, but because the tactics and mechanics of policy making in their administrations differed, the two men impressed the Soviets very differently. Tactics joined system and national fundamentals to cause the Cold War.

7

CONSENT
American Public Opinion, Congress, and the Cold War Mentality

"THE PRESIDENT'S JOB is to *lead* public opinion, not to be a blind follower," stated George Elsey, one of Harry S. Truman's chief advisers and speech writers. "You can't sit around and wait for public opinion to tell you what to do." He grew more emphatic: "In the first place, there isn't any public opinion. The public doesn't know anything about it; they haven't heard about it. You must decide what you're going to do and do it, and attempt to educate the public to the reasons for your action."[1] This unabashed stress on the president's initiative in foreign policy and the self-conscious notion that the "public" must be coaxed or "educated" into supporting what the chief executive has already decided underscore the point that the president enjoyed considerable freedom in the making of a foreign policy designed to satisfy America's fundamental needs and ideas in the tumultuous postwar international system. One student of the topic has graphically described the president as a "kind of magnificent lion who can roam widely and do great deeds so long as he does not try to break loose from his broad reservation." The "restraints" of his domain are "designed to keep him from going out of bounds, not to paralyze him in the field that has been reserved for his use."[2] Few presidents, springing as they do from the American mind and spirit, have strayed "out of bounds," and few have ever been paralyzed in efforts to achieve their self-defined "great deeds." Harry S. Truman was no exception when he attempted to meet the perceived Soviet threat and to arouse public support for his containment policies and the shaping of an American sphere of influence.

In the early years of the Cold War, public opinion and the Congress set very broad and imprecise limits on presidential activity in international affairs. Foreign policy initiative lay with the executive branch. The administration's diplomacy was not determined by the buffeting winds of public sentiment or by an obstructionist Congress. Seldom did Truman have to do what he did not want to do; seldom did he have serious trouble overcoming the obstacles of a parsimonious Congress or interest groups in order to pilot his foreign programs through either a Democratic- or Republican-controlled Capitol Hill. Congress was generally compliant, and the American people were "yea-sayers." Although Truman officials occasionally suggested that they were sensitive to or influenced by public attitudes, a search of the minutes and records of such high-level policy-making groups as the cabinet, the Committee of Three (secretaries of state, war, and navy), and the secretary of state's Staff Committee, as well as official diplomatic correspondence, does not reveal that U.S.

leaders paid much attention to American public opinion or that they were swayed by it to do something they did not wish to do.[3] President Truman charted his own foreign policy course and successfully persuaded the hesitant and reluctant to walk his path.

Some analysts, without precise evidence on how public opinion has actually affected policy, have attributed more importance to public opinion than Truman did. On the other hand, others have been skeptical of an interpretation which stresses the public's power over leaders.[4] One specialist has written that 'even though foreign policy leaders have widely underestimated their freedom of maneuver in foreign policy, they still perceive that freedom more accurately than many scholars have, and more accurately even than they themselves usually admit openly.'[5] A student of the presidency has marveled at Truman's "spacious understanding" of presidential power, despite the president's often humble, folksy explanation of his role. Truman once said, for example, that although the Constitution gave him many powers, "the principal power that the President has is to bring people in and try to persuade them to do what they ought to do without persuasion. That's what I spend most of my time doing. That's what the powers of the President amount to."[6] This self-deprecating and disingenuous statement did not accord with the facts. Truman was a maestro in drawing full tones from his constitutional strings and from his public chorus.

Truman and his advisers certainly worried about public opinion. They read the polls. They courted the ethnic vote. They buttonholed members of Congress. They warned against the dangers that could come from negative opinion. In 1947 Clark Clifford urged his boss to name the new European Recovery Program the "Truman Plan." "Are you crazy," Truman interjected. "If we sent it up to that Republican Congress with my name on it, they'd tear it apart. We're going to call it the Marshall Plan."[7] Thus Truman officials were sensitive to the public pulse, but they believed that public opinion and Congress could be persuaded and cultivated on most issues, that they were permissive rather restrictive. The president's power to create and to lead public opinion was studiously exercised. Any president can preempt the airwaves to make his case. Reporters flocked to Truman's press conferences, and as James Reston of the *New York Times* witnessed, "when the press conference ends, the scramble of reporters for the telephones is a menace to life and limb. . . ."[8] The president grabbed headlines; even his daily walks, colds, and piano playing became news.

The president exploited frightening world events in order to garner support for his foreign policy. Truman once remarked that without Moscow's "crazy" actions, "we never would have had our foreign policy . . . we never could have got a thing from Congress."[9] He exaggerated, but what he meant is illustrative: He exploited Cold War tensions through a frequently alarmist, hyperbolic, anti-Communist rhetoric which he thought necessary to ensure favorable legislative votes, to disarm his critics, and to nudge a budget-conscious Congress to appropriate funds for such programs as the Marshall Plan. "If [the Soviet threat] had never existed," remarked a colleague to Kennan, "we would have had to invent it, to create a sense of urgency we need to bring us to the point of decisive action."[10] Truman molded public opinion behind America's Cold War effort in a sometimes excitable manner, thereby intensifying Soviet-American conflict. Moscow, after all, had to respond not only to what it saw the United States doing but also to what it heard the American president say. Truman's pugnacious rhetoric also built up a momentum that came to haunt him. Truman's conservative critics reminded the president of his own extreme anti-Communist language used in the early Cold War when they later demanded that he confront the Soviet/Communist threat on all fronts at the same time with equal commitment—that, in other words, he fulfill the apparent pledge of his own tough words. Truman's style of overstatement boxed him in politically at home at the same time that it helped box out negotiations with the Soviets.

American leaders occasionally complained during and after the war about lingering American "isolationism" and bemoaned the work needed to convert it to "internationalism." During the war commentators on the American mood predicted that at war's end the GI would exchange his fatigues for isolationist garb. Reporters for *Time* magazine who asked soldiers what they thought about the war received the answer that they "never wanted to hear of a foreign country again."[11] A servicemen's indelicate ditty went this way:

> I'm tired of these Limeys and Frogs,
> I'm fed to the teeth with these Gooks, Wops, and Wogs.
> I want to get back to my chickens and hogs,
> I don't want to leave home any more.[12]

After the war W. Averell Harriman remarked that many Americans wanted nothing more than to "go to the movies and drink Coke," and Dean Acheson, concerned about a too-rapid U.S. demobilization of its armed forces, defined the administration's task in 1946 as "focusing the will of 140,-000,000 people on problems beyond our shores . . . [when] people are focusing on 140,000,000 other things. . . ."[13] Senator Wayne Morse of Oregon, a firm supporter of Truman's "hard-boiled policy" in 1945, feared that "sentimentalist groups" would once again gain control of American foreign policy.[14] "Americans can no longer sit smugly behind a mental Maginot line," Truman said just before the end of the war.[15]

Isolationism actually evaporated quickly. "Isolationism," that vague feeling that the United States should restrict its activities overseas, especially in Europe, follow an indepen-

dent or unilateral course, and mind its own business, collided
with the realities of the air age and an international system
which cast the United States in a starring role. The Pearl
Harbor attack, said Republican Senator Arthur Vandenberg
of Michigan, "ended isolationism for any realist."[16] As he put
it in early 1945, when he renounced his own "isolationism"
on the Senate floor, "I do not believe that any nation here-
after can immunize itself by its own exclusive action. . . . Our
oceans have ceased to be moats which automatically protect
our ramparts."[17] Not wishing to repeat the post-World War I
debacle wherein President Woodrow Wilson launched the
League of Nations only to have the U.S. Senate jilt it, Americans stood with Vandenberg in repudiating a failed past.
Leaders and publicists of many political persuasions lectured
the American people that the "horse-and-buggy days are
gone," for "in a world in which a man can travel from New
York to India in less time than it took Benjamin Franklin to
travel from Philadelphia to New York, the attempt to escape
into the Golden Age of normalcy is an invitation to chaos."[18]
Such lectures, joined with the fast pace of global crises and
presidential statements about the tremendous American responsibility in a world of rubble, undercut or crippled isolationist feeling. American membership in the new United Nations Organization was roundly approved. Public opinion
polls recorded that large majorities of Americans applauded
an activist foreign policy abroad.[19] Even some of the so-called
postwar isolationists, like Senator Robert Taft of Ohio, who
tried to curb American programs designed to build an economic and military shield around Western Europe, seemed
inconsistent as they shouted for American interventionism in
Asia. As the pacifist A. J. Muste once remarked, "for isolationists these Americans do certainly get around."[20] Thus,
although Truman and his officers worried about isolationism,
they did not find it an obstacle to their policy of "getting
tough."[21]

It was not "isolationism" that characterized American public opinion about Cold War events but ignorance. "Public opinion" suggests in a vague way that "the people" express themselves collectively on issues of national importance. Yet on foreign policy there was no mass public that spoke out with force or unity or that could seriously instruct or influence leaders. Most Americans read little about foreign events in their newspapers, which devoted the greater proportion of their columns to domestic topics; consequently, they were ill informed about politics abroad. When asked to list the most significant issues before the nation, Americans cataloged domestic problems. In the Truman years, labor strikes, reconversion, price controls, housing shortages, and inflation occupied Americans. "Foreign affairs!" grumbled a blue-collar worker. "That's for people who don't have to work for a living."[22]

This striking ignorance—sometimes mistaken for isolationist thought—was demonstrated in a study that the Council on Foreign Relations commissioned in March 1947. The researchers found to their dismay that three out of every ten American voters were unaware of almost every event in U.S. foreign relations. They concluded further that only a quarter of the American electorate was reasonably well informed. Sixty-five out of every one hundred voters admitted that they rarely discussed foreign affairs.[23] "There is virtually no public opinion about the Bretton Woods Conference," read one 1944 polling report. "There is no general discussion of it because there is no interest; and there is no interest because there is no comprehension of the issues. . . . Bankers and business circles are believed to be more informed than the general public, yet even these are often 'surprisingly ignorant' of the subject."[24] Other studies reported that in 1946, 43 percent of adult Americans had not followed the discussion on an American loan to Britain, that 31 percent could not even give a simple answer to a question about the purpose of the United Nations Organization, and that 58 percent had not paid attention to the major debate between the Truman administration and Henry A. Wallace that led to the latter's explosive departure from the cabinet. In a Gallup survey for September 1949, 64 percent of those polled had neither heard nor read anything about the controversial China White Paper.[25] Students of the relationship between foreign policy and public opinion have found these figures consistent with American tradition. "The mass public," James Rosenau has concluded, "is uninformed about either specific foreign policy issues or foreign affairs in general. Its members pay little, if any, attention to day-to-day developments in world politics."[26]

The evidence of ignorance or apathy suggests that leaders in Washington were permitted wide latitude and independence in making foreign policy. Elsey put it too strongly when he said, "[T]here isn't any public opinion." He would have been more accurate if he had said that it was so weak that leaders were neither educated nor moved very much by it.

There was a "public opinion" that Truman and his advisers took seriously and that they diligently sought to cultivate: the opinion of the approximately 25 percent of the American people who were attentive to foreign policy questions. Scholars have called them variously "notables," "opinion leaders," or the "foreign policy public." They constituted the small number of Americans who studied the foreign news, who traveled abroad, who spoke out. They held positions in American society that commanded authority and ensured influence—journalists, businessmen, labor leaders, intellectuals, and members of various interest and citizen groups. They produced the "public opinion" on foreign policy issues that counted. A Truman officer summarized the point: "It doesn't make too much difference to the general public what the details of a program are. What counts is how the plan is viewed by the leaders of the community and the nation."[27] Another State Department official remarked that "we read the digests, we ponder the polls, and then we are likely to be influenced by our favorite columnist."[28] The "foreign policy public" was important, too, because it could influence a wider audience. As someone put it, he "who mobilizes the elite, mobilizes the public."[29] The Truman administration happily found that the elite endorsed the president's foreign policy, further enhancing his freedom in policy making.[30]

To cement the alliance between the "opinion leaders" and the administration government officials wooed them. Interest-group executives were given flattering appointments on consulting bodies like the President's Committee on Foreign Aid, the Public Advisory Board of the Economic Cooperation Administration, and the Business Advisory Council of the Department of Commerce. They served as consultants to the American delegation at the founding meeting of the United Nations Organization in San Francisco. They were appointed to high office, as when Paul Hoffman of the Studebaker Corporation was named to head the Economic Cooperation Administration. They were invited to appear before congressional committees to state their views as "experts." They enjoyed special State Department briefings or attended special White House conferences like that for the Marshall Plan on October 27, 1947. They became participants in what some historians have called an American system of corporatism—the cooperation of elites in both the governmental and the private sectors (especially business, agriculture, and labor) to create and sustain domestic and foreign order. In this "associative state" governmental leaders and private interests share power and seek to devise regulations to produce a harmony that ensures national prosperity and security.[31] Some individuals were consulted so often or sat on so many public boards that they could truly be called "external bureaucrats."[32] The American Federation of Labor even became a propaganda organization for U.S. policy in Europe, as well as a CIA instrument for its covert operations against Communists in European trade unions.[33] All in all, the opinion leaders were courted, sometimes because their views provided new insight but largely because they represented a "public opinion" that mattered, that could be shaped to endorse Truman's Cold War policies, and that, in turn, could rally the mass public behind presidential decisions.

The major task of cultivating elite opinion fell to the State Department's Office of Public Affairs, which was organized near the end of the Second World War. This agency was designed to strengthen relations with public groups and prominent individuals. It maintained ties with more than two hundred organizations and drafted State Department responses to letters from opinion leaders. So that it could anticipate criticisms, it conducted polls and interviews with American voters and subscribed to more than a hundred newspapers and magazines. The office also sponsored an annual conference in the Department of State to which it invited about two hundred people—usually presidents of national associations. Smaller meetings of ten to thirty participants were held each week. Usually the conferees met with middle-echelon officers, but on one occasion Secretary Acheson himself addressed a small group to explain his controversial policy toward China. Director of the Office of Public Affairs Francis Russell frankly recalled that the thin line between propaganda and education was sometimes crossed.[34] Whether the office's function was education or propaganda, the chief purpose was evident: to sell the president's foreign policy to opinion leaders. That purpose was met.

A sterling example of cooperation between the government and opinion leaders came in 1947–1948, when the Committee for the Marshall Plan was organized to drum up public support for the European Recovery Program. Former Secretaries of War Henry L. Stimson and Robert Patterson joined former Assistant Secretary of State Dean Acheson to launch the committee in the fall of 1947. Working closely with the State Department, the committee staff ran newspaper ads, circulated petitions, organized letter campaigns to members of Congress, and maintained an active speakers' bureau. Groups that were asked to testify before congressional committees were supplied with prepared texts.[35] Presidential assistant Richard E. Neustadt lauded the committee as "one of the most effective instruments for public information seen since the Second World War. . . ."[36]

The administration also received help in selling its foreign aid programs from British propaganda in the United States. The head of British Information Services explained that "we have to admit at this stage of our [British] history that the United States has assumed such a dominant place in the world, and our affairs are so inextricably mixed with hers, that British policy can never be effective unless it has the tacit support and backing of the American people—or at the very least is not actively opposed to them."[37] The British publicity effort sought to persuade Americans that Britons were such worthy allies that they deserved foreign aid. When American leaders launched the Marshall Plan, they advised British officials that the money had to come from Congress. The American message was unmistakable: The British message to the American people and their representatives in Congress should be anticommunism, British self-help and sacrifice, European cooperation, and a traditional Anglo-American partnership. British Information Services in the United States, with a staff of more than two hundred, bombarded American news media with press releases, films, and speeches. American journalists were handed British Embassy guidance papers. Members of Congress enjoyed fine dinners at British expense. The British propagandists also targeted national associations like the Council on Foreign Relations, Chamber of Commerce, and Lions Clubs. They cultivated banking executives and radio commentators. Like the U.S. Department of State's public relations experts, the British publicists helped shape an American audience receptive to spending billions of dollars for an activist U.S. foreign policy.[38]

The president himself, of course, worked to shape the public opinion that his administration wanted to hear. "A politician must be in a sense a public relations man," said Truman.[39] He used techniques common to most presidencies: He spoke at times in alarmist terms, predicting dire results if a certain policy were not carried out; he appealed to patriotism to rally Americans to his banner, often recalling the sacrifices of World War II; he created awesome and frightening images of the foreign adversary. Truman simplified issues and exaggerated consequences, stirring the heart rather than the mind.[40] "That is the American way," lamented New York City lawyer and former United Nations Relief and Rehabilitation Administration official Richard Scandrett. "Things are either pure black or pure white. There are no grays."[41] Such was the case in the administration's unrelenting misrepresentations of political enemies like Henry A. Wallace. Truman and his advisers practiced a highly emotional red-baiting. To Congressman John H. Folger, the president wrote in April 1947 that Wallace "seems to have obtained his ideas of loyalty . . . from his friends in Moscow and, of course, they have no definition for that word."[42] Several months later Clark Clifford planned strategy for the 1948 presidential campaign. His advice reflected his mentor's preference: "Every effort must be made *now* jointly and at one and the same time— although, of course, by different groups—to dissuade him [Wallace] and also to identify him in the public mind with the Communists."[43]

The historian Thomas A. Bailey, author of a popular 1948 book entitled *The Man in the Street,* defended the president's efforts to "educate" an ignorant public: "Because the masses are notoriously short-sighted, and generally cannot see danger until it is at their throats, our statesmen are forced to deceive them into an awareness of their own long-term interests. . . ." He went on: "Deception of the people may in fact become increasingly necessary, unless we are willing to give our leaders in Washington a freer hand. . . . The yielding of some of our democratic control over foreign affairs is the price that we may have to pay for greater physical security."[44] Charles Bohlen explained that Cold War national security required "a confidence in the Executive where you give human nature a very large blank check."[45] Clark Clifford correctly observed that "in time of crisis the American citizen tends to back up his President."[46]

Because the American people usually rallied around their leaders during foreign policy crises and because the president usually succeeded in cultivating or manipulating public sentiment, it is not surprising that the public opinion the White House and the State Department heard largely matched the public opinion it worked to create. The administration in essence listened to the echo of its own words. "What the government hears," suggested one official, borrowing a metaphor from the navy, "is really the sound of its own screws, reflecting off its own rudder and coming up through its own highly selective sonar."[47]

Still, administration figures said that public opinion counted, that it guided their foreign policy. They were saying so ritualistically, out of habit and necessity, not because it was reality. One would expect high-level officials in a democratic-representative political system to say publicly that they believed that the public's views counted, for that is what a public audience wanted to hear. Telling the public so actually constituted another part of the effort to create friendly opinion.

American diplomats sometimes told foreign leaders that the United States could not undertake a certain policy or program because public opinion or the American people would not countenance it. In his famous acrimonious exchange with Molotov in April 1945, for example, Truman warned that Soviet behavior would affect United States policy on foreign aid to the Soviet Union because "he could not hope to get these measures through Congress unless there was public support for them."[48] Acting Secretary of State Grew told the Yugoslav foreign minister a month later that in matters of foreign policy "we were guided by public opinion" and that Yugoslavia's request for foreign aid "would to a large measure depend on the impression which the American public will gain from the policies and events in the countries recently liberated."[49] In 1947 Undersecretary of State Clayton said much the same thing in his attempt to persuade the British to join a European economic plan.[50] In all three examples, however, there is insufficient evidence to argue that the administration's reading of public opinion influenced its foreign economic policies. Such statements, it appears, more often than not represented a diplomatic device designed to press foreign officials rather than a political reality at home.[51]

Public opinion usually supported Truman's early Cold War policies, giving him a free hand. Even hostile opinion did not deter him from doing what he wanted to do. Good examples are the questions of loans to the Soviet Union and Great Britain in fall 1945. Of the respondents in a Gallup poll, 60 percent disapproved of a loan to the Soviet Union (only 27 percent approved, and 13 percent had no opinion). Another Gallup poll revealed exactly the same statistics of public opposition to a loan to Britain. The Truman administration nevertheless proceeded, in apparent violation of "public opinion," to negotiate a $3.75 billion loan to Britain, while neglecting negotiations with the Soviets, who got no loan.[52] In April 1947, shortly after his dramatic Truman Doctrine speech, the president found that a large majority of Americans believed that the problem of aid to Greece and

Turkey should be turned over to the United Nations. He never followed such a policy, again in apparent defiance of "public opinion."[53] What he and the State Department did instead was to launch an effective propaganda campaign with the message that the United Nations was an infant organization not yet ready to take on the momentous task proposed. To quiet discontent in Congress, the administration endorsed an innocuous amendment drafted by the bipartisan leader Senator Arthur H. Vandenberg and the State Department staff to the effect that the United Nations could assume the task when it was ready. "I never paid any attention to the polls myself," remembered Truman, "because in my judgment they did not represent a true cross section of American opinion. . . . I also know that the polls did not represent facts but mere speculation. . . ."[54]

When the administration said that it was responding to public opinion, it usually meant that it had to deal with a special-interest group that was one issue-oriented and that, like the president, was able to exploit public indifference or ignorance to gain its ends.[55] Thus, in one of the rare, measurable examples of successful interest-group influence, a well-organized, well-funded, and vocal Jewish American community, especially in New York, exerted considerable pressure on vote-conscious Truman in the 1948 election. He overruled his own State Department and backed the establishment of Israel (see Chapter 6). But even in this case it is not evident that Jewish lobbying for Israel was decisive in shaping administration policy. Truman's personal desire for a place for Jewish refugees, Jewish military victories against the Arabs, and the strategic position of Israel in the Middle East also persuaded the president. Israel loomed as a strategic asset in the Cold War.[56]

Even highly charged special-interest groups did not always succeed in influencing foreign policy, as the case of the Polish-Americans and U.S. policy toward Poland illustrates.

At the Teheran Conference of 1943 President Roosevelt told Premier Stalin that he could not take part in any public agreement over Polish boundaries because there were six to seven million Polish-Americans in the United States and that "as a practical man, he did not wish to lose their vote."[57] In June of the next year a State Department official (and political appointee of Roosevelt) worried about the Soviet presence in Poland and recorded in his diary that the Poles held the political balance in Illinois and Ohio and were politically potent in Detroit, Chicago, and Buffalo.[58] At the Potsdam Conference in July of the following year, President Truman mentioned that there were six million Poles in America who could be dealt with much more easily if a free election were held in Poland.[59]

Although the presidents were sensitive to this conspicuous political reality, U.S. policy toward Poland was not shaped or determined by Polish-Americans. The figure of six to seven million Polish-Americans was inflated, for it included Poles of all ages. Their voting strength was actually much less significant than the comments above suggested. Few Poles, moreover, held positions of national leadership from which to influence policy: There were no Americans of Polish descent in the Senate until well after World War II—although Michigan Senator Vandenberg spoke for them—and there were only ten to twelve Polish-Americans in the House. Also, political leadership in the Polish-American community itself was splintered, weakening its impact. Neither president respected the Polish-American Congress as an interest group; both presidents were able to reduce the effect of Polish-American opinion. FDR deftly courted Polish-American leaders in 1944 by speaking in generalities and by apparently convincing them that he agreed with them. In the election of 1944, despite differences with Roosevelt, the Poles stuck with the Democrats in overwhelming numbers. Truman grew angry with criticism from Polish-American leaders like Charles

Rozmarek that the United States had sold out Poland to the Soviets, and he paid less and less attention to them. Although Rozmarek and other leaders defected in 1948 from the Democratic ranks, Polish-Americans, as ardent Democrats, on the whole voted for Truman. In short, although the presidents and their advisers naturally worried about and courted Polish-American votes, the Polish-American community did not wield important influence in the shaping of American foreign policy.[60] Truman pursued *his* policy toward Poland.

If public opinion did not have much of an impact overall on Truman's foreign policy, can it be argued that Congress did? Congress obviously possessed powers that the amorphous public opinion lacked. In a negative and abstract sense, Congress had the power to defeat a presidential proposal. The Senate could reject a treaty if a third of its members (plus one) voted "nay," and the House of Representatives, gripping the purse strings, could refuse to appropriate funds. Both houses of Congress had the power to investigate. Administration officers had to troop into congressional hearings to answer questions from suspicious legislators, some of whom relished opportunities to denigrate "striped pants" diplomats. For a six-month period in 1947 the State Department expended more than a thousand person-days in describing and defending Truman's policies before congressional committees, and when he was secretary of state, Dean Acheson spent about one-sixth of his working days in Washington meeting with members of Congress.[61]

Congress can also create watchdog committees to oversee the execution of programs that it approved; the Senate votes on presidential appointees to diplomatic posts; the Constitution empowers the Congress to set tariffs, regulate foreign commerce and immigration, and declare war; and in extreme cases, the legislative branch can exercise its impeachment powers. In short, the separation of powers invests Congress with wide potential authority in foreign policy, and any administration—if it wishes to push its programs through the legislative process—must be alert to congressional opinion. In practice, however, Congress has been largely subservient to the president in matters of foreign policy.[62]

Most presidents have reached into well-stocked arsenals for devices to augment their powers vis-à-vis Congress. Truman was a former senator, with ten years in rank, and he utilized his status as an alumnus to gain access to the upper house. He called upon his friends there, strengthening personal contacts. As president he could be found having lunch in the Senate dining room.[63] Once, on July 23, 1947, he even entered the Senate chamber itself, prompting the presiding officer, Vandenberg, to announce that the "ex-Senator from Missouri is recognized for five minutes."[64] Besides personal lobbying, Truman attempted to persuade the larger electorate, which would, it was anticipated, in turn exercise some influence over members of Congress worried about what the folks back home were thinking. The administration could further shape favorable congressional opinion by including members of Congress directly in diplomatic negotiations. Thus Senators Robert Wagner and Charles Tobey were present at the Bretton Woods Conference, Vandenberg joined the American delegation to the United Nations Conference in San Francisco, and Vandenberg and Senator Tom Connally served at the 1946 Paris Peace Conference. Military aircraft carried members of Congress to economically hobbled postwar Europe to encourage "aye" votes for Truman-initiated recovery programs. In June 1949, just before the Senate approved American membership in NATO, Secretary of Defense Louis Johnson reminded the cabinet that a "liberal attitude in ferrying members of Congress to Europe" would be "helpful in developing support for [the] Atlantic Pact and Arms Program."[65]

Because the conduct of foreign policy has always operated in clouds of secrecy, any administration can withhold information from Congress on the ground of national security or executive privilege. "There is a point . . . when the Executive must decline to supply Congress with information," Truman wrote, "and that is when he feels the Congress encroaches upon the Executive prerogatives."[66] Congress has never been able to oversee effectively the Central Intelligence Agency, whose budget is even concealed.[67] Acheson believed that Congress was "dependent" upon the executive for knowledge of events—the "flow of papers"—and that "here knowledge is indeed power."[68]

While Truman was in office, initiative in foreign policy lay with the president. In essence, he decided which diplomatic topics the Congress acted upon. He sent requests for foreign aid; he delivered special messages; he outlined new programs. In short, as the famous saying has it, "the President proposes, the Congress disposes." What that often meant in the Truman period was that Congress gave legitimacy to what Truman had already decided. By announcing policies and then going to Congress to ask for endorsement, the president handed the legislative branch *faits accomplis*. By gaining the initiative in this way, he could exert considerable pressure on members of Congress who did not wish to be placed in the unenviable position of naysayers or neoisolationists—especially on Cold War issues which he defined in exaggerated terms as matters of national survival.

The president's March 1947 request for aid to Greece and Turkey provides a case in point. Once Truman had enunciated his "doctrine" before a joint session of Congress, many of its members hesitated to deny him his program. Senator Owen Brewster of Maine was reluctant "to pull the rug from under his feet," and Senator Leverett Saltonstall of Massachusetts said that Congress had to support the president, or "many people abroad who do not fully understand our system of government would look upon our failure as a repudiation of the President of the United States. American prestige abroad means more security and safety at home; this is to me a compelling reason.''[69] Legislative critics questioned the apparent indiscriminate globalism of the doctrine, the bypassing of the United Nations, the aid to undemocratic regimens, the salvaging of the British sphere of influence, and the cost, yet sixty-seven senators of the Republican Eightieth Congress stood with the president and only twenty-three voted against. Republican Senator Henry Cabot Lodge thought that his colleagues had to decide whether or not "we are going to repudiate the President and throw the flag on the ground and stamp on it. . . ."[70] Vandenberg was particularly alert to the relationships among the president's methods, congressional responsibilities, and American foreign policy in the Cold War:

> The trouble is that these "crises" never reach Congress until they have developed to a point where Congressional discretion is pathetically restricted. When things finally reach a point where a President asks us to "declare war" there is nothing left except to "declare war." In the present instance, the overriding fact is that the President has made a long-delayed statement regarding Communism on-the-march which *must* be supported *if* there is any hope of ever impressing Moscow with the necessity of paying any sort of *peaceful* attention to us whatever. If we turned the President down—after his speech to the joint Congressional session—we might as well either resign ourselves to a complete Communist-encirclement and infiltration or else get ready for World War No. Three.[71]

Bipartisanship was another resource for engineering congressional consent for the presidential foreign policy. Republicans, joining the president in his extreme depiction of the world crisis and the need to restore a broken world under Communist threat, muted their criticism of Truman's foreign policy, except that toward Asia. Vandenberg, one of the architects of bipartisanship, boasted in early 1949 that "during the last two years, when the Presidency and Congress represented different parties, America could only speak with unity. . . . So-called bipartisan foreign policy provided the connecting link. It did not apply to everything—for example, not to Palestine or China. But it did apply generally elsewhere." The senator concluded: "It helped to formulate foreign policy *before* it ever reached the legislative stage."[72] Vandenberg chaired the Foreign Relations Committee during the Eightieth Congress (1947–1949) and had something to say on almost every issue. He nursed presidential ambitions, became the foreign policy spokesperson for his party, and wanted to be consulted by the Truman administration. A student of the diplomatic career of Dean Acheson has concluded that Acheson "unfairly considered the Senator a superficial thinker, an egotist. . . . This egotism, Acheson believed, made it possible to manipulate Vandenberg by giving him the illusion of victory on an aspect of an issue."[73] Republican and future Secretary of State John Foster Dulles bluntly remarked that Vandenberg became the State Department's "mouthpiece" and "has no independent judgment."[74]

The Truman administration deftly flattered Vandenberg, appointing him to delegations, calling upon him for advice, applauding his Cold War patriotism, agreeing to his suggestions for appointments. During the launching of the Marshall Plan, Vandenberg said he would not support it unless a distinguished panel of citizens was appointed to study it. Truman complied and named W. Averell Harriman to head the committee. Truman wanted to make Acheson the administrator of the European Recovery Program, but Vandenberg disapproved. Truman thereupon consulted with the senator and appointed one of Vandenberg's candidates, Paul Hoffman, president of Studebaker.[75] In both cases the Marshall Plan itself was protected from serious challenge. The famous Vandenberg Resolution of 1948 was first suggested by and written in collaboration with the State Department. The document recommended that the United States associate itself with regional security pacts like that just formed in Western Europe under the Brussels Treaty. "The adoption of the Vandenberg Resolution [by a Senate vote of 64–41]," one scholar has written, "indicates once again the executive's primacy in the identification and selection of problems which occupy the foreign policy agenda of Congress and the executive."[76] All in all, Truman officials shrewdly and easily cultivated Vandenberg, disarming a potential critic and ensuring bipartisanship.

In the election of 1948 bipartisanship further greased political tracks for presidential foreign policies. As in 1944, Republican leaders pulled their punches. John Foster Dulles and Vandenberg persuaded their Republican party colleagues, including candidate Thomas Dewey, to refrain from criticizing the foreign policy of the Democratic president.[77] "One of the things I tried to keep out of the campaign was foreign policy," remembered Truman.[78] He succeeded.

"Bipartisan foreign policy is the ideal for the executive," mused Dean Acheson, "because you cannot run this damned country any other way except by fixing the whole organization so it doesn't work the way it is supposed to work. Now the way to do that is to say politics stops at the seaboard—and anyone who denies that postulate is a son-of-a-bitch and a crook and not a true patriot. Now if people will swallow that, then you're off to the races."[79] Votes in the Senate on key postwar programs reveal that the Truman administration commanded the results of the "races." The Bretton Woods agreements (World Bank and International Monetary Fund) passed 61–16, the United Nations Charter 89–2, ratification of the Italian peace treaty (1947) 79–10, assistance to Greece and Turkey 67–23, the Rio Pact 72–1, Interim Aid to Europe 86–3, the European Recovery Program 69–17, the Vandenberg Resolution 64–4, NATO 82–13, and ERP Extension 70–7. Only the favorable vote on the British loan of 1946 was close—46–33.

Most members of Congress debated how much to spend, not whether to spend. A Canadian diplomat astutely observed that the Truman administration's case for a "vigorous" foreign policy was putting doubtful senators "in the position of opening themselves to charges of lack of patriotism . . . ; they are therefore reduced to the role of critics of . . . details."[80] Sometimes they trimmed budgets and forced the executive to compromise on administrative machinery for foreign aid programs. Sometimes the president thought that he had to speak with alarm to persuade Congress to give him the votes. This was especially true with the Republican Eightieth Congress. Yet this was the same Congress that met every one of his requests for expensive foreign aid projects. Truman's tangle with what he called the "do-nothing" Eightieth Congress stemmed from domestic issues, not from questions of international relations. After Truman's stunning victory in the 1948 election, Communist Mao Zedong's 1949 triumph in China, the emergence of McCarthyism in 1950, and the outbreak of the Korean War in June of that year, bipartisanship eroded. Still, the administration, despite congressional cuts in requests for military assistance, got what it wanted from Congress, including aid to Communist Yugoslavia after Tito's break with Stalin. Acheson, no doubt a wry smile spreading across his mustachioed face, recalled that "many of those who demanded the dismissal of the Secretary of State in 1950–52 joined in passing all the major legislation he laid before the Congress. . . ."[81]

Most of the acts and treaties approved by Congress placed immense power in the hands of the president and his subordinates—to allocate funds abroad, to direct military assistance, to react quickly to crises, to order the use of nuclear weapons, to negotiate tariffs, to appoint administrators. Then, too, the president circumvented Congress by making executive agreements. Truman signed eighteen military executive agreements during his tenure—for example, those that permitted the United States to use an air base in the Azores (1947), to place troops in Guatemala (1947), and to hold bases in the Philippines.[82] In other important cases Truman simply did not go to Congress to ask for approval of his decisions. He decided to order the dropping of the atomic bombs on Hiroshima and Nagasaki on his own, and he alone possessed the awesome power thereafter to authorize the use of nuclear weapons. The Berlin blockade was met not with a congressional program but with the president's policy of an airlift. Truman never went to Congress for a declaration of war during the Korean War. It was truly a "presidential" war, but Congress voted funds time and time again to continue it. Acheson explained that the administration did not ask Congress for a war declaration because it did not want to invite hearings which might produce that "one more question in cross-examination which destroys you, as a lawyer. We had complete acceptance of the President's policy by everybody on both sides of both houses of Congress." He simply did not want to answer "ponderous questions" that might have "muddled up" Truman's policy.[83]

Thus public opinion and the Congress proved malleable, compliant, and permissive in the making of America's Cold War foreign policy. More than once President Truman successfully grasped the opportunity to free himself from political and constitutional restraints so that he could define and carry out his foreign policy preferences for dealing with the restraints and opportunities of the postwar international system. Sam Rayburn, Speaker of the House from 1940 to 1947 and again from 1949 to 1953, recognized the characteristics of an "imperial presidency" when he said that "America has either one voice or none, and that voice is the voice of the President—whether everybody agrees with him or not."[84] Indeed, the Soviets listened not to the voice of Congress or to the many voices of American public opinion but to the tough words of President Harry S. Truman.

8

SUSPICIOUSNESS
Stalin and Soviet
Foreign Policy

V-E DAY, plus two, brought the war-weary of Moscow into the streets. A noisy crowd of thousands gathered outside the American Embassy on that May 1945 day. Above, on the fourth-floor balcony, George F. Kennan waved to the throng. The demonstrators yelled wildly. Then they watched as an embassy officer ran next door to the National Hotel, requested and received a Soviet flag, and hoisted the red banner to fly beside the American Stars and Stripes. Another boisterous roar went up. Kennan went below and shouted, in Russian, "All honor to the Soviet allies." Again cheers sounded through the square.[1] The spirit of victory and alliance, the emotion derived from knowing that at last Hitler's rampage had been beaten back, welled up in the ecstatic Muscovites. But as Kennan knew well, foreign policy—especially Soviet foreign policy—was not made by "the people." How much the secretive men of the Kremlin shared that spirit and emotion and how much such positive feelings would infect postwar relations were the questions of the moment. Kennan and the embassy staff tackled those questions head-on, and scholars have devoted lifetimes to fathoming the intentions and decisions of Joseph Stalin and his Communist cohorts. Yet all the answers carry the mark of speculation, not of certainty, of guessing, not of knowing.

This chapter seeks to identify the fundamental and tactical characteristics of Soviet foreign policy in the early Cold War—those external and internal stimuli to Kremlin decisions. What were the wellsprings of Soviet behavior in the conflict-ridden international system? What domestic ideas and needs might have compelled the Soviets to build a sphere of influence in Eastern Europe, to risk breaking up the wartime alliance, and to claim great-power status? How did Soviet officials attempt to satisfy their nation's fundamental ideas and needs? How did they go about making their decisions? What was the Soviet style of diplomacy? Like Franklin D. Roosevelt, who posed the question to the Department of State, we want to understand the "Soviet psychology."[2]

Probing for the forces generating Soviet actions since the 1917 Bolshevik Revolution has been the primary, and one would have to say frustrating, function of experts called Sovietologists. During the intense Cold War, McCarthyite environment that cautioned scholars in the United States to conform to their government's official line and that welcomed the hard-line message of many Eastern European émigrés who had felt Stalinist repression directly, a strong anti-Soviet bias developed. "Cold-War ideology and politics helped shape and perpetuate an untenable scholarly consensus in the study of Soviet politics and history," one specialist has regretted. "They narrowed the range of topics and interpretations, minimized intellectual space, and made scholarly concepts hard and orthodox."[3]

If interpretive rigidity was not enough to make our understanding the Soviet Union difficult, we come to discover that trying to identify the ambitions of the Stalinist regime is akin to gazing into a crystal ball. The dizzying array of explanations demonstrates that there have been no pat answers and certainly little agreement among scholars, whatever their biases.[4] Doubt must dog any careful student of Soviet behavior. Charles Thayer, a member of the American Embassy in Moscow in the 1930s, once related a fanciful story about a Kentucky mountaineer's quest for information that illustrates how Kremlinologists must speculate about Soviet behavior:

> "Where's yer paw?" he asked the boy.
> "Gone fishin."
> "How d'ye know?"
> "Had his boots on and 'tain't rainin'."
> "Where's yer maw?"
> "Outhouse."
> "How d'ye know?"
> "Went out with a Montgomery Ward catalogue and she can't read."
> "Where's yer sister?"
> "In the hayloft with the hired man."
> "How d'ye know?"
> "It's after mealtime and there's only one thing she'd rather do than eat."[5]

The American ambassador to the Soviet Union from 1946 to 1949, Walter Bedell Smith, subscribed to the dictum of a British journalist who said that "there are no experts on the Soviet Union; there are only varying degrees of ignorance."[6] The Soviets have always been secretive about their policy-making process. The public speeches of prominent Soviet officials often seemed to be canned replicas of Communist party dogma. Kremlin officers gave little information to journalists or to foreign diplomats, and what they did release usually fell short of satisfactory explication. As of this writing, few records from the Soviet archives have been opened to researchers. The necessarily limited evidence that Sovietologists have produced to buttress their interpretations must be gleaned from Soviet press articles, public addresses, numerous but monotonous ideological tracts, summaries of the proceedings of international conferences, and a handful of memoirs. Historians have many National Security Council documents for the American side, but the records of Politburo meetings have not been revealed on the Soviet side. The rule for a careful historian is obvious: Don't claim too much. Those students of the Soviet Union who have depicted the Kremlin as a great beast, a mellowing tiger, or a neurotic bear have so argued, in other words, without the benefit of adequate and convincing evidence.[7] Their analyses may be correct, but no one can be sure. Some analysts have piled quotation upon quotation from pre-Cold War statements of V. I. Lenin or Stalin in an attempt to tap the inner core of the Kremlin, but the hazards therein are also obvious: Statements from the past, before the Cold War, were made in the historical context of a particular time and place, of an immediate issue. By necessity, a good deal of what we know about the Soviets comes from what non-Soviets have said about them. Because sources are thereby often skewed and biased, we must recognize this prejudice and guard against distortion. With all these caveats, then, we cautiously undertake in this chapter to identify the key fundamental and tactical ingredients of Soviet foreign policy.

The Soviet Union seemed eager to sustain the wartime alliance into the postwar era and to cooperate with the Rooseveltian-Churchillian scheme for spheres of influence. Stalin hoped to nurture this partnership as a mechanism for protecting and expanding Soviet interests, especially security along its borders, economic recovery from the war's heavy toll, survival of the Communist (hence Stalinist) experiment, and advancement of the case for communism around the world. An eagerness for revenge against the Germans and the Japanese (recalling the Russo-Japanese War, which the Russians soundly lost) also drove Soviet policy.[8] The Soviets worried a great deal that an Anglo-American diumvirate, powerful and anti-Soviet, would emerge after the war.[9] It seems clear that Stalin did not want war—a war that would certainly prove destructive to the Soviet Union, the Communist party, and his regime. The Soviet Union, devastated by the damage and cost of the Second World War, was simply too weak to do much more than try to keep a firm hand on Eastern Europe. On this point Kennan was consistent and insistent: "Russia's resources are already severely taxed to maintain the sphere of influence which the Soviet government has already acquired around the borders of the Soviet Union. There is no indication that Russia has the manpower or the skill to go much further in the line of dominion over other people."[10] British analysts agreed that Stalin "is, if anything, hard-headed, shrewd and cautious, particularly where the whole failure of Russian Communism is at stake."[11]

In the new postwar order Soviet officials insisted that their nation be treated as a respected equal, as one of the major powers. They deserved that rank, they claimed, by virtue of their relentless fighting and tremendous human and material losses in World War II and because of their military position in Europe at the end of the war. Longtime Soviet diplomat Maxim Litvinov complained in late 1944 that "we have never been accepted in European councils on a basis of equality. We were always outsiders."[12] Never again. They could not be taken for "fools," warned Stalin.[13] "Hitler had looked on the U.S.S.R. as an inferior country," Molotov said. "The Russians took a different view. They thought themselves as good as anyone else." The Soviet foreign minister reminded his

British counterpart that Britain's relations with "the Soviet Union must be based upon the principle of equality."[14]

Secretary of State James F. Byrnes once commented that "there is too much difference in the ideologies of the U.S. and Russia to work out a long term program of cooperation."[15] How strongly he believed this to be true we cannot know for sure, because he spent much of his brief diplomatic career working for a higher degree of cooperation. Yet he did identify an obvious tension in the Cold War and a fundamental factor in Soviet foreign policy. Soviets and Americans agreed that ideology, be it pure nineteenth-century Karl Marx, Lenin's elaborations and amendments, or Stalin's interpretations, was a Soviet mainspring. Everybody, Soviet and non-Soviet, seemed fond of quoting the past masters of Communist dogma.[16] Ambassador Smith allowed that "we always fall back on Lenin when we want an explanation of any of the phenomena of Soviet policy."[17] Another American diplomat reported in 1946 that "the Kremlin has hit [the] sawdust trail in revival of old-time Leninist religion."[18] A Soviet spokesman agreed that "an ideological war on a world scale is now being waged with unexampled ferocity."[19]

The Soviet ideology—the set of frequently articulated beliefs—was official doctrine. Cultivated by the ruling Communist party and given authority by the various agencies of the Soviet state, this dogma smacked of religious cultism, the true faith. As propaganda the ideology was broadcast around the globe; as indoctrination it was pressed upon Soviet citizens. The USSR's vice-minister of higher education declared emphatically that professors "bear a personal responsibility, not only for the standard of qualifications of graduating specialists, but also for their correct ideological training in Marxism-Leninism."[20] For Communists the tenets of their thought explained the past, present, and future. Ideology can serve a host of purposes: motive force, public relations device to rally supporters, ritualism, form of communication, symbol of continuity, rationalization for other motives, model for an ideal world, or legitimizer of policy. It provides a general guide for policy makers who, in their day-to-day deliberations, must select immediate policy courses.[21] Still, as one scholar has asked, "who can tell what the football coach who always predicts victory really believes?"[22]

The Soviet ideology betrayed a profound suspicion of non-Communist nations and their leaders.[23] In Soviet thinking the world was irrevocably divided into two competing groups: the "Soviet camp of peace, socialism, and democracy" and the "American camp of capitalism, imperialism, and war."[24] As long as both groups of nations existed, peace was impossible. Kremlin leaders saw the conflict between the capitalist and Communist worlds as a long-term struggle, deeply rooted in a dialectic of history. Capitalism, exploitative and expansionist, was the source of perpetual aggression and war. Conditions were such within the capitalist sphere that ambitious nations would always be grasping for more wealth and going to war to advance their interests. Conflict in the international system was also ensured by the class struggle within nations, by the vicious competition among capitalist states for raw materials and markets, and by the striving of colonial peoples to throw off their imperial masters. Greedy Americans and other capitalists, Communist ideologues claimed, profited from militarism, aggression, and war— "fattening on the blood of the people."[25] But the capitalist world, trapped in its unceasing conflicts, was destined to collapse. Economic havoc and depression, perhaps accompanied by war, would undercut the power of the capitalist ruling class. When economic conditions were ripe, when the capitalist leaders were down on their knees, the proletariat would seize the moment to displace them, heralding the world revolution and an end to exploitation. Communists asserted the inevitability of this scenario.

Until the dawning of this new, utopian era, however, the

Soviets faced hostile "capitalist encirclement"—the unrelenting capitalist attempt to crush the Soviet experiment, to snuff out the flame of revolution. The Soviet task, during this long but inevitable march toward a world free from capitalist iniquity, was to build the Soviet Union into a Communist bastion and a beacon for Communists elsewhere—to establish communism firmly in one country. Moscow, Stalin boasted in 1947, was "the champion of the movement of toiling mankind for liberation from capitalist slavery."[26] With the help of the irresistible theses of Marxism-Leninism, the Soviet Union could deepen the crisis in the capitalist camp and hurry the inevitable collapse by a variety of methods—from watchful waiting to "peaceful coexistence" to support for violent actions by revolutionaries. The ideology permitted flexible tactics: The end was inexorable, but the means were changeable. Thus the Soviets could even sign a pact with fascists and then join an alliance with capitalists in the Second World War. For certain, Soviets declared, revolution could not be exported. The conditions for rebellion were internal, peculiar to each nation. Finally, in this persistent struggle toward a noncapitalist utopia, everyone had to choose sides. Communist officials scoffed at neutralism or nonalignment in their rendition of the grand historical drama. "You are either with us, or against us," Stalin instructed a Chinese diplomat.[27] The ideology taught that for a long time most would be against.

One Soviet historian has found an "amazing similarity of the images" that the Soviets held of Americans and that Americans held of the Soviets. These images were one-dimensional (black and white), categorical (truth not to be doubted), stereotypical (substituting for an informed view), asynchronous (looking too much at past behavior rather than at present reality), demonized (the enemy as absolute evil), uncompromising (a duel to the death with the devil), and ideologized (made rigid by ideology).[28] Such extremist thinking was hardly conductive to a meeting of the minds through diplomacy.

Soviet ideologues turned the pages of history to find lessons that demonstrated the veracity of their theories. To them the record of capitalist hostility was evident enough: Allied military intervention in the Russian civil war and support of anti-Bolshevik forces; the creation at Versailles of a postwar cordon sanitaire of anti-Soviet states; refusal to recognize their government (Britain finally recognized it in 1924; the United States waited until 1933); and statements by leaders (like Senator Harry S. Truman) in the 1930s and early 1940s that fascists and Communists should fight each other, thereby ridding the world of two menaces. The ghost of Hitler also haunted the Soviets in the postwar period. Like Americans, they conjured up images of new Hitlers, new aggression, new wars—a replay of the 1930s. It seemed inevitable to the Soviets, following the dialectic of Marxism-Leninism, that a new round of troubles would unfold. In angrily rebuking the iron curtain speech of 1946, Stalin labeled Churchill "a firebrand of war," who reminded him "remarkably of Hitler and his friends." Would Churchill and his friends attempt another invasion like that in the World War I era? Should they, "they will be beaten, just as they were beaten twenty-six years ago."[29]

All in all, the components of the Soviet ideology told Kremlin officials that they continued to face an antagonistic world bent on extinguishing both revolution and the bearer of the torch, the Soviet Union. Because Soviet leaders felt duty-bound to preach their doctrines to others and to encourage dissident groups abroad, this ideology fed Soviet expansionism. When ideology and opportunity merged, as when Soviet troops stood guard over much of Central and Eastern Europe at the end of the war, expansionism moved from theory to reality. Although Stalin said at one point that "communism fitted Germany as a saddle fitted a cow," he also said that "whoever occupies a territory imposes on it his own social system."[30]

The essential forces behind Stalinist foreign policy seemed to be a "revolutionary romanticism" that sprang from Communist ideology and a "great-powerism" that derived from the Soviet Union's postwar status and that permitted Stalin to demand a sphere of influence.[31] The second point helps us understand another fundamental characteristic of Soviet postwar foreign policy—what in 1946 Maxim Litvinov (the Soviet foreign minister from 1930 to 1939) described as the quest for "geographical security."[32] Kennan, from his vantage point in the Moscow embassy, put the matter somewhat differently. He identified a "traditional and instinctive Russian sense of insecurity" and surmised that the Communist ideology was simply a new "vehicle" for the expression of this very Russian (as distinct from Soviet) phenomenon.[33] Although some scholars have attached more significance to ideology than to this strategic factor of national self-interest as a wellspring of Soviet behavior in the twentieth century, contemporaries thought the question of security worthy of considerable mention.[34] The Soviet concern for security seemed to have necessitated expansion or sphere building. We cannot know for sure if this drive for a secure sphere in Eastern Europe was fueled by fear or ambition, or both. But former State Department official Louis Halle appears to have made a good case for calling it "defensive expansion, an expansion prompted by the lack of natural defensive frontiers in a world of mortal danger on all sides. Where mountain-ramparts or impassable waters are lacking, sheer space must do in their stead."[35]

Since the early centuries of the Christian era the Russians have suffered invasions. Mongolian intruders from the East plundered the countryside. Genghis Khan, the thirteenth-century conqueror of Kiev, earned his infamous reputation for brutality by inflicting slaughter upon Russia. The Russians struck back, expanding their territory at the same time. From Ivan the Terrible (1533–1584) through Peter the Great (1682–1725)—who was particularly concerned about acquiring Russian access to open seas and who won a "window on Europe" by absorbing the Baltic provinces—the Russian czars enlarged their domain, in part to diminish their country's vulnerability to attack. Still, there were more invasions and wars: The Poles in the seventeenth century, like other invaders, burned Moscow, and Napoleon led his French forces into Russia during the War of 1812; the Crimean War of the 1850s and the Russo-Japanese War of 1904–1905 brought defeat to the Russians; and during World War I the Germans invaded.

The Bolsheviks, inheriting the Russian legacy, also had had to resist the invading troops of Britain, France, Japan, Italy, and the United States in 1918 and of Poland in 1920. In the harsh Brest-Litovsk Treaty of 1918, the Bolsheviks accepted a loser's peace from Germany, thereby giving up Poland, the Baltic states, and a large portion of the Ukraine— about the equivalent of the western territorial gains made since Peter the Great's day. Again, in the Second World War, Germans marched in to ravage the nation, killing millions and reducing whole sections to rubble. Never again, Stalin told Harriman, would the Soviet Union permit the Western powers to construct a cordon sanitaire in Eastern Europe to threaten Soviet security.[36] The Soviets proceeded to build their own security belt, which in Western parlance became known as the "iron curtain." As Litvinov remarked in an unusually candid criticism of his own government, the Soviets tried to grab "all they could while the going was good."[37]

The issue of postwar Poland epitomized the Soviet preoccupation with security. Poland, Soviet leaders said over and over again, was the "gateway," the "corridor," through which enemies attacked the Soviet Union. For the Soviet Union, Stalin declared, Poland was a question of "life or death."³⁸ In April 1945 he wrote Truman that Great Britain was shaping the postwar politics of Belgium and Greece because those countries were vital to British security: "I cannot understand why in discussing Poland no attempt is made to consider the interests of the Soviet Union in terms of security as well. . . ."³⁹ For Harry Hopkins, in May, Stalin repeated the point: "In the course of twenty-five years the Germans had twice invaded Russia via Poland. Neither the British nor American people had experienced such German invasions which were a horrible thing to endure. . . . It is therefore in Russia's vital interest that Poland should be strong and friendly."⁴⁰ In a public statement in March of the following year Stalin expanded the question beyond Poland when he emphasized that the Germans had also used Finland, Rumania, Bulgaria, and Hungary to invade the Soviet Union because those countries "had governments inimical to the Soviet Union."⁴¹

Why were the Soviets so determined to gain a share of the authority in managing the Dardanelles and Bosporus, the straits connecting the Black and Mediterranean seas? Stalin again pointed to national interest. "What would Britain do if Spain or Egypt were given the right to close the Suez Canal, or what would the United States Government say if some South American Republic had the right to close the Panama Canal?" Stalin asked Churchill at their 1944 Moscow meeting.⁴² No longer, the Soviet leader declared at the Yalta Conference, could the Soviets "accept a situation in which Turkey had a hand on Russia's throat."⁴³ He also told Ambassador Smith that Turkey was anti-Soviet and might permit foreign control of the straits (he thought that the Turks had done so during the war): "It is a matter of our security."⁴⁴

The Germans, Stalin prophesied, "will recover, and very quickly. Give them twelve to fifteen years and they'll be on their feet again. And this is why the unity of the Slavs is important."[45] His prediction of another war with Germany within a generation was dead wrong, but the intensity of his feeling toward that country pointed up the centrality of the strategic factor in Soviet foreign policy. "I hate Germans," Stalin remarked to Czech Prime Minister Eduard Beneš. "The Soviet Union wants nothing else than to gain allies who will always be prepared to resist the German danger."[46]

The Soviet Union's hobbled postwar economy posed another threat to survival, and the nation's economic needs seem to have constituted another—the third—fundamental ingredient in the Soviets' outward view. The Soviet Union was a "weak great power": before the war essentially a developing nation trying to establish an industrial base through rapid growth in five-year plans and after the war a devastated country facing massive reconstruction tasks.[47] "One only had to visit Russia to realize how much of its policy is affected by dire need," wrote Lucius Clay, the American military governor in Germany.[48]

Economic woes certainly explain some Soviet actions. Perhaps Soviet hyperbolic propaganda about an external enemy was stimulated by the need to rally the already burdened Soviet people to overcome the war-wrought devastation. "The emotional and physical exhaustion of the Soviet masses is a greater factor than is perhaps realized anywhere outside the USSR," the State Department informed President Truman in 1946.[49] The Soviets also sought compensation for their losses through war booty and reparations. From Manchuria they carted machinery. In Eastern Europe they confiscated property formerly owned by Germans, including equipment used for oil production in Rumania. In Hungary the Soviets gained control of the petroleum industry, some of which was German-operated in the war but owned by the Standard Oil Company of New Jersey. Trade treaties with Bulgaria, Hungary, and Rumania proved advantageous to the Soviet Union. Soviet officials also organized joint stock companies on a fifty-fifty basis with several neighboring states, and Poland was forced to ship valuable coal to the Soviet Union.[50] The Soviets, concluded a British diplomat, were pursuing an exploitative economic policy in Eastern Europe "to protect Soviet security," to gain their "rightful fruits of victory," and to ensure "reconstruction and industrialization."[51] The Soviets also insisted on large reparations from Germany and its satellites. "Reparations for Fulfillment of the Five-Year Plan" was the slogan of one Soviet planning group.[52] In their zone in Germany, Soviet officials confiscated heavy machinery and sent newly produced goods eastward. Hungary and Rumania were assessed about two hundred million dollars each in indemnities.[53] Economic needs may also explain why the Soviets intervened in Iran (for oil) and why they requested participation in a trusteeship for former Italian colonies in Africa (for uranium).[54] Finally, the U.S. chief of naval intelligence suggested in 1946 another possible expansionist effect of Russia's precarious economic status: "Maintenance of large occupational forces in Europe is dictated to a certain extent by the necessity of 'farming out' millions of men for whom living accommodations and food cannot be spared in the USSR during the current winter."[55]

Besides ideology, security, and economic needs, a fourth fundamental factor helps explain why the Soviet Union behaved as it did in world politics: military power. Derived from victories over German forces in Eastern Europe, the subsequent occupation of countries in that region, and the weakness of Soviet neighbors, this military power gave the Soviet Union regional supremacy. Unlike the United States, the Soviet Union suffered severe economic distress, had no foreign aid to dispense, and did not carry much international political weight beyond Eastern Europe. Molotov, for example, complained about the "voting game" which saw a majority at the United Nations and international conferences vote against Soviet proposals.[56] Litvinov thought it "not unreasonable for [the] USSR to be suspicious of any forum in which she would constantly be outvoted.''[57]

Yet when Americans gauged Soviet power, they did not think so much about the Soviet Union's economic deprivation or its lack of global political influence as about the huge, imposing, and battle-tested Red Army. When Secretary Byrnes mused that "somebody . . . made an awful mistake in bringing about a situation where Russia was permitted to come out of a war with the power she will have," he probably meant the power of the Red Army in Eastern Europe.[58] American military officials projected that should war break out between the United States and the Soviet Union, Red Army forces could probably march deep into Western Europe before they could be stopped and before the Soviet Union itself could be punished by American atomic attacks.[59]

The Red Army was probably the largest military grouping in Europe, and its standing, the fear it aroused in others, derived not only from its sheer size but from the fact that the Soviet Union's neighbors were so weak. The roughly half million Soviet soldiers who occupied Eastern Europe and part of Germany permitted Moscow to manipulate politics and hence to orient the foreign policies of its neighbors. The Red Army did not always have to intervene in a blatant fashion; the mere presence of troops inside a nation or near its borders carried influence and symbolized Soviet hegemony. Few could forget, as Stalin bragged in early 1946, that this was the "very army which utterly routed the German army that but yesterday struck terror into the armies of European states."[60] The Soviets also drew some measure of military power from geography. The vast landmass of the USSR, as Napoleon and Hitler had learned to their everlasting regret, could swallow invaders from the west, bitter-cold winters wearing them down. Retreating Soviet armies abandoned and even destroyed their towns, waiting for the eventual day of counterattack and retribution.

The Soviet military, however, revealed significant weaknesses, and American officials measured many of the deficiencies.[61] The Soviet navy lacked carriers and a modern fleet, a strategic air force, the atomic bomb (until 1949), and air defenses. Soviet ground forces lacked adequate motorized transportation, and troop morale was low. Roads and bridges were in terrible shape in the Soviet Union and Eastern Europe, and Soviet and Eastern European railroad track gauges were different—all obstructing transport. Much of the Soviet army's equipment was broken or obsolete; as late as 1950 half of its transportation was horse-drawn.[62] The American chief of naval intelligence suggested in 1946 that the Soviet Union was unlikely to launch a military attack because the "Red Fleet is incapable of any important offensive or amphibious operations," because "a strategic air force is practically nonexistent either in material or concept," and because "economically, the Soviet Union is exhausted. The people are undernourished, industry and transport are in an advanced state of deterioration, enormous areas have been devastated, thirty per cent of the population has been dislocated."[63] Compared with the non-Communist world, the Soviet Union was, said Kennan, the "weaker force."[64] Two years later General Lucius Clay observed that there were no signs of Soviet preparation for war, for "the Russian army was still a horse-drawn army and incapable of a blitzkrieg," and this condition explains why the Soviet military was "very circumspect" during the Berlin crisis.[65]

Western observers tended to overestimate the size of the Soviet armed forces. This happened in part because the Kremlin, secretive as always, did not publicize its own demobilization program, in part because the CIA found it difficult to penetrate the Soviet system, and in part because outsiders, in making their own military plans, tended, as always, to think the worst about the potential enemy's intentions and wherewithal. The Soviet Union, like the United States, actually demobilized its armed forces after the war. From a war-time peak of about 11.3 million persons Soviet armed forces dropped to about 2.9 million in 1948.[66] Many of the Soviet military's 175 divisions were understrength, and large numbers were performing occupation duties. The Soviets could not count on the troops of occupied nations like Poland to join them in a war. At most the Soviets had 700,000 to 800,-000 troops available for a westward attack. Since the West possessed about 800,000 as a counterforce, an approximate parity existed. Although official American analysts suggested larger figures for the size of the Soviet military, they did not expect a Soviet onslaught against Western Europe. Some politicians and the popular press, lacking the secret data of government officers or playing to the Cold War fears of the American public, downplayed Soviet demobilization, exaggerated the Soviet military threat, and inflated the numbers even more.[67] Stalin knew that his military establishment could not match up overall. In early 1948 he complained privately to Yugoslav leaders that their support for Communist rebels in the Greek civil war was dangerous to Soviet security. "What do you think, that Great Britain and the United States—the United States, the most powerful state in the world—will permit you to break their line of communication in the Mediterranean! Nonsense. And we have no navy."[68]

A working committee of the American Embassy in Moscow in 1946 delineated historical, ideological, geographic, and economic factors to explain the "dynamic, expanding" character of the Soviet Union. The committee, which included two men who later became leading academic scholars of Soviet politics (Robert Tucker and Frederick Barghoorn), advanced another fundamental ingredient, an "institutional" mainspring: totalitarianism.[69] The Soviets themselves, of course, never mentioned this characteristic. It emanated from outside observers who did not believe that Soviet fears, ideology, or economic-strategic needs were sufficient to account for the general Soviet suspiciousness of and hostility toward other nations. The Soviets, argued some analysts, exaggerated threats. Why? One highly speculative answer read that the maintenance of Stalinist totalitarianism—"a Frankenstein dictatorship worse than any of the others, Hitler included," Truman said—needed external enemies to deflect domestic criticism from the repressive regime.[70] Stalin's centralized one-man, one-party government, insisting on ideological purity and holding a monopoly of enforcing power, therefore really feared internal critics more than external capitalists. The Kremlin, goes this line of argument, heated up passions against the United States and its allies in order to silence its dissidents at home, to perpetuate its dreadful treatment of the Soviet people, and to urge the common people to accept further sacrifice. "The regime of ruthless dictatorship, of rule by police terror, imposed and maintained by Stalin from the early thirties on," concluded Thomas Whitney, a Foreign Service officer in Moscow, "required the presence of an external enemy in order that there should be justification for repression and terror."[71]

Whitney and others believed that Hitler had been a real threat to the Soviets in the 1930s but that in the late 1940s the Soviets invented the myth of "capitalist encirclement" and an "imperialist" United States as an enemy. "The basic problem," Acheson declared, "is that the very nature of the police state and of the Russian police state is such that it must continue an aggressive expansionist foreign policy. . . . It just must do that. It can't do anything else."[72] Walter Lippmann, like many others, penned an affirmative answer in 1947 to this question: "Does not the maintenance of the dictatorship in Russia depend upon maintaining a state of tension and insecurity to justify it?"[73] This speculative argument, of course, seems to have assumed a passivity on the part of the United States in the postwar period and discounted suggestions that activist American behavior might have alarmed the Soviets and influenced their decisions.

The peculiar needs and fears of the totalitarian government, it was further posited, perpetuated a Russian tradition: intense suspiciousness of all foreigners. American diplomats in Moscow frequently remarked that they were treated like potential enemies, spied upon, followed, isolated from the people, and made to suffer indignities at the hands of petty Soviet bureaucrats. Journalists had to submit all stories for clearance to capricious censors. The Soviets only reluctantly, after much obstruction, would permit American pilots to land at Soviet airfields during the war. Soviet women who had married American men were often not permitted to leave the country to join their husbands in the United States. Soviet soldiers and diplomats who had visited other nations in the course of their wartime duties came home to suspicions of disloyalty, interrogations by the secret police, and the ever-present hidden microphone. Stalin sought to detect any traces of ideological flabbiness or, worse, any evidence that the "enemy" had recruited them.[74] When Senator Wayne Morse of Oregon visited Vienna in 1946, he grew impatient with Soviet travel restrictions that held him up for an hour. "Each of these little incidents standing alone is not of great significance," he told a New York audience, "but when multiplied by many such incidents their cumulative effect helps produce the war of nerves which is developing in Europe."[75]

Even Communists in other countries were suspect. If they did not hew to the Moscow line, if they betrayed a sense of independence, if they did not wholly share the Kremlin's dark view of capitalists, and if they pursued different means from those prescribed by Stalin to reach the proletarian revolution, the totalitarian regime seemed again to be threatened, and the wayward had to be disciplined or stiff-armed. Stalin gave no aid to the Greek rebels, lectured and then broke relations with the independent Yugoslav Communist Josip

Broz Tito, and only halfheartedly supported the Communists of Mao Zedong in the Chinese civil war. Stalin "helped revolutions up to a certain point—as long as he could control them—but he was always ready to leave them in the lurch whenever they slipped out of his grasp," concluded Yugoslav Milovan Djilas after several conversations with the Soviet despot.[76] To discourage any centrifugal inclinations in the Communist world, then, Stalin exaggerated the capitalist danger.[77] In short, some have argued, totalitarian requirements necessitated international conflict.

This identification of totalitarianism as a linchpin of Soviet behavior in the Cold War, it must be repeated, rests at a higher level of conjecture than that for the other fundamental factors discussed. Assigning weights to the factors driving the Soviets' expansionist postwar course is inherently risky, but the several "fundamentals" all seem to have been ingredients in the policy mix and all were outlined by contemporaries.

Assessing the tactical factors of Soviet foreign policy also presents difficulties. The evidence is one-sided, coming from non-Soviets who sat across the negotiating table from their grim Communist counterparts. The Soviets themselves seldom commented on their own diplomatic style or method, and we can only surmise that differences in style contributed to postwar conflict. Some diplomats simply disliked other diplomats, found it nearly impossible to carry on negotiations with them, and stood back, seldom trusting. That Truman never met again with Stalin after Potsdam, that an American president did not sit down with a Soviet premier for the period 1945–1955, may not have been in itself a cause of Cold War tension, but it certainly meant that an obstacle blocked the road to diplomatic solutions. Negotiations can prove fruitless, of course, and summit conferences have often been superficial public shows of momentary cooperativeness, yet contact and communication are essential to the business of diplomacy. When they are absent—as when, for example, Harriman thought that the Soviets were "barbarians" and "world bullies" and Acheson became convinced that any discussion with the Soviets was futile—patient, low-key diplomacy gives way to name-calling, impatience, and bickering over minor matters.[78] In brief, people who do not get along cannot move negotiations along to compromise. What we can say with certainty is that the Soviet diplomatic style and its governmental structure did not serve to reduce conflict. American leaders thought that they ensured confrontation.

Stalin was the primary policy maker in a repressive state. Once, when Stalin and Harriman were discussing Poland, the ambassador warned that American public opinion, which he said the president had to listen to, would turn anti-Soviet unless an independent Polish state was established. Stalin replied that *he* had to worry about *Soviet* public opinion. Harriman shot back: "You know how to handle your public opinion."[79] Still, some internal debate did occur. Kremlin leaders, for example, apparently differed over policy toward Germany, specifically, whether to take reparations in the form of plant equipment or freshly produced goods.[80] Litvinov privately took the rare step of criticizing his government's foreign policy to an American journalist, as well as to others.[81] Eminent economist Eugene S. Varga strayed from strict Soviet ideology to argue that because of the American federal government's intervention in the economy, the anticipated postwar depression in the capitalist world might not be inevitable after all.[82] Stalin, or at least those who were privileged to be in his inner circle, apparently decided the outcome of debates and how long dissent would be tolerated. Litvinov was dropped from power, and Varga was publicly chastised and forced to recant. In the summer of 1946, moreover, Politburo member Andrei Zhdanov, apparently with Stalin's encouragement, began to push for uniformity of thought when he launched a purge of the intelligentsia that suppressed debate in agriculture and philosophy. The crackdown lasted until Zhdanov's death in 1948.[83]

Stalin's closest cohorts, a "set of inside advisers of whom we know little or nothing," reported Kennan, seemed to have been the members of the Politburo, the executive committee of the Communist party and the supreme policy-making organ.[84] "He is a decent fellow," Truman once commented about Stalin. "But Joe is a prisoner of the Politburo. He can't do what he wants to."[85] Ambassador Smith thought that the Russian leader was "chairman of the board," suggesting thereby that he had to consider the views of the other Politburo "directors."[86] Stalin was a "moderating influence" in the Kremlin, concluded Truman.[87] Indeed, some Americans believed that Stalin was not altogether a free man and that when he did exercise his authority, he attempted to curb the hostile excesses of his Politburo advisers.[88] We cannot know for sure. In any case, contemporaries and later scholars alike agree that Stalin was the prime decision maker, a secretive dictator who brooked no challenge to his authority but who at times tolerated or suffered power struggles and debates among his subordinates.[89]

Stalin himself demonstrated monstrous qualities, as evidenced by the ghastly purges of the 1930s and the terror of everyday political life in the Soviet Union. After the war, the gulags, or forced labor camps, housed large numbers of Soviet citizens. Callousness characterized his entire political career. Even his infrequent attempts at humor lent credence to the popular view that he was cold-bloodedly cruel. "Bring the machine guns. Let's liquidate the diplomats," he once joked in the presence of Charles de Gaulle, Georges Bidault, and Averell Harriman, none of whom was amused.[90] The Soviet leader was suspicious, it appears, of everyone. "He saw enemies everywhere," his daughter recalled.[91] Although some commentators speculated that Stalin was pathologically suspicious or paranoid, most contemporaries did not think him

insane or irrational.[92] Instead, they thought him a sober, if
fearful, "realist," a cautious calculator who, as he put it, preferred arithmetic to algebra.[93] Kennan wrote years later that
"merciless as he could be, and little as his purposes may have
coincided with ours, Stalin was entirely rational in his external policies. . . ."[94]

Stalin's chief negotiator, V. M. Molotov, who was the commissar for foreign affairs from 1939 to 1949 and again from
1953 to 1956 and renowned for his "extraordinary firmness"
and "pungency," received much the same assessment.[95] This
stern man, who peered through his pince-nez and "laughed
with his mouth not his eyes," was universally disliked.[96] Truman thought that labor leader John L. Lewis and Molotov
were "principal contenders for top rating as walking images
of Satan."[97] "Stone Ass," as Molotov was impolitely called,
was considered by some to be more intransigent than Stalin.
In June 1945 Harriman complained to Truman that "Molotov did not report to Stalin accurately. . . . It is also clear that
Molotov is far more suspicious of us and less willing to view
matters in our mutual relations from a broad standpoint than
is Stalin."[98] American diplomats sought to skirt Molotov, to
go directly to Stalin, who seemed more flexible. When Hopkins went to Moscow in May 1945, for example, he attempted,
through direct talks with Stalin, to change the Soviet position
on the veto in the United Nations. The Soviets wanted the
veto to cover everything, including discussion, whereas the
American position was that the veto should be used only to
strike down actions. Molotov had stood utterly firm on the
question. As Stalin listened to Hopkins and heard what Molotov had been arguing, he gruffly turned on his foreign secretary, uttered, "That's nonsense," and immediately accepted
the U.S. position.[99]

Whether observers were commenting on Stalin, Molotov,
or other Soviet officials, the pervasive judgment was that the
Soviet diplomatic style inhibited the negotiating process and

eroded goodwill. The Soviets were thought to be rude, untrustworthy, excessively suspicious, devious, unreceptive to gestures of kindness, and too dependent upon direct instructions from the Kremlin.[100] It seems that few of the experienced diplomats of the Commissariat of Foreign Affairs had survived the purges of the 1930s. Many of the new members of the diplomatic service had little university education or liberal arts background, having been schooled in technical institutes. Many had not traveled abroad and were not proficient in foreign languages.[101] Some, like Soviet Ambassador to the United Nations Andrei Vyshinsky, had been stalwarts of Stalinist ruthlessness in the purges—and Americans could not easily forget that they had blood on their hands. The polished Acheson, who found talking to the Soviets a particularly arduous trial, snidely suggested that Soviet diplomats went to schools "where naturally coarse manners were made intentionally offensive, and where the students were trained in a technique of intellectual deviousness designed to frustrate any discussion."[102] Whether so trained or whether simply crude, the Soviets developed their own "get tough" style which obstructed negotiations. To American officials, who had little bargaining experience with the Soviets before World War II, it seemed that their Soviet opposites were deliberately hindering the business of diplomacy. "They don't know how to behave," Truman remarked. "They're like bulls in a china shop. They're only twenty-five years old. We're over one hundred years old and the British are centuries older. We've got to teach them how to behave."[103]

Truman also concluded that the Soviets were "touchy," easily slighted, and oversensitive to any hint that they were not representatives of a great nation.[104] At the Potsdam Conference, for example, the British, American, and Soviet chiefs of staff gathered to discuss military questions. U.S. Admiral William Leahy rapped the gavel on the table and called the meeting "to order." The Soviet delegate, upon hearing the translation of these opening remarks, abruptly rose to his feet, grumbled that he and his colleagues had been insulted, and demanded to know who was "out of order."[105] Months later Trygve Lie, secretary-general of the United Nations, toured the devastated Soviet Union and at one luncheon bestowed what he thought was praise upon his Soviet hosts: that they ranked first in army strength, second in wealth and industry, and third in sea power. The angry Soviets interpreted these words to mean that Lie was telling them they were not a great power.[106]

The Soviets also bargained hard in negotiations. Truman saw them as "pigheaded."[107] They often repeated their positions endlessly, prolonging meetings. "Jimmy," an impatient and perturbed Truman complained to Byrnes at Potsdam after hearing a Stalin *nyet*, "do you realize that we have been here seventeen whole days. Why, in seventeen days you can decide anything!"[108] Soviet diplomats balked at compromise, perhaps fearful of having to explain any divergence from precise instructions to a suspicious Kremlin. "I must talk to my government" was a common, and annoying, utterance from Soviet diplomats at crucial moments in negotiations.[109] The seemingly timid Soviet diplomats took on the appearance of messenger boys.[110] They also threatened to walk out of meetings—and occasionally did—and they sometimes changed positions with an abruptness that baffled. They could run hot and cold; President Roosevelt noted the "Russian habit of sending him a friendly note on Monday, spitting in his eye on Tuesday, and then being nice again on Wednesday."[111] A common expression among diplomatic officers in the Moscow embassy was that when trading with the Russians, you had to buy the same horse twice because they kept bringing up points that others thought were settled.[112] Secretary Marshall deplored another Soviet tactic in negotiations: The Soviets would say to him, "You did not deny our statement so obviously it must be correct."[113] The harshest judgment was that Soviet diplomats were liars, not to be trusted.[114]

Stalin apparently described himself as a "rude old man."[115] Non-Soviet diplomats could only agree that that description was appropriate for much of the Soviet foreign service. Hugh Dalton, British chancellor of the exchequer, pronounced the Soviets a "bad mannered people." He compared them to a "pup which is not yet housetrained." Indeed, "they bounce about and bark and knock things over and misbehave themselves generally and the next day are puzzled if one is still resentful."[116] Acheson's conclusion bears repeating: "You cannot sit down with them."[117] What is more, he seldom did, for he believed that the fundamental dynamics of the Soviet Union and the tactics of its officials militated against serious accommodation in the escalating Cold War.

9

DECLINE
The Erosion of Power and the Appeal of Détente, 1950s–1980s

JOSEPH STALIN died of a stroke on March 5, 1953, suspicious to the last breath that domestic and foreign enemies were plotting against him, his autocratic state, and Soviet interests. Just a few weeks earlier, on January 20, Harry S. Truman, the American president whom Stalin found so threatening to the Soviet Union, departed the White House for his Missouri hometown after his personal popularity had plummeted and voters had repudiated his political party. Stalin's reputation for ruthlessness grew even more after his death while Americans in the years ahead elevated Truman to folk hero status. Neither Stalin nor Truman, however, could plausibly claim, in early 1953, that his postwar foreign policy had succeeded in creating global stability or in ensuring the security of his nation. Such was evident in official Washington's initial response to Stalin's death. The State Department read the event not as a chance to reduce Cold War tensions but rather as an opportunity "to sow doubt, confusion, and uncertainty" among Communists throughout the world.[1]

As Stalin's and Truman's political careers closed, the Korean War, which claimed nearly three million lives, still raged. Although the war finally ended in July 1953, its legacy included a hardening of the Cold War, especially as the United States acted on the assumptions of NSC-68. In late 1950 China had dispatched "volunteers" against American troops advancing toward its border; the blood spilled from this engagement besmeared the Sino-American relationship for decades. The restoration of Japan as a member of the U.S. sphere in Asia, which also included South Korea, Formosa (Taiwan), the Philippines, and Vietnam, was accelerated. The war induced as well more alliance building and more great-power interventions, notably in Vietnam, where radical nationalists continued their battle for independence from France. Accentuation of the ideological dimension of the Cold War counted as another outcome of the Korean War. To the end Stalin shouted warnings against "capitalist encirclement" and Truman railed against the "international Communist conspiracy."

A combination of international, national, and personal factors, as discussed in previous chapters, had merged to make the Cold War and to divide the world into spheres of influence. During the late 1940s power vacuums, massive economic disorder, civil wars, colonial revolts, disintegrating empires, newly independent states, fledgling international organizations, the atomic bomb, and a shrinking interdependent globe—all had produced severe tensions. In this unstable environment the United States and the Soviet Union sought to satisfy their particular national needs and ideas, to expand their divergent interests and principles. By the early 1950s the conflict-ridden postwar international system which emerged from the Second World War had become essentially bipolar. The two major powers had built competing spheres of influence. They had made the Cold War.

If Americans were universalist on behalf of an ideology linking peace, prosperity, democracy, and the open door, the Soviets preached a universal message of inevitable proletarian revolution. If America's political heritage championed ideals that Americans thought so superior that others should adopt them (and perhaps even be pressed to adopt them), totalitarianism and the messianic Communist mission stimulated Soviet exaggerations of an external threat and a drive to attract obedient converts to the Soviet experiment. If the Soviets conjured up the ghost of Hitler, predicting a relentless duel with the capitalist menace, Americans also drew lessons from the past that suggested a renewed struggle with Hitler-like, Red-Fascist aggression. As Americans reached for foreign outposts and markets to meet their strategic-economic needs, the Soviets found as well that their security and economy required expansionism. Whereas the Soviet Union imposed rigid authority on Eastern Europe, the United States wielded impressive economic, political, and military power on a global scale. The Soviet and U.S. spheres were quite different, especially as measured by the greater degrees of power sharing and political and religious tolerance in the American sphere, but in their expansionism both the United States and the Soviet Union unsettled the postwar world.

In the pursuit of their objectives leaders in Moscow and Washington, suspicious and distrustful of each other, conducted diplomacy with styles that stymied negotiations. The American and Soviet political systems were such that diplomacy rested in the hands of Truman and Stalin and their immediate advisers, who faced few domestic restraints and were thus able to define the character of the postwar confrontation. The autocratic Stalin governed through repression and terror; the politically astute and popularly elected Truman gained his influence from a compliant Congress and from a constitutional system that tilted in favor of presidential power. Truman could co-opt or fire his rivals; Stalin could execute or jail them. In international relations these two very different men became hard-liners who led their nations into confrontation.

Like a fast-moving glacier, the Cold War cut across the global terrain in the 1940s, scraping and grinding solid base, carving and leveling valleys, changing the topography. For nearly a half century the Cold War competition between the United States and the Soviet Union dominated the international system. Gradually the bipolar configuration gave way to a diffusion of power. Ultimately the two great powers embraced détente and ended the Cold War in the late 1980s. Like all retreating glaciers, the receding Cold War left deposits of debris and exposed an altered, scarred landscape that leaders in the 1990s struggled to measure and fathom. The previous chapters accounted for the making of the Cold War; the next two chapters explore the last several decades to explain the unmaking of the Cold War and the difficult task of defining a new global order.

Simply put, the Cold War ended because of the relative decline of the United States and the Soviet Union in the international system from the 1950s through the 1980s. The Cold War waned because the contest had undermined the power of its two major protagonists. In acts of hegemonic survival in a world of mounting challenges on several fronts, they gradually moved toward a cautious cooperation whose urgent goals were nothing less than the restoration of their economic well-being and the preservation of their diminishing global positions.

At least three sources or trends explain this gradual decline and the consequent attractions of détente. The first was the burgeoning economic costs of the Cold War. Challenges to the leadership of the two major powers from within their spheres of influence constitute the second source. The third was the emergence of the Third World, which brought new players into the international game, further diffused power, and eroded bipolarism. The three elements combined to weaken the standing of the two adversaries and ultimately to persuade Soviet and American leaders to halt their nations' descent by ending the Cold War. The Soviet Union fell much harder than the United States, but the implications of decline became unmistakable for both: The Cold War they made in the 1940s had to be unmade if the two nations were to remain prominent international superintendents.

The first source was the economic burden that the long confrontation inflicted on the United States and the Soviet Union.[2] America's impressive economic standing after the Second World War and into the 1950s went unmatched. The American economy shifted into high gear during the war while much of the rest of the world was being reduced to rubble. In the postwar years the United States used its abundant economic resources to spur the recovery of its allies and to build an international military network. The costs of maintaining and expanding its global interests climbed dramatically: $12.4 billion for the Marshall Plan, $69.5 billion for the Korean War, $22.3 billion for the Alliance for Progress, $172.2 billion for the Vietnam War. In the years from 1946 through 1987 the United States dispensed more than $382 billion in economic and military foreign aid. International organizations in which the United States was prominent, such as the World Bank, offered another $273 billion in assistance.

The United States also spent billions of dollars for CIA operations such as that at the Bay of Pigs in Cuba (1961) and for invasions like that of the Dominican Republic (1965). Support for factions in civil wars and political contests from Greece to Italy, from Chile to Nicaragua, from Angola to Somalia, from China to the Philippines—and especially in

Vietnam—drove up expenses. During 1984 to 1987 Washington sent more than $2 billion in aid just to the government of El Salvador to help that small Central American state combat an insurgency Washington called Communist. The CIA put high-ranking officials from Panama to Bolivia on the agency's payroll. Expenses also mounted for the maintenance of occupying forces in Germany, Japan, and elsewhere. U.S. Information Agency propaganda activities proved expensive, too, as witnessed by the Voice of America's $640 million expenditure in the 1970s.

Security links stretched across the globe. After the Rio Pact (1947) and NATO (1949) came the ANZUS Pact with Australia and New Zealand (1951), the defense treaty with Japan (1952), the South East Asia Treaty Organization (SEATO, 1954), and the Baghdad Pact for the Middle East (1955), which the United States supported but did not join. The rearmament of West Germany began in the early 1950s, and that half nation entered NATO in 1955. In 1959, moreover, one million Americans were stationed overseas; in 1970 the number was nearly nine hundred thousand; and by 1985 the United States still had more than half a million armed forces personnel abroad.

Alliance building, military expansion, clandestine operations, and interventionism spawned galloping defense budgets amounting to trillions of dollars over four decades. U.S. military spending stood at $13.5 billion in 1949, averaged $40 billion a year in the 1950s, rose to $54 billion in 1960 and $90 billion in 1970 (largely because of the Vietnam War), and soared to $155 billion in 1980. By 1988 the military budget alone had reached more than $300 billion. In the mid-1980s the Defense Department was spending an average of $28 million an hour, twenty-four hours a day, seven days a week. Nuclear arms development and ever more sophisticated technology drove up the cost of waging the Cold War. In 1952 the United States exploded its first thermonuclear bomb, and seven years later it launched its first intercontinental ballistic missile (ICBM). Submarine-launched ballistic missiles (SLBMs), antiballistic missiles (ABMs), cruise missiles, MX missiles, neutron bombs, stealth bombers, and President Ronald Reagan's Strategic Defense Initiative joined the relentless march toward new, expensive weapons. By 1979 the United States possessed 9,200 nuclear warheads that could be delivered by its triad of 1,054 ICBMs, 656 SLBMs, and 350 strategic bombers—more than enough nuclear capacity to destroy much of the world's population.

America's massive military spending chipped away at the nation's infrastructure, contributing to the relative decline of the United States and stimulating the movement toward Soviet-American détente. Defense spending demanded capital, which the federal government had to borrow, forcing up interest rates, which in turn slowed economic development. Persistent deficit spending by the federal government drove up the federal debt, which stood at $257 billion in 1950, $286 billion in 1960, $371 billion in 1970, and $908 billion in 1980. By 1986 the debt had reached a staggering $2.1 trillion. That year alone 19 percent of the federal budget disappeared just to pay the interest on the debt. In that same year defense gobbled up 28 percent of the budget. By comparison, 11 percent of federal expenditures went to health and Medicare, 3 percent to education, and 1 percent to environmental programs. Analysts noted that in 1984 Japan's per capita military spending came to only $102 and West Germany's to $360. In conspicuous contrast, the figure for the United States was $968.

Military spending constantly drew funds away from other categories so essential to the overall well-being of the nation—what economists call "opportunity costs." Domestic troubles mounted: lower productivity, falling savings rate, sagging agricultural sector, inadequately skilled labor force with an increasing number of functional illiterates, drug abuse, decaying cities, growing high school dropout rates, a health care system that failed to cover large numbers of people, and weak conservation programs that left the U.S. economy vulnerable to sharp swings in prices of imported raw materials. As President Jimmy Carter's national security adviser Zbigniew Brzezinski observed, the Cold War carried "painful social costs."[3]

The United States suffered relative decline, too, because other nations, especially economic rivals Japan and West Germany, invested a larger share of their budgets in *private* research and development. Substantial U.S. federal spending for *military* research and development did not create adequate "spin-offs" of technologies to the civilian economy and had the effect of drawing off scientists and technicians from the private sector to government jobs, thereby slowing technological advances in the production of commercial goods and reducing America's competitive position in international markets.[4]

The United States also became a debtor nation with a serious balance of payments problem and a widening trade deficit. In the late 1950s private overseas investments, U.S. spending for foreign aid and military activities abroad, and the American purchase of more imports than could be matched by the sale of exports precipitated a significant dollar drain. Foreigners came to hold so many U.S. dollars that they threatened the nation's gold reserves. "We're broke, anyone can topple us," Treasury Secretary John Connally told President Richard Nixon in 1971 as Washington scrambled to head off disaster.[5] That year, too, the first trade deficit since 1888 befell the United States. By the 1970s, when American sentiment for détente in the Cold War was growing, *Business Week* magazine concluded that the U.S. "colossus" was "clearly facing a crisis of the decay of power."[6] Henry Kissinger, Nixon's primary foreign policy adviser and a major influence behind détente and withdrawal from Vietnam, explained that "we were becoming like other nations in the need to recognize that our power, while vast, had limits. Our resources were no longer infinite in relation to our problems."[7] President John F. Kennedy had asserted in his 1961 inaugural address that Americans would "pay any price" and "bear any burden," but Nixon and Kissinger knew a decade later that the cost of globalism was emptying American pocketbooks.[8] Americans had "frittered" away their power, complained former Truman adviser Clark Clifford. They had reduced "this economic Gibraltar to the largest debtor nation in the world."[9]

International economic crises—high oil prices in the 1970s and massive Third World debt in the 1980s—added to America's woes. Debt-ridden nations curbed their purchases of American products and suspended debt payments. By 1985 the U.S. trade deficit had reached a remarkable $148.5 billion. Foreigners used many of the dollars they amassed to buy American companies: Japanese investors owned 7-Eleven, Fotomat, and Columbia Pictures; British buyers acquired Burger King; and German investors purchased RCA Records. Four of California's ten largest banks became Japanese-owned. "Did you hear?" went one joke. "The Japanese just bought Pearl Harbor!" Even though such foreign investment represented only a small portion of the American economy, there could be no denying that the United States seemed less able to control its own house and was more susceptible to the decisions of non-Americans.

Americans became increasingly dependent upon foreign capital to pay for their hunger for imports, to fund real estate speculation and corporate buyouts (rather than to upgrade factories, for example), and to finance the federal deficit. Americans were giving to foreigners great amounts of the nation's wealth as debt payments. By 1989 the U.S. foreign debt hit $650 billion. Americans, moreover, were not putting enough money in their savings accounts to boost investment in economic development. In 1980 the United States had the lowest personal savings rate of the "Big Seven" economies (United States, Canada, France, Italy, Japan, United Kingdom, and West Germany). Continued private American investment abroad actually made matters worse: U.S.-owned companies that set up operations abroad to take advantage of lower labor costs then exported their goods to the United States, thus aggravating the trade deficit.[10]

Although the American economy during the Cold War grew in absolute numbers, the U.S. share of the world's material resources declined relative to other nations. Analysts use different methods of computation, interpret figures differently, and sometimes cite shaky statistics or let political or ideological preferences control the "numbers game," but as somebody has put it, you do not need to be a hydraulic engineer measuring the flow to see that the water runs downhill. The signs of decline and comparative disadvantage became conspicuous. Between 1960 and 1973 the U.S. economic growth rate compared with that of all other countries was 4 percent versus 5.6 percent, and from 1973 to 1980 2 percent versus 3.6 percent. In the decade of the 1970s ninety-eight nations had higher rates of economic growth than the United States. In 1979 and 1980 the U.S. growth rate dropped to minus 0.2 percent; by comparison, Japan's stood at 4.2 percent and West Germany's at 1.8, and the world rate was 2 percent. The U.S. share of gross world product also declined: from approximately 40 percent in 1950 to about 22 percent in 1980. Japan doubled its share in the same period to 9 percent. From the 1950s to the 1980s the American share of world exports slumped while West Germany's and Japan's shares jumped. The American rate for productivity growth (output per worker) also descended; for 1950–1970 the rate was 2.68 percent, then for 1970–1980 it dropped to 1.17 percent, and for 1980–1986 it stood at 1.53 percent. For the same periods Japan's and West Germany's rates ranked higher than the

U.S. rate. The American share of world industrial production also fell, and the United States lost its lead in televisions, automobiles, semiconductors, and machine tools. In 1950 the United States produced 46 percent of the world's steel, but by 1987 the American percentage had tumbled to 11 percent, and both Japan (13.7 percent) and the European Economic Community or Common Market (17.8 percent) had surpassed the United States.

These numbers and comparisons spell relative decline, but they do not by themselves indicate how well or poorly the United States could project its power in the world. Other indicators like the extent of public consensus at home, the nature of leadership, the characteristics of the international system, the quality of production, and military readiness must join the economic statistics for a fuller appreciation of power. Nor do the numbers speak to the structural power of the United States—that is, the power to set the rules by which others have to operate in the international security system, finance, production, trade, and telecommunications.[11] But, as is suggested here, the United States found itself increasingly struggling to project power other than its military component, and its structural power also weakened.

American leaders of all political persuasions, year after year, decried the detrimental effects of the Cold War on the nation's economic well-being. The Eisenhower administration tried in the 1950s to keep military expenses down, for as Secretary of the Treasury George Humphrey remarked at a National Security Council meeting: "We might well overreach ourselves." President Dwight D. Eisenhower worried, too, about " 'busting' ourselves."[12] America faced two dangers, the former general said: "the external threat of Communism and the internal threat of a weakened economy."[13] For Eisenhower, a bloated military expenditures raised the specter of federal budgets that underfunded or neglected the domestic infrastructure and thereby undercut America's military effectiveness. A strong economy, not merely large armed forces and sophisticated nuclear equipment, he argued, was essential to effective defense. Strong nations required a well-educated, healthy citizenry and work force. He lectured that a "garrison state" threatened rather than strengthened national security.[14] "Every gun that is made, every warship launched, every rocket fired signifies, in the final sense, a theft from those who hunger and are not fed," the Republican president said. "The cost of one modern heavy bomber is this: a modern brick school in more than 30 cities."[15] In his 1961 farewell address Eisenhower warned against the "unwarranted influence" of an interlocking power elite he called the "military-industrial complex"—a coalition of military officers and defense contractors who cooperated to sustain high defense expenditures.[16] Despite his prophetic comments, an anguished Eisenhower failed to slow the arms race or escalating defense expenditures.

During the 1960s, when the Vietnam War and the Great Society programs competed for funds, the "guns versus butter" debate spotlighted the problem. Economists like Seymour Melman, in his book *Our Depleted Society*, sounded alarms.[17] Senators Hubert Humphrey, George McGovern, and William Proxmire, among many others, worried that climbing defense budgets distorted the economy. They publicized the fact that America's economic competitors were plowing funds into private research and development rather than into their militaries.[18] The civil rights leader Martin Luther King, Jr., joined many other reformers to protest the detrimental effects of the Vietnam War on the home front. He calculated that the United States spent five hundred thousand dollars to kill one Vietnamese enemy soldier but only thirty-five dollars a year to assist one American in poverty. "The promises of the Great Society," King regretted, "have been shot down on the battlefield of Vietnam."[19]

During the 1970s President Nixon, sensitive to the costs of

the Cold War and the increasing American public discontent with large budgets and high taxes, called for "burden sharing" by America's allies. One of the conservative architects of containment, George F. Kennan, bemoaned America's inattention to its domestic life. He worried about ecological ruin and the squandering of natural resources. "Foreign policy, like a great many other things," he wrote in his book *The Cloud of Danger* (1977), "begins at home."[20] With other prominent Americans Kennan advocated détente with the Soviet Union, and he admonished Washington to bring its trade and budget deficits and pell-mell defense spending under control or forfeit national greatness. What America really needed to wield continued international influence, Kennan remarked in 1985, was "self-containment."[21] About the same time the Roman Catholic Bishops of the United States sounded a familiar chord in a pastoral letter: The nuclear arms race must end because it "robs the poor and the vulnerable."[22]

To highlight Cold War spending for defense and foreign ventures and the related deteriorating American condition does not imply that the United States fell to its knees and became incapable of sustained economic growth. Despite its many domestic problems and a steady series of recessions, the United States still ranked as a wealthy, powerful nation with impressive talents and resources compared with other countries. American-owned corporations still dominated the world economy. And America's competitors had their own economic troubles. Nor does the thesis of long-term economic decline deny that the United States probably enjoyed some gains from its Cold War era spending in the form of strategic raw materials imports, markets, jobs, and technological improvements, as in 1954, for example, when the U.S. defense program funded 60 percent of IBM's computer research and development.[23]

The compelling point is that the Cold War was exceedingly

costly. With finite resources the U.S. government had to make choices. Money spent on the military and foreign interventions was not spent on building America at home. The trade-offs—fighter planes and MX missiles instead of state-of-the-art school science laboratories and job-training programs, for example—proved detrimental to the long-term health of the nation. Defense spending became "Keynesianism on steroids": The short-term effects were stimulating, but like any addiction, it produced long-term ill effects. Perhaps the money, if not devoted to military hardware, would not have been otherwise wisely invested. But it is demonstrably true that "nations that spend heavily on armaments, such as the United States and United Kingdom, have forfeited valuable gains in industrial productivity and economic growth."[24]

Measurable economic decline compelled American policy makers, however reluctantly at times, to take steps toward ending the Cold War. By relieving domestic troubles, détente seemed to offer continuation of America's world-class status. Détente might make expensive interventions and ever-growing arsenals less necessary. It also promised greater trade with both the Soviet Union and the People's Republic of China, the former hungry for American grain and the latter eager for American technology. Overall, détente might move America out of what one journalist called "Sector D"—"depression, decline, depravity, doom, denial, decay, debacle, dementia, . . . dilly-dallying, despair, . . . dysfunction, . . . doubt and disgust."[25]

The Cold War also cost the Soviet Union a great deal—indeed, much more than it cost the United States—and this burden persuaded Moscow to seek détente.[26] The Soviets began, of course, with a much lower economic base than the Americans did and had the monumental task of recovering from the devastation of the Second World War. Analysts lack full and totally reliable information on the Soviet economy and budgets, but trends are quite clear. The Soviet Union also became a big military spender, in part to catch up in the strategic arms race. In 1953 the USSR exploded its first thermonuclear bomb, and four years later it launched the first ICBM and propelled the first man-made satellite into outer space. The Soviet Union matched each American advance, and it beat the United States by four years (1968 against 1972) in creating an ABM that could knock out incoming projectiles. By the 1970s the Soviets had achieved strategic weapons parity with the United States. In 1979 the Soviets possessed 5,000 nuclear warheads that could be delivered by 1,400 ICBMs, 950 SLBMs, and 150 strategic bombers.

Foreign ventures, too, strained Soviet resources. In the 1950s Moscow began to lend funds to Third World nations— to India for a steel plant, to Egypt for the Aswan Dam. The Warsaw Pact; aid to the People's Republic of China (until halted by Moscow in the early 1960s); support for Egypt (until the Soviets were evicted in 1972), Syria, and other Middle Eastern states; and subsidies to Fidel Castro's Cuba (which averaged close to five billion dollars during the 1980s) also drew heavily on Soviet funds. North Vietnam received more than eight billion dollars in Soviet aid from 1965 to 1975.[27] The Soviet Union subsidized its Eastern European client states, probably spending at least seventeen billion dollars a year by the early 1980s. The invasions of Hungary in 1956 and Czechoslovakia in 1968 and the ten-year war in Afghanistan from 1979 to 1989 cost dearly. In 1980 alone the expense to the Soviet Union of maintaining its empire and worldwide commitments through trade subsidies, military and economic aid, interventions, and covert operations totaled approximately thirty-eight billion dollars.

The expense of the Cold War to the Soviet Union was apparent as early as the mid-1950s to Secretary of State John Foster Dulles, who explained why Moscow negotiated the treaty that, ten years after the Second World War, finally removed occupying troops from Austria. "The Soviet Union had been subjected to very heavy demands," he noted. North Korean and Vietnamese allies sought more aid. "The military requirements in the European satellite countries were heavy. The economy of the European satellite countries had been squeezed. They were restive. The whole Communist system was overextended."[28] By the early 1960s the atrophied state of the Soviet economy, not merely the Cuban missile crisis scare, explains why Nikita Khrushchev groped toward accommodation with the United States. When Undersecretary of State W. Averell Harriman met with Khrushchev in 1963, the American diplomat anticipated that the Kremlin leader would be receptive to the argument that a nuclear test ban treaty "would enable you to devote much more of your resources to civilian production."[29]

To pay for its large Red Army encamped in Eastern Europe and along the tense border with China, the considerable expansion of its navy, and its interventions, foreign aid, and nuclear weaponry, the Kremlin shortchanged the nation's domestic development. Under five-year plans, steel, automobile, oil, and electrical production registered gains from the 1940s to the 1980s, and the USSR's raw materials wealth (manganese, chrome, and more) represented fundamental strengths. But a Soviet slide became measurable. The nation's overall industrial and agricultural rates of growth slackened. In the 1950s the rate of Soviet economic growth stood at 5.9; from 1960 to 1973 the rate declined to 4.9 percent; from 1973 to 1980 the rate dropped even more to 2.6 percent; and for 1981 to 1985 the rate plummeted further to 1.9. Actually, there may have been no growth at all in this last period, according to some economists. The Soviet share of gross world product also declined.

Low productivity and shoddy craftsmanship stemmed from poor labor morale, alcoholism, high absenteeism, and a stultifying Communist party bureaucracy. "They pretend to pay us and we pretend to work" went the joke. Air and water pollution, crumbling plants, inefficient and hence dismal agricultural output, and declining life expectancy rates also plagued the Soviet Union through the Cold War decades. Shabbily manufactured tractors and trucks required inordinate maintenance; factory breakdowns and lack of spare parts slowed production. The Soviets lagged behind non-Communist nations in key technologies like computers and microcircuits. The Soviet Union had to import foodstuffs, and at times famines afflicted vast areas of the country. *"This is the political and military regime for fear of which the United States bankrupted itself in the 1980s?"* New York Senator Daniel P. Moynihan asked as he thought about why Americans had exaggerated the Soviet threat.[30]

"There are real sources of trouble" in the Soviet Union, admitted Georgi Arbatov, director of Moscow's Institute for United States and Canadian Studies. "The Cold War just prevents us from dealing with them," he explained. "Neither of us can any longer afford to squander money on fake problems, false stereotypes, and pointless suspicions. Both of us have plenty of real problems at home."[31] In 1987, for example, the Chernobyl nuclear plant accident spewed radioactive fallout across Europe and raised anew doubts about Soviet workmanship, management skills, and governmental competence. To Kremlin planners, as Mikhail Gorbachev said in 1986, a year after he came to power, "acceleration of the country's socio-economic development is the key to all our problems. . . ."[32] To save the Soviet economy, the expensive arms race had to be stopped, for military spending was eating up at least a quarter of the nation's budget.[33] Soviet foreign policy, Gorbachev announced, "is more than ever determined by domestic policy. . . . This is why we need lasting peace, predictability, and constructiveness in international relations."[34] Soviet leaders made the point again and again: Urgent needs at home demanded an end to the Cold War.

"Hegemony," one historian has written, "necessarily rests

upon both military and economic power, and the dilemma facing a maturing hegemon is that it cannot sustain both."[35] If a major power spends heavily on its military, it hurts its domestic economy; if it bleeds its economy, it is less able to sustain a competitive global position. On the other hand, if it reduces its defense spending to attend to domestic priorities, it endangers its global status, which derives in good part from military superiority. For the United States, the demands of containment compounded the problem. If, as the containment doctrine asserted, the Communist threat was global, American ramparts had to be erected everywhere. Such vigilant monitoring, and the considerable counterforce required to apply the doctrine, strained American resources. Superpower policing of the world and of empire ironically meant "permanent insecurity" for the United States because of the constant fear of falling dominoes and because "empire makes one into a worldwide target."[36] The Soviet Union, with its own brands of containment and imperialism, suffered the same fate. Ending the Cold War, Moscow and Washington officials reasoned, might stop dominoes from falling, enhance security, shield the targets, and make the hegemonic dilemma more manageable.

In addition to the economic burden of the Cold War, another significant source accounted for the great powers' decline and their movement toward détente: challenges to their hegemony from independent-minded client states and allies. Some allies, such as West Germany and France, advanced détente on their own. Others made so much trouble that the hegemonic powers welcomed détente as a means to discipline them—Moscow's eagerness to build Soviet-American cooperation as a counterweight to China, for example. The two great powers also embraced détente as a means to reassert mastery, as in the 1970s, when Moscow hoped that the United States would accept the Soviet Union's preeminent influence in Eastern Europe and Washington hoped that détente would create a great-power "equilibrium" that would help reduce radical revolution in the American sphere.[37] Sometimes détente afforded a great power an apparent opportunity to exploit division within a sphere in order to contain or weaken its adversary. The USSR, for example, attempted to encourage France to spoil U.S. plans for Western Europe, and the United States played its "China card" against the Soviet Union.

The theme of challenges from within spheres is well documented in the Soviet case.[38] The Soviet Union's control of its Eastern European empire had always been troublesome and incomplete—witness Tito's challenge to Stalin in 1948. In the 1950s nationalist stirrings continued to destabilize the Soviet empire. In mid-1953 East Germans rebelled against their Soviet masters, who crushed the revolt. Then, in 1956, after Khrushchev had denounced Stalin, called for "peaceful coexistence" with the West, and suggested that Moscow would tolerate different brands of communism, Eastern Europeans seized the apparent political space granted them. Poles rioted and sacked the offices of the secret police and Communist headquarters. The Polish military quelled the rebellion, but Moscow had to accept a Polish leader it had once ostracized for being too Titoist. The Soviets, to relieve their own economic burden, even tolerated U.S. aid to Poland for years. In Hungary the revolution against the Soviets elicited a far stronger response from the Kremlin. Hungarians rebelled in the streets, and local revolutionary councils helped shape an anti-Soviet government. Rather than permit a member of its Warsaw Pact to slip away, Moscow smashed the Hungarian uprising. However much this use of brutal force may have secured the Soviet grip on Eastern Europe in the short term, it proved a hollow victory, revealing the deteriorating hold of the Soviet Union on its European sphere of influence that would be dramatically loosened in the 1980s under renewed pressures for independence.

The Sino-Soviet split also weakened Soviet power.[39] The Soviet Union had never satisfied Chinese expectations for foreign aid and had often shipped inferior quality products to its Communist ally. Mao Zedong's government harshly rejected the Soviet call for peaceful coexistence, competed with the Soviets for influence in Vietnam, and frightened Kremlin leaders by seemingly going to the brink during the Quemoy/Matsu crises of the 1950s. Beijing officials also complained that the Soviets would not share nuclear weapons with them (the Chinese exploded their first atomic device in 1964) and resented the Soviet Union's wooing of China's enemy India. The schism opened wide in the late 1950s and early 1960s, prompting the cutoff of Soviet assistance, and in 1969 it exploded into violence along the shared border. Although each side claimed the other was prostituting Marxism-Leninism, the rupture stemmed fundamentally from "deep national antagonisms, a power clash of opposing national interests."[40] In the early 1970s, when Beijing began to pursue accommodation with the United States (its "America card") to counter its rival, Moscow saw détente with Washington as a potential check on the People's Republic of China. When in the next decade China undertook a modernization program that promised a stronger economy, the anxious Soviets decided to open talks with their erstwhile Asian ally.[41] Soviet troubles with allies, then, eroded bipolarism and sped the process of ending the Cold War.

The United States, too, faced challenges from within its far-flung sphere of influence, although with less disarray than that experienced by the Soviets. Europe became for Americans a source not only of friends but also of rivals, who themselves marched in the direction of ending the Cold War.[42] Marshall Plan and NATO allies eagerly sought valuable assistance from the United States and thrived economically, but they chafed under the U.S. influence that accompanied the aid. Many Europeans became alarmed by the American push for German rearmament, by the provocative U.S. march to the Chinese border in Korea, by U.S. strictures on trade with Communist states, and by the extremism of McCarthyism. These developments raised "doubts" in Europe "as to the wisdom of American leadership."[43] Throughout the 1950s and after, America's European partners reached for more independence from the United States as their recovery from the depredation of war progressed.

Charles de Gaulle's France became a particularly nettlesome ally. After de Gaulle's ascendency in 1958, he sought to restore French glory and power, guide Europe, reduce the influx of American investment and cultural influence, and steer an independent course in the Cold War. Even before the imposing French general took power, Paris had vetoed the American-sponsored European Defense Community because it might serve as a potential vehicle for rearming Germany. France helped organize the Common Market and then blocked British membership in the new trading group because, to de Gaulle, Britain had become America's Trojan horse. He disparaged the "two hegemonies," *both* the United States and the Soviet Union, and encouraged Third World nations to evade their grasp.[44] France promoted European integration as a tool to diminish American influence on the Continent. For this reason "Washington always feared that a unified Europe—if it were truly independent—could be dangerous."[45] France developed its own nuclear capacity in 1960. Six years later de Gaulle withdrew his nation from the NATO military structure and required the removal of alliance bases from French territory. Like many other European allies, France also violated American restrictions on trade with Communist countries.

As much as de Gaulle criticized U.S. foreign policy, his distrust of the Soviet Union kept him from trying to push the United States out of Europe. De Gaulle "fears both the hegemony of the U.S. and its disengagement," pointed out the

French ambassador to the United States.[46] Overall, de Gaulle's impact was considerable: He reduced American influence in Western Europe by fracturing the alliance, and his concerted, independent effort to mend fences with Moscow advanced détente with the Soviet Union.

Although Great Britain remained America's staunchest ally, it, too, proved difficult for Washington policy makers, and the intermittent discord further diminished U.S. influence in the Atlantic alliance. Against American advice, London maintained relations with the People's Republic of China. Worse still, Britain joined France and Israel in a military attack upon Egypt in 1956 without informing Washington before the assault. During this Suez crisis President Eisenhower bitterly chastised America's renegade allies and applied economic coercion against Britain to force its withdrawal from Egypt. More tussles with all three allies lay ahead. During the 1973 Arab-Israeli War, for example, American allies in Europe became much more concerned about ensuring the flow of oil from Arab nations than about Israel's security, a major U.S. objective; Britain even denied the United States use of its bases in Cyprus. Israel and the United States later became so divided on Middle East issues that they sometimes sounded more like enemies than close friends. In 1981, for example, after Washington strongly disapproved Israel's sudden annexation of the Golan Heights, the territory it had seized from Syria in the Six-Day War of 1967, the Israeli prime minister shot back: "Are we a banana republic?" Then, when Americans protested the Israeli bombing of suspected Palestine Liberation Organization camps in Lebanon, Israeli Prime Minister Menachem Begin wagged his finger once more and recalled the American killing of civilians in Vietnam: "You don't have a right, from a moral perspective, to preach to us."[47]

Such expressions of independence by allies became common during the Vietnam era, when NATO partners failed to support the long U.S. war in Southeast Asia. The British, complained the always pungent President Lyndon B. Johnson, could at least have sent a platoon of bagpipers. The Atlantic alliance was further rent when two NATO members, Turkey and Greece, battled each other in disputed Cyprus. Dissension within the Atlantic alliance swelled further as Europeans questioned American reliability and judgment. They feared that the United States might drag NATO partners into an unwanted war in Asia or that Americans might fail to protect Western Europe from a Soviet attack lest American countermeasures in Europe invite a Soviet nuclear onslaught against the United States itself. Some jittery Europeans also believed that American policy makers preferred to use European territory as a nuclear battleground. Under the weight of such strains the American sphere of influence in Europe progressively frayed.

The nationalism and independent decision making of West Germany also shook the American sphere and advanced détente. Many West Germans scorned Americans when the United States did not knock down the Berlin Wall after it went up in 1961, and Chancellor Konrad Adenauer became suspicious that Moscow and Washington would cut deals at Germany's expense. Soon France and Germany seemed to be competing to see which could first establish détente with the Soviet Union. When Willy Brandt became chancellor in 1969, the Federal Republic of Germany displayed unusual independence by making overtures to Moscow. Brandt's Eastern policy *(Ostpolitik)* led in 1970 to a Soviet-German nonaggression treaty, which especially reduced friction over Berlin. Two years later, in an early gesture toward reunification, the two Germanys opened diplomatic channels. Kissinger bristled at this "new form of classic German nationalism," but he nonetheless endorsed Brandt's efforts because most allies did. "We could best hold the Alliance together," he recalled, "by accepting the principle of détente. . . ."[48]

Greatly expanded Western European trade with and investment in the Soviet sphere of influence beginning in the late 1940s also drew back the "iron curtain" in a seemingly irreversible process of economic détente. After the divisive Suez crisis, for example, America's European allies sought more energy independence from the Middle East—and from the United States. The Soviet Union, to Washington's dismay, became an alternative oil and natural gas source. When Europeans set out in the 1980s to build a natural gas pipeline from Western Europe to Siberia, the United States made a futile and ill-advised attempt to scuttle the project. Tempers flared once again within the Atlantic alliance, leading to further discord and a reduced U.S. position in Europe.[49] At the same time supranational structures, like the European Economic Community (organized in 1959) and the Conference on Security and Cooperation in Europe (formed in 1973), demonstrated the growing initiative of Western European governments. U.S. officials continued to say they welcomed European unity, but they sensed that integration was actually supplanting American supremacy.

The diminution of America's power could be measured even in the most conspicuous arena of its hegemony—Latin America.[50] Pan-Americanism and the Organization of American States had long served as instruments of U.S. influence in the region, much to the regret and annoyance of Mexicans, Argentines, and others who resisted North American paternalistic guidance. Latin Americans gave only lukewarm support to the United States in the Korean War; only Colombia contributed troops to the United Nations forces, and few hemispheric states met their pledges to increase production of strategic materials. In 1954 a leftist, nationalist government in Guatemala challenged North American property interests and U.S. hemispheric leadership. The CIA plotted intervention and overthrew the Guatemalan upstarts. In 1958 anti-Yankee demonstrations so threatened Vice President Richard Nixon's life and his goodwill trip to South America that Eisenhower launched Operation Poor Richard as a contingency should Nixon have to be rescued from Venezuela. This deployment of U.S. military power only heightened tensions. The following year Panamanian nationalists rioted after U.S. officials had rebuffed their efforts to fly Panama's flag in the Canal Zone; another uprising in 1964 left four American soldiers and twenty-four Panamanians dead.

Other signs of hemispheric independence became evident when Venezuela helped found the Organization of Petroleum Exporting Countries (OPEC) and nationalized American-owned oil companies. American-owned multinational corporations faced higher taxes, terrorism, expropriation, and regulations on the hiring of nationals (Argentina, for example, required that at least 85 percent of management and other high-level personnel in foreign-owned firms be Argentine).[51] During the Vietnam War, when the United States appeared "unreliable as a security partner," Brazil began to import weapons from European suppliers; later it developed its own profitable weapons-exporting business.[52] U.S. hegemony in the Western Hemisphere had rested in part on U.S. dominance in arms production and weapons sales. Washington witnessed another setback in the 1970 election of the Marxist President Salvador Allende in Chile and in Peru's defiant 1970s purchases of Soviet MiGs. The 1979 victory of the radical Sandinistas over the longtime U.S. ally Anastasio Somoza in Nicaragua and Argentina's selling of grain to the Soviet Union in 1980 during a U.S.-imposed embargo against the Soviets provided further evidence of diminished U.S. power in the hemisphere. Although the CIA helped depose Allende in 1973, this American success and the U.S. military interventions in the Dominican Republic (1965), Grenada (1983), and Panama (1989) attested not to U.S. strength but to the loosening of its imperial net. Western Hemispheric nations, overall, boldly questioned the "hegemonic presumption" of the United States.[53]

The most serious defiance to the United States came from Cuba's Fidel Castro. After years of civil war against U.S. ally Fulgencio Batista, Castro's rebel army finally forced the dictator from Havana in January 1959. The emergence of the radical Cuban Revolution rocked Washington while at the same time it buoyed other Latin American nationalists to seek alternatives to their U.S.-backed regimes and capitalist models of economic development. The CIA jumped into action once again. The covert agency's clumsy attempts to depose and assassinate Castro faltered, especially in the disastrous Bay of Pigs operation, but these activities, sabotage, and an economic embargo prompted Cuba to appeal for assistance from a Soviet Union more than willing to exacerbate U.S. woes in its sphere. One result was the Cuban missile crisis of 1962, which seemed to threaten nuclear war after the Soviets had recklessly placed medium-range missiles on the Caribbean island to deter an expected U.S. attack.[54] The United States erected a naval blockade around Cuba and went to the brink of war to get the rockets out. Castro survived the crisis, consolidated his power, and promised revolution all over Latin America. Cuba remained a Soviet ally, although Havana frequently followed an independent foreign policy. Cuban-American hostility persisted despite some steps toward improved relations in the 1970s.[55]

As he cultivated détente in the early 1970s, President Nixon identified five power centers in the world: the United States, the Soviet Union, China, Japan, and the Common Market. Under détente, he declared, each center should maintain order among smaller states in its region of responsibility. Because the "five great economic superpowers will determine the economic future," Nixon explained, "and, because economic power will be the key to other kinds of power, [they will determine] the future of the world. . . ."[56] For the United States, détente seemed to offer opportunities to determine the future—to discipline its Latin American sphere under a global system of great-power management and to deter Soviet inroads or assistance to rebel groups like the insurgent Sandinistas in Nicaragua by threatening to withdraw the economic benefits the Soviets sought from détente. Détente beckoned as a means to reestablish U.S. control of its most traditional sphere. In 1984 the President's Commission on Central America warned that if the United States ever revealed symptoms of decline in its own neighborhood, it would experience the "erosion of our power to influence events worldwide that would flow from the perception that we were unable to influence vital events close to home."[57]

If the erosion of American and Soviet power stemmed from the fracturing of their spheres, so, too, was it due to the rise of the Third World.[58] After the Second World War a cavalcade of colonies broke from their imperial rulers. From 1943 to 1989 no fewer than ninety-six countries gained independence and entered the international system as new states. Many liberations came in the 1950s and 1960s—among them Libya (1951), Sudan, Morocco, and Tunisia (1956), and Ghana (1957). In 1960 alone eighteen new African nations became independent; 1962 and 1975 each saw seven more newborn nations. Diplomats in the early 1960s, Undersecretary of State George W. Ball recalled, necessarily had to focus "on problems involving the bits and pieces of disintegrating empires."[59]

At first analysts tagged them "backward" or "underdeveloped nations," then shifted to less disparaging terms, like "developing" or "emerging states." Soon they became known as the "Third World," a general term applied to those parts of the global community belonging neither to the "First World" of the United States and its allies in the capitalist "West" nor to the "Second World" of the Soviet Union and its allies in the Communist "East." The Third World nations were largely nonwhite, nonindustrialized, poor, and located in the southern half of the globe (thus sometimes called the "South"). Many of them became unstable, plagued by civil wars, dictatorial rulers, tribal, ethnic, and class rivalries, drought, poverty, and economies dependent upon the sale of only one commodity. To the alarm of Washington, some of them launched social revolutions and embraced socialist models of development. On the minds of American leaders, too, was the growth of newly industrialized nations in the Third World, like South Korea and Brazil, that challenged the United States in world markets.

When many Third World nations formed a nonaligned movement to challenge the two Cold Warriors and to press for an end to their dangerous competition, the international system fragmented, bipolarism eroded, and the relative power of the United States and the Soviet Union diminished accordingly. After the 1955 Bandung Conference, many Third World nations in Asia, Africa, and the Middle East declared their neutralism in the Cold War. Third World expressions of alienation from the two superpowers came in many other forms, including Pan-Arabism and Muslim fundamentalism, the Group of 77 in the United Nations, and the movement for a law of the sea treaty to ensure that rich seabed minerals, a "common heritage of mankind," did not become a source of profit for commercial mining companies alone.[60]

By sheer force of numbers Third World states became a formidable bloc in world forums. The United States gradually became isolated in the United Nations. In the Security Council, for example, the United States, losing the majority vote its sphere members had long provided, had to cast its first veto in 1970, and by the 1980s it was averaging four vetoes a year. The United States became the largest caster of nay votes in the General Assembly, where it frequently had to contend with setbacks like the 108–9 vote to condemn its invasion of Grenada. In the 1950s General Assembly members voted 70 percent of the time with the United States; in the 1970s the coincidence rate fell to 30 percent, and by the early 1980s to 20 percent.[61] In the late 1970s the United States actually pulled out of the International Labor Organization and in the early 1980s out of the UN Educational, Scientific, and Cultural Organization in attempts to weaken international agencies where Third World influence had come to flourish.

Third World nations also threw the American-designed liberal, capitalist order on the defensive in the 1970s by demanding a New International Economic Order in which the industrialized nations of the "North" would share their wealth with the "South" through tariff revision, technology transfers, stable and higher prices for raw materials, and increased economic assistance. Developing nations also demanded a greater voice in the World Bank, International Monetary Fund (IMF), and General Agreement on Tariffs and Trade (GATT). "The object is to complete the liberation of the Third World countries from external domination," to gain "economic liberation" by changing the "structure of power," explained Tanzania's President Julius K. Nyerere.[62] U.S. officials complained that many Third World governments criticized the United States for acting self-interested while they themselves indulged in corruption, imposed tyrannies, warred against one another, and lavished their nations' scarce resources on military weaponry. Nonetheless, through its persistent appeal for a new economic order and nonalignment, the Third World destabilized the Cold War international system. Once, in 1974, after Henry Kissinger had expounded on the virtues of hemispheric community, a Colombian diplomat bluntly challenged him: "Latin America's community is the Third World."[63] "I feel we are at a watershed," Kissinger observed a year later. "We're at a period of extraordinary creativity or a period when really the international order came apart politically, economically and morally."[64]

The United States and the Soviet Union coveted alignment

with Third World states, for they could supply strategic minerals, market and investment opportunities, votes in the United Nations, intelligence posts, and military bases. Conflicts in the developing nations drew the United States and the Soviet Union into prolonged, costly interventions that further taxed precious resources. Each major power claimed that the other was exploiting Third World turmoil, and the emerging nations became adept at playing the two superpowers off against each other, even extracting money from both. The contest for the allegiance of the emerging states spurred foreign aid programs, covert plots, and military interventions. The United States tended to support the propertied classes, while the Soviets endorsed insurgents, radicals, or Third World leaders who criticized the United States. Populous and neutralist India became a hotly contested prize, not only because it represented a testing ground for competing models of development and political principles but also because India bordered the one nation that Moscow and Washington could agree was threatening both—the People's Republic of China. As much as the Cold War behemoths pressed nonaligned Third World countries like India to abandon their neutralism, they could not halt the movement. "We will not be subjected," boomed Egypt's Gamal Abdul Nasser, "either by West or East."[65]

All of this tugging and pulling jolted the international system. Sometimes U.S. officials felt compelled to compromise with Third World nationalism to retain some influence, as in 1978, when President Carter negotiated canal treaties with Panama that provided for both the return of the waterway to Panama and the endorsement of a continued U.S. security role on the isthmus. The United States, however, never became isolated from the Third World and retained hefty instruments of influence. America did not turn into the "pitiful, helpless giant" that Nixon said it might if the United States lost the Vietnam War.[66] Although the Third World's share of gross world product rose, Third World peoples remained desperately poor, wracked by high infant mortality, unemployment, disease, and illiteracy rates. Third World nations never shed their dependency upon outsiders. Still, developing, neutralist nations presented tenacious challenges to great-power management of the international order. The Third World vigorously, if not always successfully, challenged what Senator J. William Fulbright once called America's "arrogance of power."[67] And U.S. economic problems—high interest rates, indebtedness, and trade imbalances—undercut the American "capacity to lead" the Third World because the United States became less able to provide debt relief and urgently needed development capital.[68] International affairs became more fluid, more unpredictable, less secure, and less manageable.

Détente was born in part as a response to this disorderly, pluralistic world. With the United States suffering Third World setbacks in Vietnam, Iran, Nicaragua, and elsewhere, and the Soviet Union stumbling in Egypt and Afghanistan, among other places, Washington and Moscow looked less and less like superpowers. The declining powers in this transforming international system sought to hold their positions by moving from confrontation to cooperation. Détente seemed to promise a restoration of great-power control, a reassertion of great-power tutelage. If détente was embraced as a means to reduce the costs of the Cold War and to meet challenges from sphere members, it also became attractive as a means to deal with the volatile Third World. As President Jimmy Carter once said, Americans had to put their "inordinate fear of Communism" behind them in order to address long-term Third World crises.[69] For the United States, détente with the Soviet Union also offered a "fulcrum or base from which to exert American diplomatic leverage" in the Third World.[70] In 1990, during the Gulf War, when Soviet-American cooperation marshaled a worldwide condemnation of Iraq after it had invaded neighboring Kuwait, Secretary of State James Baker expressed what leaders before him had been saying about the virtues of détente: "When the United States and the Soviet Union lead, others are likely to follow."[71]

For a number of reasons, then—Cold War economic burden, challenges from allies, and the rise of the Third World—the United States and the Soviet Union suffered decline, although the latter slumped far more than the former. The retirement of the Cold War near the close of the twentieth century seemed to provide hope for the restoration of lost status.

10

END
Toward a
Post-Cold War Order

THE UNITED STATES and the Soviet Union, bedeviled by Cold War-induced economic problems, independent-minded allies, and contentious Third World nations, gradually moved in fits of truculence and accommodation toward détente and the ultimate end of the Cold War. By the late 1960s, remembered Henry Kissinger, America had to operate "in much more complex conditions than we had ever before faced." That time "marked the end of the period of American predominance based on overwhelming nuclear and economic supremacy." Indeed, he continued, "the Soviet nuclear stockpile was inevitably approaching parity. The economic strength of Europe and Japan was bound to lead them to seek larger political influence. The new, developing nations pressed their claims to greater power and participation." If the world further "tilted against us," he feared, America's strong, if no longer preeminent, position in the international balance of power would falter. In this unsettled environment, détente became ever more attractive.[1] Détente did not mean that Soviet-American rivalry would cease, but rather that judicious great-power cooperation, located somewhere between hostile obstructionism and friendly coexistence, would reduce world tensions. Moscow and Washington cautiously endorsed détente as a process to stem the erosion of their power.

The two adversaries moved haltingly toward easing the Cold War; reversals often followed advances, and the positive steps sometimes came as much from fears of military imbalances and nuclear war as from economic or domestic worries. The process actually began gingerly in the 1950s; it came to fruition dramatically in the early 1990s. Soviet-American summit conferences in 1955, 1960, and 1961 produced little agreement, especially on the issues of divided Berlin and the arms race. But after the 1962 missile crisis the two powers installed a hot line for better communication during crises and signed the Test Ban Treaty (1963), which outlawed tests in the atmosphere, in outer space, and underwater. The Vietnam War obstructed accommodation for much of the 1960s, but significant strides toward improving relations came early in the next decade, when the Nixon administration opened relations with the People's Republic of China and negotiated with the Soviet Union the SALT-I strategic arms control and the ABM treaties. Nixon's Vietnamization program to facilitate U.S. extrication from the war in Southeast Asia signaled another effort to advance détente and trim the costs of the Cold War. President Carter's SALT-II Treaty followed in 1979. Although the U.S. Senate never ratified this agreement, in protest against the Soviet invasion of Afghanistan, both Moscow and Washington honored the accord.

Regional conflicts in which the two major powers backed opposing sides began to undermine détente after the mid-

1970s: Angola, Ethiopia-Somalia, Afghanistan, and Central America. After first savaging détente, because "we thought we were playing catch-up ball" with the Soviets, and denying that large defense budgets would strain the American economy, Reagan administration officials ended up in 1987 signing with Moscow an agreement eliminating intermediate-range nuclear forces in Europe (INF Treaty).[2] Talks on reducing strategic nuclear weapons and conventional forces also proceeded. The Cold War era seemed to be winding down.

Soviet President Mikhail Gorbachev, more than anyone else in a position of power, boldly sought to calm the icy winds of the Cold War. To overcome his nation's economic stagnation and salvage something of the Soviet Union's slipping international status, Gorbachev launched *perestroika* (economic restructuring) and *glasnost* (political liberalization). For reform and recovery to succeed, however, Moscow had to make several critical decisions that ensured an end to the Cold War. Because the Soviets had to obtain capital from and economic cooperation with Western Europe and the United States for *perestroika* to work, Moscow had to improve "the atmosphere of the dialogue with America."[3] To signal that they were, in fact, serious about halting the Cold War and that a new environment favorable to economic linkages was being created, the Soviets had to jettison completely their failed ten-year occupation of Afghanistan and help settle regional conflicts in Africa and Central America. To relieve the overburdened Soviet budget, Gorbachev had to reduce assistance to Third World nations; in 1989, for example, Moscow halted arms shipments to the leftist Sandinista government in Nicaragua that the United States had been trying to overthrow.[4] To cut Cold War military expenses, the Gorbachev government had to seek arms control agreements with the United States and even unilaterally reduce Soviet military forces.

To attract Western economic assistance, the Soviets also had to resolve one of the long-standing issues of the Cold War: their domination of neighbors. They had to permit self-determination for Eastern Europe and East Germany. Gorbachev decided to let Eastern Europe go because the USSR could no longer pay the price necessary to keep the rebellious region in check and because letting it go improved chances for détente with the United States and thus for Soviet economic revival. Whether or not Gorbachev expected Eastern Europe "to crumble like a dry Saltine cracker in just a few months," he nonetheless spurred the process.[5] His reforms set loose a chain reaction that seemed to leave the United States a spectator rather than a prime mover.[6] The collapse of hard-line Communist governments in Poland, Hungary, Czechoslovakia, and Rumania in the revolutions of 1989 and the dramatic razing of the Berlin Wall in November were followed the next year by the fusing of the two Germanys. "We want to lead," remarked a West German official in the language of an independent great power. "Perhaps in time the United States will take care of places like Central America, and we will handle Eastern Europe."[7] In 1990, too, the Baltic republics of Latvia, Lithuania, and Estonia took their first and ultimately successful steps toward full independence.

In 1991 the Union of Soviet Socialist Republics itself came apart in a flurry of declarations of independence and autonomy by individual republics, including the largest, Russia. Positioned perilously between traditionalists and reformers, Gorbachev tried to hold the middle ground and proposed a less centralized confederation. Then, in late summer, antireform, hard-line Communists arrested him in a coup that seemed to prefigure "another totalitarian dusk" and a return to frigid Soviet-American relations all too familiar in the Cold War.[8] But brave Muscovites rallied in the streets, stoutly refusing to let their recent reform history be reversed. The conspirators faced two choices: Gun down thousands of protesting citizens or abandon their putsch. The unpopular hardliners quit after only three days. Russian President Boris Yeltsin emerged triumphant. He and other ardent reformist politicians soon denounced communism and Gorbachev left office. The USSR dissolved into a new Commonwealth of Independent States, its economy unstrung, its army and KGB (secret police) discredited, its empire in Europe independent, and its worldwide allies adrift without further foreign aid or ideological affinity. The Cold War seemed over once and for all.

Some observers celebrated America's containment doctrine and substantial U.S. military outlays as having forced the Soviets to back down and out of the Cold War.[9] Although American foreign policies obviously prompted expensive Soviet countermeasures and compounded the problems of the Soviet economy, that simple proposition lacks explanatory power and ignores the high costs the United States itself paid to implement containment. There were more persuasive explanations. One was the failure of the Communist system itself. Crippling state interventionism and a corrupt, self-perpetuating party bureaucracy clogged the command economy. Denied incentives, a demoralized people learned how not to work. The political terror imposed by the authoritarian regime stifled initiative and suppressed innovative thinking.

A second explanation points to a new generation of Soviet leaders who emerged to challenge this suffocating system. Gorbachev at age fifty-four symbolized the generational change when he came to power in 1985; he replaced a series of hard-line, incapacitated old men—Leonid Brezhnev, Yuri Andropov, Konstantin Chernenko—and looked to a new future. Another explanation was the long-term economic underdevelopment of the Soviet Union. Historians have demonstrated that the economies of both czarist Russia and the Soviet Union have suffered from recurring natural disasters, wars, the tenacious debilitation of a once-enslaved peasantry, and the disruptions that necessarily arise from revolutionary ferment. Fourth, Eastern Europeans themselves, not Americans, rolled back the Soviet sphere. For the Soviets, the tenacity and courage of Lech Walesa's Solidarity movement in Poland and Vaclav Havel's "velvet revolution" in Czechoslovakia raised the costs of clinging to empire. Perhaps a fifth factor was the ethnic diversity of the Soviet Union that had long been threatening to tear the nation apart. However complex the explanation, the conclusion is inescapable: The Soviet Union was rocked by substantial disorder at home, and ending the Cold War became an appealing way to relieve it.

U.S. entry into the Persian Gulf War of 1990 and 1991, following Iraq's brutal invasion and annexation of oil-rich Kuwait, exposed a core feature of the immediate post-Cold War international order: the U.S. drive to recoup lost influence, to reestablish credibility, to reaffirm a counterrevolutionary posture, to reassert the great-power status that the prolonged Cold War had eroded. If President Jimmy Carter had sought a fresh start after the Vietnam War and President Ronald Reagan had called for a "national reawakening," President George Bush claimed that the new war in the Middle East was the first post-Cold War "test of our mettle." The president claimed that "recent events have surely proven that there is no substitute for American leadership" in the world. And "let no one doubt our staying power."[10] The *Wall Street Journal* welcomed the outbreak of war because a U.S. victory "lets America, and above all its elite, recover a sense of self-confidence and self-worth."[11] During Operation Desert Storm proud Americans ballyhooed the destructive power of their high-tech air war, the credibility of their military forces, the skill with which an international coalition was created, and the swiftness of victory. "This is the end of the decline," cheered an official of the conservative American Enterprise Institute.[12]

The justification for America's resurgent great-power leadership was no longer anticommunism but rather the promotion of democracy and the blocking of aggression—a "substitute rationale for globalism."[13] In a world moving from Cold War to hot peace, Bush lifted Theodore Roosevelt's big stick once again to reclaim a global policeman's role for the United States, while at the same time the president spoke in Wilsonian tones about American exceptionalism. The drive for U.S. hegemony, now propelled by the need to restore American prestige and power after the Cold War, remained constant from the old world order to the new.

In some ways international relations at the start of the post-Cold War era did not look that much different from world affairs in the late 1940s. In the tumultuous international systems of both periods power was in the process of being redistributed. Leaders' fears of chain reactions that the anarchy characteristic of all systems could set loose continued from one era to the next. At both times the United States ranked as a great power, especially with military strength other states could not match. The nuclear arms race, although tamed by the great powers under détente, still troubled leaders who warned against nuclear proliferation and knew that nuclear arsenals in the United States and the Soviet Union remained large enough to incinerate Earth.

Habits of thought embedded themselves, and deeds became institutionalized. One axiom suggests that when government officials do not know what to do, they do what they know. Foreign policy bureaucracies tend to shun "intellectual retooling," perpetuating the familiar wisdom of the past.[14] Some prominent Americans who had lived their lives in a Cold War setting continued to sniff a Soviet trick. Former President Richard Nixon, still claiming headlines after ignoble resignation for his "Watergate" crimes two decades earlier, warned that in a reformed Soviet Union the United States "may well face a stronger, more confident, more dangerous adversary."[15]

When the Cold War retired, it seemed that the enormous

defense spending could at last be shifted as a "peace dividend" to America's ailing domestic front to improve education, the cities, health, the environment, and the nation's economic competitiveness and to relieve the destitution of more than thirty million very poor Americans. In the euphoric mood after spectacular triumph in the Persian Gulf War of 1991, some Americans wondered: "If we can make the best smart bomb, can't we make the best VCR?"[16] Others urged a Marshall Plan for America itself now that the enemy was economic malaise at home. Yet President George Bush, declaring an urgent U.S. police role in a disorderly world, resisted significant cuts in the military budget and seemed only mildly interested in what he sometimes called "domestic stuff."[17] Even as the Cold War receded, then, its great-power monuments of rigid thinking, demonization and exaggeration of the enemy (so evident in depictions of Iraq's brutal dictator Saddam Hussein), imperial presidency, high military budgets, avoidance of diplomacy with obnoxious adversaries, and military prowess persisted to make the new world order seem an awful lot like the old.

But much had changed. By the 1990s all three worlds were breaking up.[18] The First World was dividing into trading blocs and rivals—North America, Japan, and the Economic Community in Europe. "Effective, usable power has been shifted from the nuclear musclemen to the more agile trading states," one analyst observed.[19] In the Second World communism was disintegrating, Moscow was relinquishing its power in Eastern Europe and Germany, and the several Soviet republics became independent. The Third World, too, was fragmenting: into Newly Industrializing Countries (NICs), oil-rich nations, and the Fourth World (the poorest of nations). Power in the world became more diffused also because of the proliferation of nonstate actors. International businesses made decisions that states could not always control. The internationalization of information, advances in communications technology, and the availability of inexpensive equipment like tape recorders and VCRs undercut governments' attempts to manage information and silence critics. And more than two thousand international nongovernmental organizations commanded attention on human rights, the environment, and other issues.[20]

A conspicuous difference between the 1940s and 1990s, of course, was the end of the Cold War. The Cold War was the defining characteristic of the international system for more than four decades. The long confrontation had been at root a bipolar contest over spheres of influence between the United States and the Soviet Union, both of which, to wage the Cold War, developed massive nuclear weaponry, built competing alliances, and espoused rival ideologies. But by the early 1990s the spheres were breaking up. The Warsaw Pact disintegrated and NATO's status became uncertain, and the new Russia, desperate for assistance, developed links with the European Economic Community and the World Bank. The two powers also were taking serious steps to reduce the danger of nuclear weapons. And ideology seemed less central to and less divisive in world politics. Neither the United States nor Russia seemed any longer to count the other as an inevitable, inveterate enemy.

Different at the end of the twentieth century, too, was the reduced international standing of the United States. Analysts debated whether the United States still ranked as a hegemonic power. Although a military giant quite willing to project that power, as evidenced by Bush's wars in Panama and the Persian Gulf, the United States, measured in terms of its relative economic power, shaky infrastructure, flagging competitiveness, and loss of influence to other nations, had declined. Whereas Truman era Americans had touted their hegemonic status, some Americans at the close of the Cold War speculated about the U.S. "swan song as the great world superpower" and mused that the overmilitarized United

States and Soviet Union were like two "dinosaurs" that faced, if not extinction, perilous futures.[21]

In sharp contrast with the "declinists," other Americans, tagged "revivalists," heralded the emergence of a unipolar world with the United States standing prominently at the top—a triumphant Pax Americana.[22] In his 1991 State of the Union address, Bush spoke buoyantly of America's "defining hour."[23] After U.S. and coalition forces had pummeled Iraq in the Persian Gulf War, the president chided critics who doubted the quality of American education and production. "Well, don't you believe it," he told Congress. "The America we saw in [Operation] Desert Storm was first-class talent."[24] In January 1992 Bush lashed out at "gloomsayers" and "prophets of doom." "We won the Cold War, and we will win the competitive wars," he claimed.[25] That is just what leaders of declining nations have always said through history, rebutted the doubters. They always deny that they are in trouble, take little action, and thus ensure that the process of decline will persist—in this case the decline spawned by the Cold War.

Although it became fashionable to say that America had won "the sucker and won it big," and it became evident that democratization and capitalism were ascending, the Cold War actually had no winners.[26] Both the United States and the Soviet Union had spent themselves into weakened conditions. Both had paid tremendous prices for making and waging the Cold War. That is why President Gorbachev launched his restructuring programs and why President Bush, echoing Carter and Reagan, made the case for American "renewal" and "renewed credibility."[27] Each major power, in groping for an end to the Cold War, was seeking structures of stability at home and abroad to stem the decline—and collapse—that other complex societies had suffered in the past.[28]

It seemed unlikely that international relations, even if they hardened once more, would ever again approach the depth of

Cold War frigidity. "There is little chance," Mikhail Gorbachev himself remarked in 1990, "that either side could revive the 'enemy image' that used to fuel the Cold War and confrontation."[29] Still, little is immutable in world affairs, and successes are often short-lived. As geologists know, glaciers can refreeze.

NOTES

ABBREVIATIONS IN THE NOTES

DSB   *Department of State Bulletin* (Washington, D.C.)

DSR   U.S. Department of State Records, Washington, D.C.

FOC   Foreign Office Correspondence, Public Record Office, London, England

FRUS   U.S. Department of State, *Foreign Relations of the United States* (Washington, D.C.)

HSTL   Harry S. Truman Library, Independence, Missouri

JCS   Joint Chiefs of Staff (U.S.)

LC   Library of Congress, Washington, D.C.

NA   National Archives, Washington, D.C.

PPP   *Public Papers of the President of the United States* (Washington, D.C.)

PRO   Public Record Office, London, England

SWNCC   State-War-Navy Coordinating Committee (U.S.)

PREFACE

1. Winston S. Churchill to Harry S. Truman, January 29, 1946, Box 115, President's Secretary's File, Harry S. Truman Papers, HSTL.

CHAPTER 1. RUBBLE: THE WORLD IN 1945

1. Quoted in Oscar Jacobi, "Berlin Today," *New York Times Magazine,* September 24, 1944, p. 5.
2. Charles M. W. Moran, *Churchill: Taken from the Diaries of Lord Moran* (Boston, 1966), pp. 290–91; Hastings Ismay, *The Memoirs of General, the Lord Ismay* (London, 1960), p. 402; David Dilks, ed., *The Diaries of Sir Alexander Cadogan, 1938–1945* (New York, 1971), pp. 763–64.
3. Quoted in Moran, *Churchill,* p. 291.
4. Harry S. Truman, *Memoirs* (Garden City, N.Y., 1955–1956; 2 vols.), I, 341.
5. For Berlin, see Michael Balfour and John Mair, *Four-Power Control in Germany and Austria* (London, 1956), pp. 7–8; Lucius D. Clay, *Decision in Germany* (Garden City, N.Y., 1950), pp. 21, 31–32; Eugene Davidson, *The Death and Life of Germany* (New York, 1959), p. 66; Dilks, *Diaries,* pp. 761–764; Ismay, *Memoirs,* pp. 401–402; Richard Mayne, *Recovery of Europe, 1945–1973* (Garden City, N.Y., 1973), pp. 34–45; Moran, *Churchill,* pp. 288–91; Robert Murphy, *Diplomat Among Warriors* (Garden City, N.Y., 1964), pp. 257, 264; Alexander Werth, *Russia at War, 1941–1945* (New York, 1964)), pp. 890, 892; *New York Times,* July 5, 1945; Jacobi, "Berlin," p. 5; *Life,* XIX (July 23, 1945), 19–27.
6. Clay, *Decision,* p. 21.
7. Quoted in Moran, *Churchill,* p. 289.
8. Benjamin V. Cohen to Charles C. Burlingham, August 11, 1945, Box 2, Burlingham Papers, Harvard Law School Library, Cambridge, Mass.
9. Murphy, *Diplomat,* p. 257.
10. Moran, *Churchill,* p. 289.
11. Quoted in W. D. Jacobs, "Where Do the People Live?," *Commonweal,* XLIII (January 18, 1946), 354.
12. Clay, *Decision,* p. 16. For conditions in Germany, see ibid., pp. 15–16, 31–32; Mayne, *Recovery,* pp. 35–45; Balfour and Mair, *Four-Power,* pp. 7–14; Jacobs, "Where?," pp. 354–55.
13. Quoted in Marquis Childs, "London Wins the Battle," *National Geographic,* LXXXVIII (August 1945), 129. For Britain, see ibid., pp. 129–52; Balfour and Mair, *Four-Power,* p. 12; and Dilks, *Diaries,* p. 607.

14. For Europe, see UN General Assembly, *Preliminary Report of the Temporary Sub-Commission on Economic Reconstruction of Devastated Areas* (London, 1946); United Nations Relief and Rehabilitation Administration, European Regional Office, *Post-War Public Finance in Greece* (London, 1947), pp. 1–2; Francis F. Lincoln, *United States' Aid to Greece, 1947–1962* (Germantown, Tenn., 1975), p. 53; George Woodbridge et al., *The History of the United Nations Relief and Rehabilitation Administration* (New York, 1950; 3 vols.), II, 94–97, 138–39; Jon V. Kofas, *Intervention and Underdevelopment: Greece during the Cold War* (University Park, Pa., 1989), pp. 8–10; "Allies Enter Vienna," *Life*, XIX (September 3, 1945), 34; Thomas R. Henry, "Tale of Three Cities," *National Geographic*, LXXXVIII (December 1945), 641–69; "Building Damage and Reconstruction in France," *Monthly Labor Review*, LXI (November 1945) 925–29; R. G. Hawtrey, "The Economic Consequences of the War," in Arnold J. Toynbee, ed., *The Realignment of Europe* (London, 1955), pp. 36–51; Katharine Duff, "Italy," ibid., pp. 440–41; James Edward Miller, *The United States and Italy, 1940–1950* (Chapel Hill, N.C., 1986), p. 151; Mayne, *Recovery*, pp. 35–45; Gordon Wright, *The Ordeal of Total War* (New York, 1968), pp. 234–67; Alan S. Milward, *War, Economy and Society, 1939–1945* (Berkeley, Calif., 1977); House of Representatives, Committee on International Relations, *Problems of World War II and Its Aftermath* (executive session hearings; historical series; Washington, D.C., 1976), vol. I, part 2, pp. 465–94.
15. Paul K. French, "William E. Brown, Dean of UVM's Medical College, 1945–52: An Oral History Interview," *Vermont History*, XLI (Summer 1973), 170.
16. Stephen D. Kertesz, *Between Russia and the West: Hungary and the Illusions of Peacemaking, 1945–1947* (Notre Dame, Ind., 1984), pp. 20–21.
17. John Hersey, "Home to Warsaw," *Life*, XVIII (April 9, 1945), 16, 19.
18. Irving Brant, quoted in Richard C. Lukas, *Bitter Legacy: Polish-American Relations in the Wake of World War II* (Lexington, Ky., 1982), p. 33.
19. For Poland, see Woodbridge, *UNRRA*, II, 200–02; Stanislaw Jankowski, "Warsaw: Destruction, Secret Town Planning, and Postwar Reconstruction," in Jeffrey M. Diefendorf, ed., *Rebuilding Europe's Bombed Cities* (New York, 1990), pp. 79–80.
20. Arthur Bliss Lane, *I Saw Poland Betrayed* (Boston, c. 1948 [1965]), pp. 4, 9.
21. B. V. Sokolov, "On the Relationship of Losses in Personnel and Military Equipment on the Soviet-German Front during the Great Fatherland War," *Voprosy Istorii*, no. 9 (September 1988), 116–126 (in Russian).

22. For conditions in the USSR, see Diary, November 10, 1944, vol. 49, Henry L. Stimson Papers, Yale University Library, New Haven, Conn.; "First Monthly Report," by Marshall MacDuffie (Chief, UNRRA Mission to Ukraine), April 2, 1946, Box 59,000, UNRRA Records, United Nations Library, New York; Statement by Richard Scandrett (n.d., but 1946), Box 58,000, ibid.; Woodbridge, *UNRRA*, II, 231–32; Werth, *Russia*, pp. 350–53; John R. Deane, *The Strange Alliance* (New York, 1947), pp. 3–7; William McNeill, *America, Britain, Russia* (London, 1953), pp. 441n, 670; Thomas P. Whitney, *Russia in My Life* (London, 1963), pp. 65, 69, 101–02; Harry Schwartz, *Russia's Postwar Economy* (Syracuse, 1947); Isaac Deutscher, *Stalin* (New York, 1973), pp. 573–75; Thomas G. Paterson, *Soviet-American Confrontation: Postwar Reconstruction and the Origins of the Cold War* (Baltimore, 1973), p. 34; V. Lelchuk et al., *Short History of Soviet Society* (Moscow, 1971), pp. 309–16; *New York Times*, February 9, 1946; Vera Micheles Dean, "Russia's Internal Economic Problems," *Foreign Policy Reports*, XXIII (July 1, 1947), 98–106; Dmitri Volkogonov, *Stalin: Triumph and Tragedy*, trans. Harold Shukman (New York, 1991), p. 504.

23. Quoted in Harrison Salisbury, *Russia on the Way* (New York, 1946), p. 318.

24. W. Averell Harriman and Elie Abel, *Special Envoy to Churchill and Stalin, 1941–1946* (New York, 1975), p. 257.

25. Werth, *Russia*, p. 353.

26. Lelchuk, *Short History*, p. 312.

27. Joy Davidman, ed., *War Poems of the United Nations* (New York, 1943), p. 33.

28. Frederick Brainin, "The Refugees' Testament," ibid., p. 6.

29. Mayne, *Recovery*, pp. 36–37.

30. John W. Dower, *War without Mercy: Race & Power in the Pacific War* (New York, 1986), pp. 296–99; Stanley Karnow, *In Our Image: America's Empire in the Philippines* (New York, 1989), p. 333.

31. For China at war's end, see Woodbridge, *UNRRA*, II, 371–72, 388, 412–45; Pendleton Hogan, "Shanghai After the Japs," *Virginia Quarterly Review*, XXII (January 1946), 91–108; Arthur Bryant, *Triumph in the West* (Garden City, N.Y., 1959), p. 506; Dower, *War*, pp. 295–296; Jonathan D. Spence, *The Search for Modern China* (New York, 1990), p. 496.

32. Davidman, *War Poems*, pp. 54–55.

33. For Japan, see *New York Times*, September 1, 1945; Douglas MacArthur, *Reminiscences* (New York, 1964), p. 280; Robert J. Donovan, *Conflict and Crisis* (New York, 1977), p. 69; William J. Sebald, *With MacArthur in Japan* (New York, 1965), pp. 39–41; Alfred C. Oppler, *Land Reform*

in Occupied Japan: A Participant Looks Back (Princeton, N.J., 1976), p. 17; Peter Calvocoressi and Guy Wint, *Total War* (New York, 1972), chs. 20–21.

34. Masuo Kato quoted in Michael S. Sherry, *The Rise of American Air Power* (New Haven, 1987), p. 281.

35. Sebald, *With MacArthur*, p. 39.

36. Otis Carey, ed., *War-Wasted Asia: Letters, 1945–46* (Tokyo, 1975), p. 61.

37. For accounts of Hiroshima, see John Hersey, *Hiroshima* (New York, 1946); John Tolland, *The Rising Sun* (New York, 1970); William L. Laurence, *Dawn over Zero* (New York, 1946).

38. Michihiko Hachiya, *Hiroshima Diary*, trans. Warner Wells (Chapel Hill, N.C., 1955), p. 6.

39. These figures, a total of 1945 and post-1945 deaths caused by the bombings, follow the Committee for the Compilation of Materials on Damage Caused by the Atomic Bombs in Hiroshima and Nagasaki, *Hiroshima and Nagasaki: The Physical, Medical, and Social Effects of the Atomic Bombings* (New York, 1981), pp. 113–15.

40. Quoted in Gregg Herken, *The Winning Weapon* (New York, 1980), pp. 20–21n.

41. Eduard Mark, " 'Today Has Been a Historical One': Harry S. Truman's Diary of the Potsdam Conference," *Diplomatic History*, IV (Summer 1980), 324; Truman, *Memoirs*, I, 421.

42. Quoted in Hermann Rauschning, *The Voice of Destruction* (New York, 1940), p. 5.

43. Transcript of Proceedings, "American Foreign Policy," June 4, 1947, Box 93, Records of the U.S. Mission to the United Nations, NA. Emphasis added.

44. Melvyn P. Leffler explores "national security" in an essay of that title in Michael J. Hogan and Thomas G. Paterson, eds., *Explaining the History of American Foreign Relations* (New York, 1991), pp. 202–13.

45. Theodore H. White, *In Search of History: A Personal Adventure* (New York, 1979), p. 224.

46. For the United States, see Jack Goodman, ed., *While You Were Gone* (New York, 1946); Department of Commerce, Bureau of the Census, *Historical Statistics of the United States* (Washington, D.C., 1975); Richard Polenberg, *War and Society: The United States, 1941–1945* (Philadelphia, 1972); Richard E. Lingeman, *Don't You Know There's a War On?* (New York, 1970); John M. Blum, *V Was for Victory* (New York, 1976); Geoffrey Perrett, *Days of Sadness, Years of Triumph: The American People, 1939–1945* (Baltimore, 1974); John B. Rae, *Climb to Greatness: The American Aircraft Industry, 1920–1960* (Cambridge,

Mass., 1968); "Picture of the Week," *Life*, XIX (August 13, 1945), 26–27; "The Meaning of Victory," *Life*, XIX (August 27, 1945), 34.

47. Quoted in "The Talk of the Town," *The New Yorker*, XXI (September 1, 1945), 17.

48. Quoted in Eric Goldman, *The Crucial Decade—and After, 1945–1960* (New York, 1971), p. 14.

49. Quoted in Daniel Yergin, *Shattered Peace* (Boston, 1977), p. 298.

50. "It's Wonderful," *Fortune*, XXXII (October 1945), 125.

51. Allan Nevins, "How We Felt About the War," in Goodman, *While*, p. 23.

52. V. M. Molotov, *Problems of Foreign Policy: Speeches and Statements, April 1945–November 1948* (Moscow, 1949), pp. 209–14.

53. Quoted in Eric A. Johnston, "My Talk with Joseph Stalin," *Reader's Digest*, XLV (October 1944), 3.

54. Quoted in Harriman and Abel, *Special*, p. 277.

55. Truman, *Memoirs*, I, 341.

56. "Americans Hope for U.S. of Europe," *Saturday Evening Post*, CCXVII (April 7, 1945), 112.

CHAPTER 2. CONFLICT: THE POSTWAR
INTERNATIONAL SYSTEM

1. Herman Finer, in "What Are the Implications of President Truman's Speech?," *University of Chicago Round Table*, no. 469 (March 16, 1947), p. 8.

2. Dean Acheson, *Present at the Creation* (New York, 1969).

3. For the international system, see Kenneth N. Waltz, *Theory of International Politics* (Reading, Mass., 1979); Raymond F. Hopkins and Richard W. Mansbach, *Structure and Process in International Politics* (New York, 1973); Robert J. Art and Robert Jervis, eds., *International Politics: Anarchy, Force, Imperialism* (Boston, 1973); Marshall R. Singer, *Weak States in a World of Power* (New York, 1972); Bruce M. Russett, *Power and Community in World Politics* (San Francisco, 1974); Hans J. Morgenthau, *In Defense of the National Interest* (New York, 1951) and *Politics Among Nations*, 4th ed. (New York, 1967); Robert Gilpin, *War and Change in World Politics* (Cambridge, Eng., 1981); Michael Mandelbaum, *The Fate of Nations* (New York, 1988); Ole R. Holsti, "International Relations Models" and Stephen Pelz, "Balance of Power," in Hogan and Paterson, *Explaining*, pp. 57–88, 111–40.

4. Quoted in Yergin, *Shattered*, p. 223.

5. Quoted in Joseph M. Jones, *The Fifteen Weeks* (New York, 1955), p. 141.
6. For U.S. power, see Chapter 4 below. For hegemony, see Thomas J. McCormick, "World Systems," in Hogan and Paterson, *Explaining*, p. 93, and Thomas J. McCormick, *America's Half-Century* (Baltimore, 1989), pp. 4–7. For a contrary view, that a balance of power rather than U.S. hegemony prevailed, see Joseph S. Nye, Jr., *Bound to Lead: The Changing Nature of American Power* (New York, 1990), pp. 69–73.
7. Quoted in Robert Donovan, *Tumultuous Years* (New York, 1982), p. 176.
8. Stanley Hoffmann, "A View from at Home: The Perils of Incoherence," *Foreign Affairs*, LVII (No. 3, 1978), 468.
9. Paul Kennedy, *The Rise and Fall of the Great Powers* (New York, 1987), p. 515.
10. See Paterson, *Soviet-American;* McCormick, *America's Half-Century;* Fred L. Block, *The Origins of International Economic Disorder* (Berkeley, Calif., 1977); Alan S. Milward, *The Reconstruction of Western Europe, 1945–51* (London, 1984); Michael J. Hogan, *The Marshall Plan* (New York, 1987); Imanuel Wexler, *The Marshall Plan Revisited* (Westport, Conn., 1983).
11. Quoted in Lloyd C. Gardner, *Architects of Illusion* (Chicago, 1970), p. 54.
12. See, for example, John Iatrides, *Revolt in Athens* (Princeton, N.J., 1972) and ed., *Greece in the 1940s* (Hanover, N.H., 1981); Lars Baerentzen et al., eds., *Studies in the History of the Greek Civil War* (Copenhagen, 1987); Spence, *Search;* Michael M. Boll, *Cold War in the Balkans* (Lexington, Ky., 1984); Pjotr Wandycz, *The United States and Poland* (New York, 1980); Ronald Tiersky, *French Communism, 1920–1972* (New York, 1974); Tony Judt, *Resistance and Revolution in Mediterranean Europe, 1938–1948* (London, 1989); Miller, *United States and Italy;* Phyllis Auty, *Tito* (New York, 1970); Anthony Polonsky, "Stalin and the Poles, 1941–7," *European History Quarterly*, XVII (October 1987), 453–92.
13. For decolonization, see Rupert Emerson, *From Empire to Nation* (Cambridge, Mass., 1960); Rudolf von Albertini, *Decolonization* (Garden City, N.Y., 1971); William Roger Louis, *Imperialism at Bay* (New York, 1978) and *The British Empire in the Middle East* (New York, 1984); L. S. Stavrianos, *Global Rift* (New York, 1981); Robert J. McMahon, *Colonialism and Cold War: The United States and the Struggle for Indonesian Independence* (Ithaca, N.Y., 1981); Gary R. Hess, *The United States' Emergence as a Southeast Asian Power, 1940–1950* (New York, 1987); Christopher Thorne, *The Issue of War* (New York, 1985); Gabriel Kolko, *Confronting the Third World* (New York, 1988); Douglas Little,

"Cold War and Colonialism in Africa: The United States, France, and the Madagascar Revolt of 1947," *Pacific Historical Review*, LIX (November 1990), 527–52; Scott L. Bills, *Empire and Cold War: The Roots of US-Third World Antagonism, 1945–1947* (New York, 1990); other works cited below.

14. Michael H. Hunt and Steven I. Levine, "The Revolutionary Challenge to Early U.S. Cold War Policy in Asia," in Warren I. Cohen and Akira Iriye, eds., *The Great Powers in East Asia, 1953–1960* (New York, 1990), p. 14.

15. Quoted in Lloyd C. Gardner, *Approaching Vietnam: From World War II through Dienbienphu, 1941–1954* (New York, 1988), p. 25.

16. Quoted ibid., p. 72.

17. Quoted in Christopher Thorne, *Allies of a Kind* (London, 1978), p. 594.

18. September 26, 1947, report quoted in Robert J. McMahon, "Toward a Postcolonial Order: Truman Administration Policies toward South and Southeast Asia," in Michael J. Lacey, ed., *The Truman Presidency* (New York, 1989), p. 348.

19. Quoted in H. W. Brands, *India and the United States* (Boston, 1990), p. 47.

20. Ambassador Jerome Huddle and Nehru quoted in H. W. Brands, *The Specter of Neutralism* (New York, 1989), pp. 22, 23.

21. NSC-48 (December 1949) quoted in Dennis Merrill, *Bread and the Ballot: The United States and India's Economic Development, 1947–1963* (Chapel Hill, N.C., 1990), p. 44.

22. "Appraisal of U.S. National Interests in South Asia," SANACC 360/14, March 30, 1949, Box 65, SWNCC Records, Records of Interdepartmental and Intradepartmental Committees, NA.

23. Quoted in Diane Shaver Clemens, *Yalta* (New York, 1970), p. 48.

24. John D. Hickerson Oral History Interview, HSTL.

25. Quoted in Robert C. Hilderbrand, *Dumbarton Oaks: The Origins of the United Nations and the Search for Postwar Security* (Chapel Hill, N.C., 1990), p. 127.

26. For the United Nations, see Thomas M. Campbell, *Masquerade Peace: America's UN Policy, 1944–1945* (Tallahassee, 1973); Robert A. Divine, *Second Chance* (New York, 1967); Hilderbrand, *Dumbarton Oaks;* George T. Mazuzan, *Warren T. Austin at the U.N., 1946–1953* (Kent, Ohio, 1977).

27. Harold Urey quoted from *Collier's*, in Wesley T. Wooley, *Alternatives to Anarchy* (Bloomington, Ind., 1988), p. 6.

28. Spencer R. Weart, *Nuclear Fear: A History of Images* (Cambridge, Mass., 1988), p. 106.

29. Harold D. Lasswell, *Power and Personality* (New York, 1948), p. 180.

30. Henry L. Stimson and McGeorge Bundy, *On Active Service in Peace and War* (New York, 1947), pp. 634–43.

31. John H. Herz, *International Politics in the Atomic Age* (New York, 1959), p. 104.

32. Bernard Brodie, ed., *The Absolute Weapon* (New York, 1946).

33. The columnist Max Lerner quoted in Paul Boyer, *By the Bomb's Early Light* (New York, 1985), p. 34.

34. The case for the stabilizing impact of nuclear weapons is made in John Lewis Gaddis, *The Long Peace* (New York, 1987), pp. 229–31, and John Lewis Gaddis, "Great Illusions, the Long Peace, and the Future of the International System," in Charles W. Kegley, Jr., ed., *The Long Postwar Peace* (New York, 1991), pp. 25–55. Critical essays on the thesis by Michael Brecher and Jonathan Wilkenfeld and John A. Vasquez, among others, are found in Kegley, *Long Postwar Peace*. Also skeptical are Vladimir O. Pechatnov, "New Myths in Soviet-U.S. Relations," in Donald R. Kelley and Hoyt Purvis, eds., *Old Myths and New Realities in United States-Soviet Relations* (New York, 1990), pp. 53–54; Stephen Van Evera, "Primed for Peace: Europe after the Cold War," *International Security*, XV (Winter 1990–1991), 7–57.

35. David Holloway, *The Soviet Union and the Arms Race*, 2d ed. (New Haven, Conn., 1984), p. 27.

36. See especially Alan Henrikson, "'The Map as an 'Idea': The Role of Cartographic Imagery during the Second World War," *American Cartographer*, II (April 1975), 19–53;

37. Lester Markel, "Opinion—A Neglected Instrument," in Lester Markel et al., *Public Opinion and Foreign Policy* (New York, 1949), p. 4.

38. Department of State, *The Development of Foreign Reconstruction Policy* (Washington, D.C., 1947), p. 12.

39. "Notes for Address at the Wings Club," May 5, 1947, Box 158, Dwight D. Eisenhower Pre-Presidential Papers, Dwight D. Eisenhower Library, Abilene, Kan.

40. N. L. Englehardt, Jr., *Toward New Frontiers of Our Global World* (New York, 1943), p. 10.

41. Quoted in James Eayers, *In Defence of Canada: Peacemaking and Deterrence* (Toronto, 1972), p. 332.

42. David Dilks, "The British View of Security: Europe and a Wider World, 1945–1949," in Olav Riste, ed., *Western Security: The Formative Years* (Oslo, Norway, 1985), p. 32.

43. Stimson and Bundy, *On Active*, p. 652. See also *FRUS, 1946*, I, 1161, 1166; *DSB*, XIII (November 4, 1945), 709.

CHAPTER 3. SPHERES:THE QUEST FOR
INFLUENCE TO 1947

1. "A Conversation at the United States Ambassador's Residence, Moscow, on 17th December, 1945," CAB 133/82, Cabinet Records, PRO; *FRUS, 1945,* II, 629.
2. Quoted in Robin Edmonds, *Setting the Mould: The United States and Britain, 1945–1950* (New York, 1986), p. 27; Denis Smith, *Diplomacy of Fear: Canada and the Cold War, 1941–1948* (Toronto, 1988), p. 120.
3. Quoted in Edmonds, *Setting,* p. 28.
4. Murphy, *Diplomat,* p. 164.
5. Quoted in Yergin, *Shattered,* p. 61.
6. Adam B. Ulam, *Expansion and Coexistence: Soviet Foreign Policy, 1917–73,* 2d ed. (New York, 1974), p. 437.
7. For spheres of influence, see Geddes W. Rutherford, "Spheres of Influence: An Aspect of Semi-Suzerainty," *American Journal of International Law,* XX (April 1926), 300–25; Frederick L. Schuman, "Spheres of Influence," *Encyclopedia of the Social Sciences* (New York, 1944; 15 vols.), XIV, 297–99; Walter Lippmann, *U.S. War Aims* (Boston, 1944); "Sphere of Influence Arrangements Among the European Powers, 1871–1945," Office of Intelligence Research Report No. 4693, June 30, 1948, Box 8, Charles Bohlen Files, DSR.
8. "Introduction," in Riste, *Western,* p. 11.
9. Warren F. Kimball, ed., *Churchill & Roosevelt: The Complete Correspondence* (Princeton, N.J., 1984; 3 vols.), III, 203.
10. Charles S. Maier, "The Politics of Productivity: Foundations of American International Economic Policy after World War II," *International Organization,* XXXI (Autumn 1977), 630.
11. *FRUS, 1895,* Part I, p. 558.
12. Cordell Hull, *Memoirs* (New York, 1948; 2 vols.), II, 1314–15.
13. Quoted in Robert Dallek, *Franklin D. Roosevelt and American Foreign Policy, 1932–1945* (New York, 1979), p. 456.
14. *FRUS: The Conferences at Cairo and Tehran, 1943,* pp. 530–32; Willard Range, *Franklin D. Roosevelt's World Order* (Athens, Ga., 1959), p. 174. For Roosevelt's views, see Robert A. Divine, *Roosevelt and World War II* (Baltimore, 1969); Herbert Feis, *Churchill, Roosevelt, Stalin* (Princeton, 1957); Edward M. Bennett, *Franklin D. Roosevelt and the Search for Victory* (Wilmington, Del., 1990); Warren F. Kimball, *The Juggler: Franklin D. Roosevelt as Wartime Statesman* (Princeton, 1991).
15. *FRUS, 1944,* I, 166; Kimball, *Churchill,* II, 767.
16. Quoted in Robert L. Messer, "Paths Not Taken: The United States De-

partment of State and Alternatives to Containment, 1945–1946," *Diplomatic History*, I (Fall 1977), 303n.

17. Quoted in Yergin, *Shattered*, p. 43. For the contrary perspective that Roosevelt did not accept spheres, see Lynn E. Davis, *The Cold War Begins* (Princeton, N.J., 1974), pp. 37, 140–43; Thomas T. Hammond, ed., *Witnesses to the Origins of the Cold War* (Seattle, 1982), p. 294.

18. Such was probably also his intention in getting the Declaration of Liberated Europe—a pledge of free elections—accepted at the Yalta Conference. Fraser J. Harbutt, *The Iron Curtain: Churchill, America, and the Origins of the Cold War* (New York, 1986), pp. 87–88.

19. Quoted in Julian G. Hurstfield, *America and the French Nation, 1939–1945* (Chapel Hill, N.C., 1986), p. 215; Charles de Gaulle, *The War Memoirs of Charles de Gaulle: Unity, 1942–44* (New York, 1959), p. 270.

20. Quoted in Gabriel Kolko, *The Politics of War* (New York, 1968), p. 142.

21. Winston S. Churchill, *Triumph and Tragedy* (Boston, 1953), p. 227. See also Albert Resis, "The Churchill-Stalin 'Percentages' Agreement on the Balkans, Moscow, October 1944," *American Historical Review*, LXXXIII (April 1978), 368–87.

22. Graham Ross, *The Foreign Office and the Kremlin: British Documents on Anglo-Soviet Relations, 1941–45* (Cambridge, Eng., 1984), p. 176.

23. Navy cable, Harriman to the President, October 10, 1944, Box 187, W. Averell Harriman Papers, LC; *FRUS, 1944*, IV, 1009.

24. Kimball, *Churchill*, III, 371.

25. Quoted in Divine, *Second*, p. 84.

26. Clemens, *Yalta*, p. 263; John Lewis Gaddis, *The United States and the Origins of the Cold War, 1941–1947* (New York, 1972), pp. 163–64.

27. *FRUS, 1945*, V, 821–22.

28. Akira Iriye, *The Cold War in Asia* (Englewood Cliffs, N.J., 1974), p. 96.

29. *FRUS, Berlin*, II, 450.

30. George F. Kennan, *Memoirs, 1925–1950* (Boston, 1967), p. 260.

31. *FRUS, 1944*, IV, 1009.

32. *FRUS, Berlin*, I, 262.

33. Quoted in Arthur Schlesinger, Jr., "Origins of the Cold War," *Foreign Affairs*, XLVI (October 1967), 28.

34. Quoted in Richard J. Walton, *Henry Wallace, Harry Truman, and the Cold War* (New York, 1976), pp. 104, 107. See also Henry A. Wallace, "The Path to Peace with Russia," *New Republic*, CXV (September 30, 1946), 401–06; Ronald Radosh and Leonard P. Liggio, "Henry A. Wallace and the Open Door," in Thomas G. Paterson, ed., *Cold War Critics* (Chicago, 1971), pp. 76–113.

35. Quoted in Messer, "Paths," p. 302.

36. H. Stuart Hughes, "The Second Year of the Cold War: A Memoir and an Anticipation," *Commentary*, XLVIII (August 1969), 29.
37. George F. Kennan to Charles Bohlen, January 26, 1945, Box 8, Bohlen Files.
38. Kennan, *Memoirs*, p. 256. For Charles Bohlen's dissent from Kennan's frank spheres approach, on the ground that the American public, especially people of Eastern European descent, would protest, see T. Michael Ruddy, *The Cautious Diplomat: Charles E. Bohlen and the Soviet Union, 1929–1969* (Kent, Ohio, 1986), pp. 32–33; David Mayers, *George Kennan and the Dilemmas of US Foreign Policy* (New York, 1988), pp. 94–96.
39. Lippmann, *U.S. War Aims*, p. 88. See also Walter Lippmann, "A Year of Peacemaking," *Atlantic Monthly*, CLXXVII (December 1946), 35–40.
40. J. C. Donnelly, Minutes, "Supplementary to Weekly Political Summary," July 16, 1944, AN 2829/20/45, Foreign Office Correspondence, PRO.
41. For the distinction between "open" and "exclusive" spheres, see Eduard M. Mark, "The Interpretation of Soviet Foreign Policy in the United States, 1928–47" (Ph.D. dissertation, University of Connecticut, 1978), pp. 135–37, 190–95, 205–06, 229–30, 267–69, 295.
42. *FRUS, 1945*, V, 232.
43. Ibid., p. 843.
44. "United States: Dominant Considerations in Judging a Soviet Regional Policy in Eastern Europe," March 15, 1944, Special Subcommittee on Problems of European Organization of the Advisory Committee on Postwar Foreign Policy, Box 85, Harley A. Notter Files, DSR; Minutes, March 3, 1944, Box 84, ibid. For thoughts similar to those of Bohlen, see William T. R. Fox, *The Super-Powers* (New York, 1944), p. 97; Sumner Welles, *The Time for Decision* (New York, 1944), pp. 332–33.
45. Harry Hopkins statement to Stalin, *FRUS, Berlin*, I, 38.
46. "Note by Sir Archibald Clark Kerr on a discussion between the Prime Minister and the Soviet Ambassador at No. Downing Street on May 18, 1945," Premier 3, 396/12, Prime Minister's Office Records, PRO.
47. Thomas Inglis (Office of Naval Intelligence), quoted in Barton J. Bernstein, "American Foreign Policy and the Origins of the Cold War," in Barton J. Bernstein, ed., *Politics and Policies of the Truman Administration* (Chicago, 1970), p. 40.
48. Charles Bohlen lecture, April 28, 1948, Box 6, Bohlen Files.
49. *FRUS, 1944*, IV, 989.
50. Russell D. Buhite, "Soviet-American Relations and the Repatriation of Prisoners of War, 1945," *The Historian*, XXXV (May 1973), 384–97.
51. Truman paraphrased by Edward Stettinius, in Thomas M. Campbell and

George C. Herring, eds., *The Diaries of Edward R. Stettinius, Jr., 1943–1946* (New York, 1975), p. 318.

52. *FRUS, 1944,* IV, 993.
53. Walter Brown Notes, July 22, 1945, Folder 602, James F. Byrnes Papers, Clemson University Library, Clemson, S.C.
54. John Hickerson, *FRUS, 1945,* IV, 408.
55. Charles Bohlen lecture, July 10, 1947, Box 10, Bohlen Files.
56. Commerce, *Historical Statistics,* pp. 870, 903, 905.
57. Gerald K. Haines, "Under the Eagle's Wing: The Franklin Roosevelt Administration Forges an American Hemisphere," *Diplomatic History,* I (Fall 1977), 373–88; J. Fred Rippy, *Globe and Hemisphere* (Chicago, 1958).
58. Walter LaFeber, ed., *The Dynamics of World Power: Eastern Europe and the Soviet Union* (New York, 1973; 4 vols., edited by Arthur M. Schlesinger, Jr.), II, 84.
59. Quoted in David Green, "The Cold War Comes to Latin America," in Bernstein, *Politics,* p. 164.
60. Memorandum for the Use of the Mediterranean Fleet, "United States Policy toward Saudi Arabia," November 8, 1946, Box 1812, Loy Henderson Files, DSR. See also Aaron D. Miller, *Search for Security: Saudi Arabian Oil and American Foreign Policy, 1939–1949* (Chapel Hill, N.C., 1980).
61. *FRUS, 1944,* III, 103.
62. Quoted in Thorne, *Issue,* p. 206.
63. *PPP, Truman, 1945,* p. 203.
64. Quoted in Thorne, *Allies,* p. 458.
65. A British official quoted in Hilderbrand, *Dumbarton,* p. 171.
66. Quoted in Llewellyn Woodward, *British Foreign Policy in the Second World War* (London, 1962), p. 531n.
67. Harriman and Abel, *Special,* p. 517. Truman quoted in Thorne, *Allies,* p. 659.
68. Edwin O. Reischauer, *The United States and Japan* (Cambridge, Mass., 1950), pp. 40, 45, 48.
69. Quoted in Robert D. Warth, "Stalin and the Cold War: A Second Look," *South Atlantic Quarterly,* LIX (Winter 1960), 9. See also Michael Schaller, *The American Occupation of Japan* (New York, 1985), p. 18; Howard B. Schonberger, *Aftermath of War: Americans and the Remaking of Japan, 1945–1952* (Kent, Ohio, 1989), pp. 45–46; Marc S. Gallicchio, *The Cold War Begins in Asia* (New York, 1988), p. 116.
70. James F. Byrnes, *Speaking Frankly* (New York, 1947), p. 102.
71. Dean Rusk, *As I Saw It* (New York, 1990), p. 123.

72. Harry Howard Oral History Interview, HSTL.
73. *DSB*, XIII (November 4, 1945), 710. See also ibid., XIV (March 10, 1946), 357–58, and Charles Bohlen to Walter Lippmann, February 17, 1948, Box 57, Walter Lippmann Papers, Yale University Library, New Haven, Conn.
74. Former Ambassador to the Soviet Union Joseph Davies wrote in his diary for September 22, 1945: "The Russians want to find out whether we will apply one rule for our security in the Pacific and refuse to apply the same rule in Europe where the Soviets similarly need it in their interest. . . . They also want to know whether, for reasons of security, the Panama Canal is to be controlled by the United States, while similar security against attack is to be denied them at their back door—the Dardanelles and the Straits." Diary, Box 22, Joseph Davies Papers, LC. See also Vera Micheles Dean, "Is Russia Alone to Blame?," *Foreign Policy Bulletin*, XXV (March 8, 1946), 1–2.
75. Quoted in Yergin, *Shattered*, p. 150.
76. Quoted in Clemens, *Yalta*, p. 152.
77. Miller, *United States and Italy*, pp. 156–60.
78. *FRUS, Berlin*, II, 358–359, 362.
79. See James L. Gormly, *From Potsdam to the Cold War: Big Three Diplomacy, 1945–1947* (Wilmington, Del., 1990); Michael M. Boll, *Cold War in the Balkans: American Foreign Policy and the Emergence of Communist Bulgaria, 1943–1947* (Lexington, Ky., 1984).
80. Philip E. Mosely, "Soviet-American Relations since the War," *Annals of the American Academy of Political and Social Science*, CCLXIII (May 1949), 202.
81. Quoted in Harriman and Abel, *Special*, p. 538.
82. Molotov, *Problems*, pp. 210–216. See also Joseph F. Harrington and Bruce J. Courtney, *Tweaking the Nose of the Russians: Fifty Years of American-Romanian Relations, 1940–1990* (Boulder, Colo., 1991), p. 43; *Soviet Press Translations*, I (November 1946), and III (January 15, 1947); *FRUS, Berlin*, II, 303, 365.
83. Truman, *Memoirs*, I, 412.
84. *FRUS, 1946*, VII, 499.
85. For Iran, see Paterson, *Soviet-American*, pp. 177–83; Mark H. Lyttle, *The Origins of the Iranian-American Alliance, 1941–1953* (New York, 1987).
86. Truman, *Memoirs*, I, 552.
87. H. Freeman Matthews to Dean Acheson, February 11, 1946, Box 2, H. Freeman Matthews Files, DSR. See also *FRUS, 1946*, VI, 695.
88. See the speech in LaFeber, *Eastern Europe*, pp. 191–99.
89. William O. McCagg, Jr., *Stalin Embattled, 1943–1948* (Detroit, 1978), pp. 217–27; Werner G. Hahn, *Postwar Soviet Politics* (Ithaca, N.Y., 1982), pp. 22–23.

90. John M. Blum, *The Price of Vision: The Diary of Henry A. Wallace* (Boston, 1973), p. 547.
91. "Political Situation in the United States," February 17, 1946, AN 423/1/45, FOC.
92. B. E. T. Gage, Minutes, ibid.
93. *FRUS, 1946*, VI, 706.
94. Harbutt, *Iron Curtain*, pp. 151–208.
95. Paraphrase by Sir Maurice Peterson, "Interview between His Majesty's Ambassador and Stalin," May 28, 1946, N6984/140/38, FOC.
96. Walter Bedell Smith, *My Three Years in Moscow* (Philadelphia, 1950), p. 50.
97. Quoted in Robert J. Donovan, *Conflict and Crisis* (New York, 1977), p. 213.
98. Blum, *Price*, p. 536.
99. Piers Dixon, *Double Diploma* (London, 1968), p. 212.
100. Herkin, *Winning*, pp. 171–91.
101. "Narrative of U.S. Naval Forces, Europe, 1 September 1945 to 1 October 1946," Command Files, Naval Historical Center, Old Navy Yard, Washington, D.C.; Memorandum of Conversation by James Riddleberger, September 7, 1946, Box 2, Matthews Files, DSR.
102. "Quarterly Summary of U.S. Naval Forces Eastern Atlantic and Mediterranean," October 1, 1946–April 1, 1947, Command Files, Naval Historical Center.
103. John Gimbel, *Science, Technology, and Reparations: Exploitation and Plunder in Postwar Germany* (Stanford, Calif., 1990).
104. Jean E. Smith, ed., *The Papers of Lucius D. Clay: Germany, 1945–1949* (Bloomington, Ind., 1974; 2 vols.), I, 213.
105. *DSB*, XV (July 28, 1946), 170; John Gimbel, "Die Vereinigten Staaten, Frankreich und der Amerikanische Vertragsentwurf zur Entmilitarisierung Deutschlands: *Vierteljahrshefte für Zeitgeschichte* (1974), pp. 258–86; Yergin, *Shattered*, pp. 225–30.
106. *FRUS, 1946*, VII, 840–41.
107. Melvyn P. Leffler, "Strategy, Diplomacy, and the Cold War: The United States, Turkey, and NATO, 1945–1952," *Journal of American History*, LXXI (March 1985), 807–25. A work which exaggerates the Soviet threat to Turkey and basically reflects the official U.S. perspective is Bruce R. Kuniholm, *The Origins of the Cold War in the Near East* (Princeton, N.J., 1980).
108. *New Times* (Moscow), January 1, 1947. For the harsher Soviet tone which became noticeable in April 1946, see "Interpretive Report on Soviet Policy Based on the Press for April 1 to 28, 1946," by American Embassy in Moscow, April 30, 1946, Box 1384, Moscow Post Files, DSR; Maurice Peterson to Ernest Bevin, July 22, 1946, 861.00/7-2246, DSR; British Embassy, Moscow, "Soviet Union Quarterly Report, July–September,

1946," October 22, 1946, Box 1384, Moscow Post Files; *New Times,* March 15, May 1, May 15, June 1, August 1, 1946; White House Daily Summary, May 21 and August 16, 1946, DSR; "Interpretive Report on Soviet Policy Based on the Press for May, 1946," June 13, 1946, Box 1384, Moscow Post Files.

109. "The Novikov Telegram, Washington, September 27, 1946," *Diplomatic History,* XV (Fall 1991), 527–37. See discussion of its meaning, ibid., pp. 539–63; "A Soviet 'Long Telegram'?," *U.S. Institute for Peace Journal,* III (October 1990), 8–9.

110. White House Daily Summary, November 21, 1946, DSR.

111. Reinhold Niebuhr, "The Fight for Germany," *Life,* XXI (October 1946), 65.

112. Department of Commerce, *Foreign Aid by the United States Government, 1940–1951* (Washington, D.C., 1952); Paterson, *Soviet-American.*

113. *FRUS, 1946,* VII, 223.

CHAPTER 4. POLARIZATION: THE COLD WAR, 1947–1950

1. "Public Information Program on United States Aid to Greece," March 3, 1947, SWNCC FPI 30, Box 88, SWNCC Records.

2. *PPP, Truman, 1947,* pp. 176–80.

3. Ambassador to Turkey Edwin C. Wilson in Senate, Committee on Foreign Relations, *Legislative Origins of the Truman Doctrine* (executive session hearings; historical series; Washington, D.C., 1973), p. 52.

4. Mr. Ross to Dean Rusk, March 19, 1947, U.S. Mission to the United Nations Records.

5. "X," "The Sources of Soviet Conduct," *Foreign Affairs,* XXV (July 1947), 581.

6. Princeton Seminar Transcript, July 8–9, 1953, Box 64, Dean Acheson Papers, HSTL.

7. Studies of the Truman Doctrine, Greece, and Turkey include John O. Iatrides, *Revolt;* Iatrides, *Greece in the 1940s;* Lars Baerentzen, *Studies;* Kuniholm, *Origins;* Wittner, *American Intervention;* Howard Jones, *"A New Kind of War": America's Global Strategy and the Truman Doctrine in Greece* (New York, 1989); Melvyn P. Leffler, "From the Truman Doctrine to the Carter Doctrine: Lessons and Dilemmas of the Cold War," *Diplomatic History,* VII (Fall 1983), 245–66.

8. Walter Lippmann, *The Cold War* (New York, 1947), pp. 11–12, 14, 38, 50–52.

9. Walter Lippmann to William Knowland, September 21, 1949, Box 82, Series III, Lippmann Papers.

10. Hoffmann, "A View," 468; Robert W. Tucker, *The Radical Left and American Foreign Policy* (Baltimore, 1971), pp. 108–09.

11. Escott Reid quoted in Smith, *Diplomacy of Fear*, p. 199.

12. Hogan, *Marshall Plan;* Paterson, *Soviet-American;* Milward, *Reconstruction;* Wexler, *Marshall Plan;* Melvyn P. Leffler, "The United States and the Strategic Dimensions of the Marshall Plan," *Diplomatic History,* XII (Summer 1988), 277–306.

13. "Report of the Special Ad Hoc Committee," SWNCC-360, April 21, 1947, Box 65, SWNCC Records.

14. House of Representatives, Committee on International Relations, *Foreign Economic Assistance Programs* (executive session hearings; historical series; Washington, D.C., 1976), vol. IV, part 2, p. 38.

15. *FRUS, 1947,* III, 232.

16. House of Representatives, Committee on Foreign Affairs, *Emergency Foreign Aid* (hearings; Washington, D.C., 1947), p. 122.

17. *PPP, Truman, 1948,* p. 234.

18. White House Summary, July 3, 1947, DSR.

19. Secretary's Weekly Summary, July 14, 1947, DSR. Apparently this is also what the Soviet archives reveal as Moscow's reason for jilting the Marshall Plan. See M. M. Narinskii, "Consolidation of the Cold War, 1945–1950: Theses," Seminar on the Origins of the Cold War Sponsored by the U.S. Institute of Peace and the USSR Ministry of Foreign Affairs, Moscow and Washington, D.C., June and July, 1990, p. 1.

20. Margaret Carlyle, ed., *Documents on International Affairs, 1947–1948* (London, 1952), pp. 129–30.

21. Quoted in John Gimbel, *The Origins of the Marshall Plan* (Stanford, 1976), p. 263.

22. Senate, Committee on Foreign Relations, *Foreign Relief Aid: 1947* (executive session hearings; historical series; Washington, D.C., 1973), p. 153.

23. "Powerlessness" is the theme of Josef Becker and Franz Knipping, eds., *Power in Europe? Great Britain, France, Italy and Germany in a Postwar World, 1945–1950* (Berlin, 1986).

24. Quoted in Foreign Office Minutes on the Political Situation in the United States, August 20, 21, 1945, AN2505/4/45, FOC; Louis, *Imperialism,* p. 550.

25. Harriman and Abel, *Special,* p. 531.

26. The Palestine/Israel question is also discussed below in Chapter 7.

27. Quoted in Robert M. Hathaway, *Great Britain and the United States: Special Relations since World War II* (Boston, 1990), p. 21.

28. Quoted in Alan Bullock, *Ernest Bevin: Foreign Secretary, 1945–1951* (London, 1983), p. 203. For other works on the sometimes strained but nonetheless enduring Anglo-American relationship, see Randall B. Woods, *A Changing of the Guard: Anglo-American Relations, 1941–*

1946 (Chapel Hill, N.C., 1990); David Reynolds, "A 'Special Relationship'? America, Britain and the International Order since the Second World War," *International Affairs* (London), LXII (Winter 1985–86), 1–20; Wm. Roger Louis and Hedley Bull, eds., *The "Special Relationship": Anglo-American Relations since 1945* (Oxford, 1986).

29. Quoted in René Girault, "The French Decision-Makers and Their Perception of French Power in 1948," in Becker and Knipping, *Power*, p. 61.

30. Quoted in Hans-Jürgen Schröder, "The Economic Reconstruction of West Germany in the Context of International Relations, 1945–1949," ibid., p. 313.

31. Robert Frank, "The French Dilemma: Modernization with Dependence or Independence and Decline," ibid., pp. 263–80.

32. Diary, November 23, 1948, Lippmann Papers. Friction with France is also discussed in Hogan, *Marshall Plan*, pp. 195–96.

33. The "Third Force" issue is developed throughout Becker and Knipping, *Power*. See especially Bernd-Jürgen Wendt, "Europe between Power and Powerlessness," p. 545.

34. See Chapter 9 below.

35. Secretary's Weekly Summary, May 19, 1947, DSR; "Guidance on Military Aspects of United States Policy . . . International Control of Atomic Energy," by Joint Strategic Survey Committee for JCS, JCS 1764/1, July 14, 1947, Box 166, Central Decimal File 471.6, JCS Records; Secretary's Weekly Summary, December 15, 1947, DSR; *FRUS, 1948*, V, part 1, 119–20.

36. "The Position of the United States with Respect to Soviet-Directed World Communism," NSC-7, March 30, 1948, National Security Council Records, Modern Military Branch, NA.

37. *FRUS, 1947*, III, 691.

38. Tony Judt, "Introduction," in Judt, *Resistance*, pp. 1–28; David Travis, "Communism and Resistance in Italy, 1943–8," ibid., pp. 103–04; McCagg, *Stalin*, pp. 213, 267–268, 307–308; Edward Mortimer, *The Rise of the French Communist Party, 1920–1947* (London, 1984), p. 358; Donald L. M. Blackmer, *Unity in Diversity: Italian Communism and the Communist World* (Cambridge, Mass., 1968), pp. 14–15; M. Adereth, *The French Communist Party* (Manchester, Eng., 1984), p. 134; Paolo Spriano, *Stalin and the European Communists* (London, 1985).

39. Miller, *United States and Italy*, pp. 213–49.

40. Clark Clifford and the act quoted in Senate, Select Committee to Study . . . Intelligence Activities, *Foreign and Military Intelligence*, book I (Washington, D.C., 1976), pp. 143–44.

41. Ibid., p. 144; John Ranelagh, *The Agency: The Rise and Decline of the CIA* (New York, 1986), pp. 121, 133, 137–38; Trevor Barnes, "The Se-

cret Cold War: The C.I.A. and American Foreign Policy in Europe, 1946–1956: Part I," *Historical Journal*, XXIV (June 1981), 399–415; Rhodri Jeffreys-Jones, *The CIA and American Democracy* (New Haven, 1989); Harry H. Ransom, *The Intelligence Establishment* (Cambridge, Mass., 1970), ch. IV; Harry Rositzke, *The CIA's Secret Operations* (New York, 1977), pp. 18–20; John Prados, *Presidents' Secret Wars* (New York, 1986), pp. 26–90; William M. Leary, *Perilous Missions: Civil Air Transport and CIA Covert Operations in Asia* (University, Ala., 1984).

42. Secretary's Weekly Summary, July 7, 1947, DSR; Clinton P. Anderson, *Outsider in the Senate* (New York, 1970), pp. 70–71; George C. Herring, "The Truman Administration and the Restoration of French Sovereignty in Indochina," *Diplomatic History*, I (Spring 1977), 97–117; Clark M. Clifford, "A Viet Nam Reappraisal," *Foreign Affairs*, XCVII (July 1969), 603; McMahon, *Colonialism;* McMahon, "Toward"; "Military Aid Priorities," SANACC 360/11, Subcommittee for Rearmament, August 18, 1948, SWNCC Records; *FRUS, 1948*, V, 655–56; Gerald K. Haines, *The Americanization of Brazil* (Wilmington, Del., 1989), p. 46.

43. Major General Curtis LeMay's 1947 report quoted in David A. Rosenberg, "American Atomic Strategy and the Hydrogen Bomb Decision," *Journal of American History*, LXVI (June 1979), 67.

44. "Guidance for the Preparation of a Joint Outline War Plan," Joint Staff Planners to Joint War Plans Committee, August 29, 1947, 381-USSR, Box 37B, JCS Records; "Broiler," by Joint Strategic Plans Group, JSPG 496/1, November 8, 1947, ibid. The planners code-named their various "war plans," 1946–1948, Pincher, Broiler, Bushwacker, and Grabber.

45. Kennan, *Memoirs*, p. 401.

46. John D. Hickerson Oral History Interview, HSTL.

47. Quoted in Princeton Seminar transcript, October 10–11, 1953, Box 65, Acheson Papers.

48. Margaret Truman, *Harry S. Truman* (New York, 1973), p. 359.

49. "American-Russian Relations," Records of Groups, vol. XIV, Council on Foreign Relations Files, New York.

50. J. Samuel Walker, " 'No More Cold War': American Foreign Policy and the 1948 Soviet Peace Offensive," *Diplomatic History*, V (Winter 1981), 75–91.

51. For Germany and the Berlin crisis, see Bruce Kuklick, *American Policy and the Division of Germany* (Ithaca, N.Y., 1972); John H. Backer, *Priming the German Economy: American Occupational Policies, 1945–1948* (Durham, N.C., 1971); John Gimbel, *The American Occupation of Germany* (Stanford, 1968); Manuel Gottlieb, *The German Peace Settlement and the Berlin Crisis* (New York, 1960); Avi Shlaim, *The United States and the Berlin Blockade, 1948–1949* (Berkeley, 1983); Paterson,

Soviet-American, ch. 11; Leffler, "Strategic Dimensions"; Hannes Ado-meit, *Soviet Risk-Taking and Crisis Behavior* (London, 1982), chs. 6–10.

52. *FRUS, 1948*, IV, 1073–1112; Henry W. Brands, Jr., "Redefining the Cold War: American Policy toward Yugoslavia, 1948–1960," *Diplomatic History*, XI (Winter 1987), 41–53.

53. Josip Broz Tito, "On Certain International Questions," *Foreign Affairs*, XXXVI (October 1957), 77.

54. Great Britain, France, Belgium, Luxembourg, Netherlands, Denmark, Italy, Norway, Iceland, Portugal, Canada, and the United States were the original members. Greece and Turkey joined in 1952; West Germany entered NATO in 1955. For the Brussels Pact and NATO, see other works cited in this chapter and Brunello Vigezzi, "Italy: The End of a 'Great Power' and the Birth of a 'Democratic Power,'" in Becker and Knipping, *Power*, pp. 76–80; Pierre Melandri and Maurice Vaisse, "France: From Powerlessness to the Search for Influence," ibid., p. 465; Escott Reid, *Time of Fear and Hope: The Making of the North Atlantic Treaty, 1947–1949* (Toronto, 1977); Ennio Di Nolfo, ed., *The Atlantic Pact Forty Years Later* (Berlin, 1991); Martin H. Folly, "Breaking the Vicious Circle: Britain, the United States, and the Genesis of the North Atlantic Treaty," *Diplomatic History*, XII (Winter 1988), 59–77; Lawrence S. Kaplan, *The United States and NATO: The Formative Years* (Lexington, Ky., 1984); Lawrence S. Kaplan, *NATO and the United States* (Boston, 1988); Lawrence S. Kaplan, *A Community of Interests: NATO and the Military Assistance Program, 1948–1951* (Washington, D.C., 1980); Timothy Ireland, *Creating the Entangling Alliance* (Westport, Conn., 1981); Joseph Smith, ed., *The Origins of NATO* (Exeter, Eng., 1990). Also see Chester Pach, Jr., *Arming the Free World: The Origins of the United States Military Assistance Program* (Chapel Hill, N.C., 1991).

55. Quoted in Hixson, *Kennan*, pp. 80. See also Ruddy, *Cautious*, pp. 85–91.

56. House, *Foreign Economic Assistance*, part 2, vol. IV, p. 25; *FRUS, 1948*, III, 183.

57. Senate, Committee on Foreign Relations, *North Atlantic Treaty* (hearings; Washington, D.C., 1949), p. 213; *FRUS, 1948*, III, 40.

58. Acheson in Princeton Seminar transcript, October 10–11, 1953, Box 65, Acheson Papers.

59. Senate, *North Atlantic Treaty*, pp. 213–14.

60. Quoted in Walter LaFeber, *America, Russia, and the Cold War, 1945–1990*, 6th ed. (New York, 1991), p. 84.

61. Cominform bulletin quoted in Marshall D. Schulman, *Stalin's Foreign Policy Reappraised* (New York, 1966), p. 94.

62. *FRUS, 1946*, VI, 704.

63. Thomas G. Paterson, *Meeting the Communist Threat: Truman to Reagan* (New York, 1988), pp. 60–63.
64. Interview with Dean Acheson, February 17, 1955, Box 1, Memoirs File, Post-Presidential Files, HSTL.
65. Quoted in David McLean, "American Nationalism, the China Myth, and the Truman Doctrine: The Question of Accommodation with Peking, 1949–1950," *Diplomatic History*, X (Winter 1986), 32.
66. *FRUS, 1949*, VIII, 388.
67. *FRUS, 1950*, VII, 1368.
68. Vladislav Zubok, "Consolidation of the Cold War, 1945–1950," Seminar on the Origins of the Cold War, p. 8.
69. Russell D. Buhite and Wm. Christopher Hamel, "War for Peace: The Question of an American Preventive War against the Soviet Union, 1945–1955," *Diplomatic History*, XIV (Summer 1990), 367–84.
70. David A. Rosenberg, "U.S. Nuclear Stockpile, 1945 to 1950," *Bulletin of the Atomic Scientists*, XXXVIII (May 1982), 25–30; Roger Dingman, "Atomic Diplomacy during the Korean War," *International Security*, XIII (Winter 1988–1989), 52.
71. Shulman, *Stalin's*, pp. 104–38; Ulam, *Expansion*, pp. 498–503.
72. Acheson, *Present*, pp. 378–79.
73. *DSB*, XXII (June 26, 1950), 1038.
74. Ibid., 1037; ibid., XXII (March 20, 1950), 427–28.
75. Gregg Herken, *Counsels of War*, expanded ed. (New York, 1987), pp. 54–59; Mayers, *Kennan*, pp. 305–09.
76. Quoted in McGeorge Bundy, *Danger and Survival: Choices About the Bomb in the First Fifty Years* (New York, 1988), pp. 209.
77. Quoted in R. Gordon Arneson, "The H-Bomb Decision," *Foreign Service Journal*, XLVI (May 1969), 27.
78. NSC 48/2 quoted in Roger Dingman, "1950: The Fate of a Grand Design," *Pacific Historical Review*, XLVII (August 1978), 465. See also Hess, *United States' Emergence*, pp. 311–32.
79. McMahon, "Toward," p. 354. Douglas Pike has found that the Soviet Union was only minimally involved in Indochinese affairs in the late 1940s. See his *Vietnam and the Soviet Union* (Boulder, Colo., 1987).
80. Michael Schaller, "Securing the Great Crescent: Occupied Japan and the Origins of Containment in Southeast Asia," *Journal of American History*, LXIX (September 1982), 392–414; Ronald McGlothlen, "Acheson, Economics, and the American Commitment in Korea, 1947–1950," *Pacific Historical Review*, LVIII (February 1989), 23–54.
81. NSC-68, "United States Objectives and Programs for National Security," April 14, 1950, *FRUS, 1950*, I, 237–92. See Samuel F. Wells, Jr.,

"Sounding the Tocsin: NSC-68 and the Soviet Threat," *International Security*, IV (Fall 1979), 116–58; Paterson, *Meeting*, pp. 52–53.

82. Edward W. Barrett in Princeton Seminar Transcript, October 10–11, 1953, Box 65, Acheson Papers.

83. Recent scholarship emphasizes a civil war in Korea between the Communist Kim Il Sung government of the North and the American-backed Syngman Rhee government in the South, as well as factionalism within the North. Robert R. Simmons, *The Strained Alliance: Peking, Pyongyang, Moscow and the Politics of the Korean Civil War* (New York, 1975); Bruce Cumings, *The Origins of the Korean War* (Princeton, 1981, 1990; 2 vols.); John Merrill, *Korea: The Peninsular Origins of the War* (Newark, Del., 1989); Barton J. Bernstein, "The Truman Administration and the Korean War," in Lacey, *Truman*, pp. 410–44.

84. Nikita Khrushchev, *Khrushchev Remembers* (Boston, 1970), pp. 367–69.

85. Zubok, "Consolidation," p. 8. One scholar argues that there was no Chinese-Soviet discussion of a North Korean invasion before it occurred and that China itself did not know of Kim's plans. Vladimir Petrov, in "Behind the Scenes: Stalin, Mao Zedong, and the Korean War," Kennan Institute for Advanced Russian Studies, *Meeting Report* (Washington, D.C., November 6, 1989).

CHAPTER 5. ACTIVISM: AMERICAN IDEOLOGY,
ECONOMIC-STRATEGIC NEEDS, AND POWER

1. Transcript, Eric Sevareid's "A Conversation with Dean Acheson," CBS Television Network, September 28, 1969.

2. Acheson in House, *Foreign Economic Assistance*, vol. IV, part 2, p. 38.

3. *DSB*, XX (February 6, 1949), 157.

4. For "core values," see Leffler, "National Security," pp. 202–13.

5. *PPP, Truman, 1945*, pp. 433–34.

6. Samuel Rosenman, ed., *Public Papers of Franklin D. Roosevelt* (New York, 1938–1950; 13 vols.), XIII, 595.

7. *DSB*, XIV (May 19, 1946), 831.

8. *FRUS, 1946*, VI, 708.

9. *DSB*, XII (May 27, 1945), 979.

10. *PPP, Truman, 1947*, p. 167.

11. Quoted in Paterson, *Soviet-American*, p. 5.

12. *DSB*, XVI (June 15, 1947), 1160.

13. Ibid., XXII (April 22, 1945), 738. For the "peace and prosperity" concept, see Paterson, *Meeting*, pp. 18–34.

14. Truman on Point Four in *PPP, Truman, 1949*, 329–33. For the mission-

ary zeal but disappointing results of this program, see Paterson, *Meeting*, pp. 147–58.

15. For the antirevolutionary theme, see Michael H. Hunt, *Ideology and U.S. Foreign Policy* (New Haven, 1987), chs. 4–5.

16. Quoted in Henry H. Adams, *Harry Hopkins: A Biography* (New York, 1977), p. 398.

17. Hunt, *Ideology*, ch. 3.

18. Arthur Schlesinger, Jr., "America: Experiment or Destiny?," *American Historical Review*, LXXXII (June 1977), 518. Denis Brogan wrote in 1952 that "probably the only people in the world who now have the historical sense of inevitable victory are the Americans." Brogan, "Illusions of American Omnipotence," *Harper's*, CCV (December 1952), 21–28.

19. For the missionary, expansionist character of the American self-image, see Jonathan Daniels, *White House Witness* (Garden City, N.Y., 1975), p. 222; O. Edmund Clubb, *The Witness and I* (New York, 1974), p. 16; Tucker, *Radical*, pp. 69, 74; J. William Fulbright, "Reflections: In Thrall to Fear," *The New Yorker*, XLVII (January 8, 1972), 41–62; William A. Williams, *The Tragedy of American Diplomacy* (New York, 1962), pp. 9–10.

20. Quoted (1947) in John Lewis Gaddis, "The Insecurities of Victory: The United States and the Perception of the Soviet Threat after World War II," in Lacey, *Truman*, p. 267n. See also Kennedy, *Rise*, pp. 360–61.

21. Gaddis Smith, *Dean Acheson* (New York, 1972), p. 416.

22. *Congressional Record*, XC (1944), Appendix, p. 265.

23. For the historical imperative, see Ernest R. May, *"Lessons of the Past"* (New York, 1973); Michael Roskin, "From Pearl Harbor to Vietnam: Shifting Generational Paradigms and Foreign Policy," *Political Science Quarterly*, LXXXIX (Fall 1974), 563–88.

24. Cabinet Meeting, August 31, 1945, Notes on Cabinet Meetings, Connelly Papers. Byrnes in *DSB*, XIV (March 24, 1946), 482; Truman in Blum, *Price*, p. 602.

25. Quoted in Woods, *Changing*, p. 251.

26. Truman, *Memoirs*, I, 119, 121.

27. Minutes, April 30–May 1, 2, 1946, 34th Annual Meeting of the Chamber of Commerce, Chamber of Commerce Library, Washington, D.C.

28. *Wall Street Journal*, June 25, 1941.

29. Les K. Adler and Thomas G. Paterson, "Red Fascism: The Merger of Nazi Germany and Soviet Russia in the American Image of Totalitarianism, 1930's–1950's," *American Historical Review*, LXXV (April 1970), 1046–64.

30. *PPP, Truman, 1947*, p. 238.
31. Carl T. Durham to John A. Buchanan, March 25, 1947, Folder 773, Carl T. Durham Papers, University of North Carolina Library, Chapel Hill.
32. Deane, *Strange*, p. 4.
33. George F. Kennan, "Overdue Changes in Our Foreign Policy," *Harper's*, CCXIII (August 1956), 28.
34. David M. Potter, *People of Plenty: Economic Abundance and the American Character* (Chicago, 1954).
35. For data here and below, see Paterson, *Soviet-American*, ch. 1.
36. Willard L. Thorp in Department of State, *Problems of United States Foreign Economic Policy* (Washington, D.C., 1947), p. 3.
37. John Snyder to the President, "Comments on Draft of the Economic Report of the President," n.d., OF 396, Truman Papers.
38. Committee for Economic Development, *International Trade, Foreign Investment, and Domestic Employment* (New York, 1945), p. 10; Johnston in B. C. Forbes, ed., *America's Fifty Foremost Business Leaders* (New York, 1948), p. 226.
39. *PPP, Truman, 1946*, p. 354.
40. Senate Committee on Foreign Relations, *European Recovery Program* (hearings; Washington, D.C., 1948), p. 369.
41. *DSB*, XXI (September 12, 1949), 401.
42. "Report of the Group on American Interests in Foreign Countries," October 15, 1945, vol. VIII, Special Committee Investigating Petroleum Resources, U.S. Senate Records, NA; Petroleum Administrator Harold Ickes quoted in Herbert Feis, *Three International Episodes: Seen from E.A.* (New York, 1966 [c. 1947]), p. 99. See also *DSB*, XIII (August 5, 1945), 175.
43. Feis, *Three*, p. 97. See also Herbert Feis, *Petroleum and American Foreign Policy* (Stanford, 1944); David A. Rosenberg, "The U.S. Navy and the Problem of Oil in a Future War: The Outline of a Strategic Dilemma, 1945–1950," *Naval War College Review*, XXIX (Summer 1976), 53–64; Bernard Brodie, *Foreign Oil and American Security* (New Haven, 1947), p. 1.
44. Michael S. Sherry, *Preparing for the Next War: American Plans for Postwar Defense, 1941–45* (New Haven, 1977), p. 206.
45. Quoted in Joseph Jones, *A Modern Foreign Policy for the United States* (New York, 1944), p. 25.
46. "Statement of the Effect of Atomic Weapons on National Security and Military Organization," JCS 1477/10, March 31, 1946, Box 166, Central Decimal File 471.6, JCS Records.
47. *FRUS, 1946*, I, 1144 (with maps).
48. Ibid., 1180–82.

49. Quoted in Robert G. Albion and Robert H. Connery, *Forrestal and the Navy* (New York, 1962), p. 170.
50. Telephone conversation, Senator Claude Pepper and James Forrestal, March 24, 1947, Box 91, James Forrestal Papers, Princeton University Library, Princeton, N.J.
51. Morgenthau, *Politics*, p. 25. See also Melvyn P. Leffler, *A Preponderance of Power: National Security, the Truman Administration, and the Cold War* (Stanford, 1992).
52. Quoted in Sherry, *Planning*, p. 57.
53. NSC-51 (March 29, 1949), quoted in McMahon, *Colonialism*, p. 310.
54. *Economist*, CLII (May 24, 1947), 785.
55. Thorne, *Allies*, p. 502.
56. Earl of Halifax to Ernest Bevin, August 9, 1945, AN 2560/22/45, FOC.
57. Quoted in Thorne, *Allies*, p. 515.
58. *FRUS, 1944*, IV, 931.
59. Francis Williams, *Twilight of Empire: Memoirs of Prime Minister Clement Attlee* (New York, 1962), p. 134.
60. Andrei Zhdanov, *The International Situation* (Moscow, 1947), pp. 11–12.
61. M. J. Brown, "The Foreign Policy of the United States," *Yearbook of World Affairs, 1948* (London, 1948), p. 39.
62. Senate, *European Recovery*, p. 2.
63. Department of State, *Peace, Freedom, and World Trade* (Washington, D.C., 1947), p. 5.
64. "Remarks by the President to the Group Meeting at the White House," draft, October 27, 1947, OF 426, Truman Papers.
65. John G. Stoessinger, *The United Nations and the Superpowers*, 2d ed. (New York, 1970), p. 10; Harlan Cleveland, "U.S. Learns the Politics of the Veto," *New York Times*, January 18, 1976.
66. Edward T. Rowe, "The United States, the United Nations, and the Cold War," *International Organization*, XXV (Winter 1971), 59–78; Frederick H. Gareau, *The Cold War, 1947 to 1967* (Denver, 1969); Koko, *Politics*, pp. 467–79.
67. Senate, Committee on Foreign Relations, *Assistance to Greece and Turkey* (hearings; Washington, D.C., 1947), p. 37.
68. For U.S. participation in the World Bank and International Monetary Fund, see Paterson, *Soviet-American*, ch. 7; Alfred E. Eckes, Jr., *A Search for Solvency: Bretton Woods and the International Monetary System, 1941–1947* (Austin, 1975). Harry White, quoted in Lloyd C. Gardner, *Aspects of New Deal Diplomacy* (Madison, Wis., 1964), p. 290.
69. *PPP, Truman, 1945*, pp. 404–06.
70. See, for example, Thomas B. Inglis, "Basic Factors in World Relations,"

February 1947, Office of Naval Intelligence, Strategic Plans Division Records, Office of Chief of Naval Operations, Box 110 (A-14), Naval Historical Center.

71. Kenneth J. Hagan, *This People's Navy* (New York, 1990), p. 333.
72. *PPP, Truman, 1945*, p. 432.
73. Review by T. M. P. in *New York Times Film Reviews, 1913–1968* (New York, 1970; 6 vols.), III, 1947. See also Bob Thomas, *Walt Disney: An American Original* (New York, 1976), pp. 183–86.
74. "Statement by W. A. Harriman," September 8, 1947, Folder C2-1, President's Air Policy Commission Records, HSTL.
75. Commerce, *Historical Statistics*, p. 1141.
76. See Richard F. Haynes, *The Awesome Power: Harry S. Truman as Commander-in-Chief* (Baton Rouge, 1973), pp. 120–25; Yergin, *Shattered*, pp. 270–71.
77. Warner R. Schilling, "The Politics of Defense: Fiscal 1950," in Warner R. Schilling, Paul Y. Hammond, and Glenn H. Snyder, *Strategy, Politics, and Defense Budgets* (New York, 1962), p. 30.
78. Walter Millis, ed., *The Forrestal Diaries* (New York, 1951), pp. 350–51.
79. Diary, October 5, 1945, Harold Smith Papers, Franklin D. Roosevelt Library.
80. Dwight D. Eisenhower to Bernard Baruch, June 14, 1946, Box 166. Central Decimal File 471.6, JCS Records. See also William Leahy to Bernard Baruch, June 11, 1946, Bernard Baruch Papers, Princeton University Library; Admiral C. W. Nimitz to Bernard Baruch, ibid.
81. *FRUS, 1945*, V, 923.
82. Quoted in Barton J. Bernstein, "The Quest for Security: American Foreign Policy and International Control of Atomic Energy, 1942–1946," *Journal of American History*, LX (March 1974), 1015. See also Barton J. Bernstein, "Roosevelt, Truman, and the Atomic Bomb, 1941–1945: A Reinterpretation," *Political Science Quarterly*, XC (Spring 1975), 23–69.
83. Quoted in Lisle Rose, *After Yalta* (New York, 1973), p. 124.
84. David Alan Rosenberg, "U.S. Nuclear Stockpile, 1945 to 1950," *Bulletin of Atomic Scientists*, XXXVIII (May 1982), 25–30; Rosenberg, "Reality and Responsibility: Power and Process in the Making of United States Nuclear Strategy, 1945–68," *Journal of Strategic Studies*, IX (March 1986), 39.
85. Quoted in Rosenberg, "U.S. Nuclear," p. 27.
86. Melvyn P. Leffler, "Was 1947 a Turning Point in American Foreign Policy?," in L. Carl Brown, ed., *Centerpiece: American Diplomacy since World War II* (New York, 1990), p. 38.
87. Byrnes seemed to worry, too, that the Soviets would want to be present at

the test site. Cabinet Meeting, March 22, 1946, Notes on Cabinet Meetings, Connelly Papers. The Bikini test was delayed until July.

88. Quoted in Donovan, *Conflict*, p. 130.

89. For a contrary interpretation, see Adam Ulam's statement that "I don't think we realized how strong we were," in House of Representatives, Committee on Foreign Affairs, *The Cold War: Origins and Development* (hearings; Washington, D.C., 1971), p. 20, and his *The Rivals* (New York, 1971), which finds an "era of American omnipotence" but also argues that Americans did not attempt to use their power, especially their atomic power.

90. Cabinet Meeting, October 12, 1945, Notes on Cabinet Meetings, Connelly Papers (Byrnes's comment was in reference specifically to the UN Food and Agriculture Organization); John Foster Dulles to Geoffrey Parsons, June 16, 1947, John Foster Dulles Papers, Princeton University Library. See also Howard K. Smith, *The State of Europe* (New York, 1949), pp. 70, 92–94. Arnold Toynbee referred to the " 'invisible empire' which the United States has built up through its commerce, the size of which we sometimes might not appreciate," in "British Foreign Policy," Discussion Meeting Report, March 13, 1947, Records of Groups, vol. XIV, Council on Foreign Relations Files.

91. Universal military training was not instituted. Cabinet Meeting, September 7, 1945, Notes on Cabinet Meetings, Connelly Papers.

92. Jones, *A Modern*, p. 33.

CHAPTER 6. TOUGHNESS: TRUMAN'S STYLE OF DIPLOMACY

1. Harriman and Abel, *Special*, p. 440.

2. Archibald Clark-Kerr to W. Averell Harriman, April 13, 1945, Box 1372-B, Moscow Post Files.

3. Quoted in Clinton Rossiter, *The American Presidency* (New York, 1956), p. 10.

4. Arthur M. Schlesinger, Jr., *The Imperial Presidency* (Boston, 1973), p. 381.

5. Franz Schurmann, *The Logic of World Power* (New York, 1974), p. 17.

6. Harriman and Abel, *Special*, pp. 94, 367.

7. Kimball, *Churchill*, III, 359.

8. Memorandum, W. B. Brown to Mr. Coombs, April 11, 1952, Box 25, President's Materials Policy Committee Records, HSTL.

9. Kennan, *Memoirs*, p. 290.

10. Quoted in Yergin, *Shattered*, p. 82. See also Andrei Vyshinsky's comment: "The death of Roosevelt had disturbed Soviet leaders. They knew

ROOSEVELT, and knew what to expect. They did not know TRUMAN or what his attitude would be." Diary-Journal, July 15, 1945, Box 18, Davies Papers.

11. *FRUS, 1945,* II, 247.
12. Harriman and Abel, *Special,* p. 268.
13. Senate, *Legislative Origins,* p. 95.
14. *New York Times,* October 13, 1971.
15. Harriman and Abel, *Special,* p. 170.
16. Kimball, *Churchill,* I, 421.
17. Harriman and Abel, *Special,* p. 228. Also p. 362.
18. Some historians cite a Roosevelt letter to Churchill of April 6, 1945, to argue that FDR himself was moving toward a "tougher" stance vis-à-vis the Soviet Union just before he died. But as Warren F. Kimball has pointed out, that letter was written by hard-liner Admiral William D. Leahy, not by FDR. The president himself wrote a letter on April 10, two days before his death, in which he told Churchill that problems with the Soviets usually straightened out and that he and Churchill should "minimize the general Soviet problem as much as possible. . . ." Kimball, *Juggler,* pp. 179–80.
19. Charles E. Bohlen, *Witness to History, 1929–69* (New York, 1973), p. 213.
20. Truman, *Memoirs,* 81–82.
21. Harriman and Abel, *Special,* pp. 452, 454; Truman quoted in Gaddis, *United States and Origins,* p. 205.
22. Moran, *Churchill,* p. 306.
23. Anthony Eden quoted in Thorne, *Allies,* p. 245; Stimson quoted in Donovan, *Conflict,* p. 20. Truman's style is a theme in William E. Pemberton, *Harry S. Truman: Fair Dealer & Cold Warrior* (Boston, 1989).
24. Handwritten notes by George Elsey, March 2, 1948, Box 20, George Elsey Papers, HSTL. Elsey also remembered that Truman "did have something of a quick temper and snapped back, sometimes too fast, in press conferences on domestic as well as foreign matters." George Elsey Oral History Interview, HSTL.
25. Quoted in Donovan, *Conflict,* pp. 58–59.
26. Michael J. Cohen, *Truman and Israel* (Berkeley, 1990), pp. 7–10, 275–76; Arnold A. Offner, "Harry S Truman as Parochial Nationalist," in Thomas G. Paterson and Robert J. McMahon, eds., *The Origins of the Cold War,* 3d ed. (Lexington, Mass., 1991), p. 52.
27. "Note of the Prime Minister's Conversation with President Truman at Luncheon, July 18, 1945," by Winston Churchill, Premier 3, 430/8 Prime Minister's Office Records; Churchill ("takes no") quoted in Charles L. Mee Jr., *Meeting at Potsdam* (New York, 1975), p. 75.

28. Quoted in Truman, *Truman*, p. 269.
29. Robert Ferrell, ed., *Dear Bess: The Letters from Harry to Bess Truman, 1910–1959* (New York, 1983), p. 519.
30. Dana Wilgress quoted in Smith, *Diplomacy of Fear*, p. 118.
31. Quoted in Walton, *Wallace*, p. 36.
32. Felix Frankfurter to Charles C. Burlingham, November 12, 1948, Box 5, Burlingham Papers.
33. For more favorable accounts of Truman's style than given here, see John Lewis Gaddis, "Harry S. Truman and the Origins of Containment," in Frank J. Merli and Theodore A. Wilson, eds., *Makers of American Diplomacy* (New York, 1974), pp. 493–520; Alonzo L. Hamby, "The Mind and Character of Harry S. Truman," in Lacey, *Truman*, pp. 19–53.
34. Rusk, *As I Saw It*, p. 155; Clark Clifford with Richard Holbrooke, "Serving the President: The Truman Years—I," *The New Yorker*, LXVII (March 25, 1991), 52.
35. Truman paraphrased in Blum, *Price*, p. 373; Herken, *Winning*, p. 16.
36. Quoted in Yergin, *Shattered*, p. 72.
37. Campbell and Herring, *Diaries*, p. 325.
38. Quoted in Truman, *Truman*, p. 358.
39. Truman also said in 1941: "If we see that Germany is winning the war we ought to help Russia, and if Russia is winning we ought to help Germany, and in that way let them kill as many as possible, although I don't want to see Hitler victorious under any circumstances. Neither of them think anything of their pledged word." *New York Times*, June 24, 1941.
40. Blum, *Price*, pp. 440–41.
41. For Truman's misuse of history, see J. Garry Clifford, "Harry Truman and Peter the Great's Will," *Diplomatic History*, IV (Fall 1980), 371–85.
42. Quoted in Thomas G. Paterson, "Potsdam, the Atomic Bomb, and the Cold War: A Discussion with James F. Byrnes," *Pacific Historical Review*, XLI (May 1972), 228.
43. Blum, *Price*, p. 475.
44. *FRUS, 1944*, IV, 997. Italics added.
45. Diary, April 26, 1945, Oscar Cox Papers, Roosevelt Library.
46. Quoted in Gaddis, "Truman," p. 500.
47. "Memorandum on Secretary of State Byrnes' Diplomacy with Regard to the Soviet Union," by C. M. Richardson Dougall, September 1946, RP 4, Foreign Policy Studies Branch, Division of Policy Research, DSR.
48. Journal, July 16, 1945, Box 18, Davies Papers.
49. For these ambassadors, see Paterson, *Soviet-American Confrontation*, pp. 120–36; Martin Weil, *A Pretty Good Club: The Founding Fathers of the U.S. Foreign Service* (New York, 1978), pp. 194–97; John O. Iatrides, *Ambassador MacVeagh Reports: Greece, 1933–1947* (Princeton, 1980).

50. Quoted in May, *"Lessons,"* pp. 27, 29.

51. Kennan, *Memoirs*, p. 564.

52. May, *"Lessons,"* pp. 30–31.

53. Harry S. Truman to James F. Byrnes, September 24, 1946, Folder 52, Byrnes Papers.

54. Diary, October 17, 1947, Box 2, Felix Frankfurter Papers, LC.

55. Truman, *Memoirs*, I, 552.

56. Notes from interview with Harry S. Truman, August 30, 1949, Notebooks, Box 85, Jonathan Daniels Papers, University of North Carolina Library.

57. For the uneasy Byrnes-Truman relationship, see Robert Messer, *The End of an Alliance: James F. Byrnes, Roosevelt, Truman, and the Origins of the Cold War* (Chapel Hill, N.C., 1983).

58. *Vital Speeches*, XII (October 1, 1946), 739.

59. Quoted in Truman, *Truman*, pp. 317–18.

60. *PPP, Truman, 1946*, p. 431. Emphasis added.

61. Ibid., *Truman, 1948*, p. 189.

62. Handwritten notes by George Elsey, (n.d. but March 1948), Box 20, Elsey Papers.

63. *PPP, Truman, 1948*, pp. 182–86.

64. Cohen, *Truman and Israel*, pp. 277–80.

65. *FRUS, 1948*, V, part 2, 975.

66. Ibid., 1490.

67. Ibid., 1131.

68. For the view that bureaucracies are really subordinate to the president, see Stephen D. Krasner, "Are Bureaucracies Important? (Or Allison Wonderland)," *Foreign Policy*, no. 7 (Summer 1972), 159–79; Robert J. Art, "Bureaucratic Politics and American Foreign Policy: A Critique," *Policy Sciences*, IV (1973), 467–90; James Nathan, "The Roots of the Imperial Presidency: Public Opinion, Domestic Institutions, and Global Interests," *Presidential Studies Quarterly*, V (Winter 1975), 63–74. For a contrary view, that bureaucracies can shape or even dominate policy making, see Graham T. Allison, "Conceptual Models and the Cuban Missile Crisis," *American Political Science Review*, LXII (September 1969), 689–718, and his *Essence of Decision* (Boston, 1971). The general question is explored in J. Garry Clifford, "Bureaucratic Politics," in Hogan and Paterson, *Explaining*, pp. 141–50.

69. Clark Clifford to Herbert Feis, July 16, 1953, Box 36, Elsey Papers.

70. Acheson, *Present*, p. 254; Elsey Oral History Interview.

71. Memorandum for Files by David D. Lloyd, December 3, 1949, Chronological File, David D. Lloyd Papers, HSTL.

72. Paterson, *Meeting*, pp. 147–58.

73. Richard E. Neustadt, *Presidential Power: The Politics of Leadership* (New York, 1960), p. 10. Italics in original.
74. Walter Bagehot quoted ibid., p. 34. Italics in original.
75. Quoted in Truman, *Truman*, p. 290.
76. Truman, *Memoirs*, II, 442.
77. *PPP, Truman, 1946*, p. 102.
78. Richard A. Barnet, *Intervention and Revolution* (New York, 1968), p. 23.
79. James C. Thomson, Jr., "On the Making of U.S. China Policy, 1961–9: A Study in Bureaucratic Politics," *China Quarterly*, no. 50 (April–June 1972), p. 222; Thomson's review of Clubb's *Witness and I* in *New York Times Book Review*, February 23, 1975, pp. 1–2.
80. See Leslie H. Gelb and Morton H. Halperin, "Diplomatic Notes: The Ten Commandments of the Foreign Affairs Bureaucracy," *Harper's Magazine*, CCXLIV (June 1972) 28–37.
81. Irving L. Janis, *Victims of Groupthink* (Boston, 1972).
82. For a discussion of this tradition, see James C. Thomson, Jr., "Getting Out and Speaking Out," *Foreign Policy*, no. 13 (Winter 1973–1974), pp. 49–69.
83. Chester Bowles to Joseph Davies, February 22, 1946, Box 5, Chester Bowles Papers, Yale University Library.
84. George McGhee Oral History Interview, HSTL.
85. *New Times* (Moscow), June 1, 1946.
86. Ibid., June 6, 1947.
87. Memorandum, December 10, 1943, Box 39, Isador Lubin Papers, Roosevelt Library.
88. Quoted in Gaddis, *United States and Origins*, p. 243.
89. Hickerson Oral History Interview, HSTL.

CHAPTER 7. CONSENT: AMERICAN PUBLIC OPINION, CONGRESS, AND THE COLD WAR MENTALITY

1. Elsey Oral History Interview, HSTL.
2. Rossiter, *American Presidency*, p. 52.
3. The cabinet meeting minutes are located in the Connelly Papers, HSTL. The records of the secretary's Staff Committee and the Committee of Three are found in the NA. This chapter has been informed by studies of the relationship between public opinion, presidential leadership, and foreign policy: Blair Bolles, "Who Makes Our Foreign Policy," Foreign Policy Association *Headline Series*, no. 62 (March–April 1947), pp. 5–86; Markel, *Public Opinion;* Bernard C. Cohen, *The Influence of Non-Gov-*

ernmental Groups on Foreign Policy Making (Boston, 1959); Bernard C. Cohen, *The Public's Impact on Foreign Policy* (Boston, 1973); Bernard C. Cohen, "The Relationship between Public Opinion and Foreign Policy Maker," in Melvin Small, ed., *Public Opinion and Historians* (Detroit, 1970), pp. 65–80; Melvin Small, "Public Opinion," in Hogan and Paterson, *Explaining,* pp. 165–76; Walter LaFeber, "American Policy-Makers, Public Opinion, and the Outbreak of the Cold War, 1945–50," in Yōnosuke Nagai and Akira Iriye, eds., *The Origins of the Cold War in Asia* (New York and Tokyo, 1977), pp. 43–65; Gabriel A. Almond, *The American People and Foreign Policy* (New York, 1950); James N. Rosenau, *National Leadership and Foreign Policy* (Princeton, N.J., 1963); James N. Rosenau, *Public Opinion and Foreign Policy* (New York, 1961); William R. Caspary, "U.S. Public Opinion during the Onset of the Cold War," *Peace Research Society (International) Papers,* IX (1968), 25–46; Doris A. Graber, *Public Opinion, the President, and Foreign Policy* (New York, 1968); Ralph B. Levering, *The Public and American Foreign POlicy, 1918–1978* (New York, 1978); Richard J. Barnet, *The Rockets' Red Glare: When America Goes to War—the Presidents and the People* (New York, 1990).
4. For scholars who attribute influence to public opinion, see, for example, Thomas A. Bailey, *Man in the Street* (New York, 1948) and Gaddis, *United States and Origins.*
5. Cohen, "Relationship," p. 79.
6. Rossiter, *American Presidency,* p. 122.
7. Quoted in Truman, *Truman,* p. 353. Clark Clifford corroborates this vignette in Clark M. Clifford, "The Presidency as I Have Seen It," in Emmet John Hughes, ed., *The Living Presidency* (New York, 1973), p. 318.
8. James Reston, "The Number One Voice," in Markel, *Public Opinion,* p. 66.
9. Quoted in Neustadt, *Presidential Power,* p. 50.
10. Quoted in Barton Gellman, *Contending with Kennan: Toward a Philosophy of American Power* (New York, 1984), p. 97.
11. Quoted in Carl L. Becker, *How New Will the Better World Be?* (New York, 1944), p. 25.
12. Quoted in Perrett, *Days,* p. 418.
13. Harriman and Abel, *Special,* p. 531; *DSB,* XIV (June 16, 1946), 1045.
14. Senator Wayne Morse to Andrew Comrie, October 22, 1945, Box S-4, Wayne Morse Papers, University of Oregon Library, Eugene, Ore.
15. Quoted in Divine, *Second,* p. 280.
16. Arthur H. Vandenberg, Jr., ed., *The Private Papers of Senator Vandenberg* (Boston, 1952), p. 1.

17. *Congressional Record*, XCI (January 10, 1945), 166.
18. Becker, *How New*, p. 43. See also Lester Markel, "Opinion—A Neglected Instrument," in Markel, *Public Opinion*, p. 4.
19. Almond, *American People*, pp. 76, 84, 208, 248; George H. Gallup, *The Gallup Poll: Public Opinion, 1935–1971* (New York, 1972; 3 vols.), I, 534.
20. Quoted in Justus D. Doenecke, "The Strange Career of American Isolationism, 1944–1954," *Peace and Change*, III (Summer–Fall 1975), 80. In 1942 the British minister in the Washington embassy, Sir Ronald Campbell, offered an explanation: "There are among the isolationists a type of people who I can easily imagine proceeding from their isolationist reasoning to a stage where they will satisfy themselves that in order to isolate themselves properly the United States must rule the roost." Quoted in Thorne, *Allies*, p. 139.
21. For a similar conclusion, which argues that Truman officials were surprised that isolationism was weak, see May, *"Lessons,"* p. 49.
22. Quoted in Martin Kriesberg, "Dark Areas of Ignorance," in Markel, *Public Opinion*, p. 54.
23. Markel, "Opinion," p. 9.
24. Quoted in Woods, *A Changing*, p. 137.
25. Gallup, *Gallup Poll*, I, 561, 604; II, 852; Leonard S. Cottrell, Jr., and Sylvia Eberhart, *American Opinion on World Affairs in the Atomic Age* (Princeton, N.J., 1948), pp. 13–14.
26. Rosenau, *Public Opinion*, p. 35.
27. Quoted in Kensuke Yanagiya, "The Renewal of ERP: A Case Study" (unpublished paper, Public Affairs 520-D, Woodrow Wilson School of Public and International Affairs, Princeton University, 1952), p. 20.
28. Quoted in Markel, "Opinion," p. 31.
29. Almond, *American People*, p. 138.
30. See, for example, Ronald Radosh, *American Labor and United States Foreign Policy* (New York, 1969); Thomas G. Paterson, "The Economic Cold War: American Business and Economic Foreign Policy, 1945–1950" (unpublished Ph.D. dissertation, University of California, Berkeley, 1968); H. Schuyler Foster, "American Public Opinion and U.S. Foreign Policy," *DSB*, XLI (November 30, 1959), 796–803.
31. Michael J. Hogan, "Corporatism," in Hogan and Paterson, *Explaining*, pp. 226–36.
32. Chadwick F. Alger, "The External Bureaucracy in United States Foreign Affairs," *Administrative Science Quarterly*, VII (June 1962), 50–78.
33. Ronald L. Filipelli, *American Labor and Postwar Italy, 1943–1953: A Study of Cold War Politics* (Stanford, 1989), pp. xiii, 113–17.
34. Francis Russell Oral History Interview, HSTL.

35. Paterson, *Soviet-American*, pp. 221–22; Harold Stein Oral History Interview, HSTL.

36. Neustadt, *Presidential Power*, p. 49.

37. William Edwards quoted (1948) in Caroline Anstey, "Foreign Office Publicity, American Aid and European Unity: Mobilising Public Opinion, 1947–1949," in Becker and Knipping, *Power*, pp. 375–76.

38. Ibid., pp. 379–82.

39. Quoted in Manfred Landecker, *The President and Public Opinion* (Washington, D.C., 1968), p. 64.

40. The historian Robert A. Divine has concluded that from 1940 to 1960 presidents usually manipulated foreign policy subjects to gather votes: "[P]residential candidates . . . play politics with foreign policy; they exploit crises overseas. . . ." *Foreign Policy and U.S. Presidential Elections, 1940–1948* (New York, 1974), p. ix.

41. Richard Scandrett to Phyllis Auty, October 25, 1948, vol. 20-A, Richard Scandrett Papers, Cornell University Library.

42. Truman to Folger, April 19, 1947, Box 141, President's Secretary's File, Truman Papers.

43. Clark Clifford, memorandum for the President, November 17, 1947, Box 21, Clark Clifford Papers, HSTL.

44. Bailey, *Man*, p. 13.

45. Ibid., p. 6.

46. Quoted in Walton, *Wallace*, p. 301.

47. Charles Frankel, quoted in Cohen, *Public's Impact*, pp. 178–79.

48. *FRUS, 1945*, V, 257.

49. Memorandum of Conversation, May 30, 1945, vol. 7, Conversations, Joseph Grew Papers, Houghton Library, Harvard University.

50. *FRUS, 1947*, III, 281.

51. See Cohen, "Relationship," for points in this paragraph.

52. Gallup, *Gallup Poll*, I, 530, 535.

53. Ibid, p. 639.

54. Truman, *Memoirs*, II, 177. Theodore C. Sorensen, one of President John F. Kennedy's chief aides, has written that "democratic government is not a popularity contest; and no President is obligated to abide by the dictates of public opinion. . . . Public opinion is often erratic, inconsistent, arbitrary, and unreasonable . . . [and] it rarely speaks in one loud, clear, united voice. . . . He [the president] has a responsibility to lead public opinion as well as respect it—to shape it, to inform it, to woo it, and win it. It can be his sword as well as his compass. *Decision-Making in the White House* (New York, 1963), pp. 45–46.

55. Almond, *American People*, p. 86.

56. *FRUS, 1948*, V, 546–47; Cohen, *Truman and Israel*, pp. 275–81.

57. *FRUS: Conferences at Cairo and Teheran,* p. 594.
58. Diary, June 13, 1944, Box 5, Breckinridge Long Papers, LC.
59. *FRUS, Berlin,* II, 206.
60. Peter M. Irons, "The Test Is Poland: Polish Americans and the Origins of the Cold War," *Polish-American Studies,* XXX (Autumn 1973), 5–63; John N. Cable, "Vandenberg: The Polish Question and Polish-Americans, 1944–1948," *Michigan History,* LVII (Winter 1973), 296–310; Jack L. Hammersmith, "Franklin Roosevelt, the Polish Question, and the Election of 1944," *Mid-America,* LXIX (January 1977), 5–17; Divine, *Foreign Policy,* pp. 110–12, 143; Louis L. Gerson, *The Hyphenate in Recent American Politics and Diplomacy* (Lawrence, Kan., 1964), pp. 138–40, 150–52, 161; Stephen A. Garrett, "Eastern European Ethnic Groups and American Foreign Policy," *Political Science Quarterly,* XCIII (Summer 1978), 301–23.
61. Markel, "Opinion," p. 24; Dean Acheson, *A Citizen Looks at Congress* (Westport, Conn., 1974 [c. 1956]), p. 65.
62. In addition to works cited above on the presidency, see for Congress and the foreign policy process: James A. Robinson, *Congress and Foreign Policy-Making,* rev. ed. (Homewood, Ill., 1967); Arthur Schlesinger, Jr., "Congress and the Making of American Foreign Policy," *Foreign Affairs,* LI (October 1972), 78–113; Robert Dahl, *Congress and Foreign Policy* (New York, 1950); Holbert N. Carroll, *The House of Representatives and Foreign Affairs,* rev. ed. (Boston, 1966); Daniel S. Cheever and H. Field Haviland, Jr., *American Foreign Policy and the Separation of Powers* (Cambridge, Mass., 1952); Francis O. Wilcox, *Congress, the Executive, and Foreign Policy* (New York, 1971).
63. Reston, "Number One Voice," p. 72.
64. Quoted in Floyd M. Riddick, "The First Session of the Eightieth Congress," *American Political Science Review,* XLII (August 1948), 683.
65. Cabinet Meeting, June 9, 1949, Notes on Cabinet Meetings, Connelly Papers. See also Ithiel de Sola Pool, Suzanne Keller, and Raymond A. Bauer, "The Influence of Foreign Travel on Political Attitudes of American Businessmen," *Public Opinion Quarterly,* XX (Spring 1956), 161–75.
66. Truman, *Memoirs,* II, 454.
67. Paterson, *Meeting,* pp. 234–55.
68. Acheson, *A Citizen,* p. 53.
69. "Should Truman's Greek and Turkish Policy Be Adopted: A Radio Discussion," *University of Chicago Roundtable,* April 20, 1947, pp. 7, 2.
70. Senate, *Legislative Origins,* p. 142. See also ibid., pp. 46, 132, 133, 136; Representative Francis Case to Harry S. Truman, May 10, 1947, Box 1278, OF 426, Truman Papers; *Congressional Record,* XCIII (April

16, 1947), 3484–85; *New York Times*, March 18, 1947; Susan M. Hart-
mann, *Truman and the 80th Congress* (Columbia, Mo., 1971), pp. 60,
63, 64.

71. Arthur Vandenberg to Bruce Barton, March 24, 1947, Box 2, Arthur
    Vandenberg Papers, University of Michigan Library, Ann Arbor, Mich.

72. Vandenberg, *Private Papers*, pp. 550–51. Emphasis added.

73. Smith, *Acheson*, p. 407. See also Dean Acheson, "Senator Vandenberg
    and the Senate," in James D. Barber, ed., *Political Leadership in Ameri-
    can Government* (Boston, 1964), pp. 74–83.

74. Diary, November 21, 1948, Lippmann Papers.

75. Paterson, *Soviet-American*, pp. 222–24; Neustadt, *Presidential Power*,
    pp. 52–53.

76. Robinson, *Congress*, p. 46.

77. For the election of 1948, see Michael A. Guhin, *John Foster Dulles: A
    Statesman and His Times* (New York, 1972), pp. 54–55, 160–61; Louis
    Gerson, *John Foster Dulles* (New York, 1967), pp. 52–53; Divine, *For-
    eign Policy*, pp. 167–276; Robert A. Divine, "The Cold War and the
    Election of 1948," *Journal of American History*, LIX (June 1972), 90–
    110.

78. Truman, *Memoirs*, II, 211.

79. Quoted in Theodore A. Wilson and Richard D. McKinzie, "White House
    versus Congress: Conflict or Collusion? The Marshall Plan as a Case
    Study" (unpublished paper, annual meeting of the Organization of Amer-
    ican Historians, 1973), p. 2.

80. Quoted in Smith, *Diplomacy of Fear*, p. 207.

81. Acheson, *A Citizen*, p. 75. See also Smith, *Acheson*, pp. 142, 252, 408–
    09; Bradford Westerfield, *Foreign Policy and Party Politics* (New
    Haven, 1955).

82. Loch Johnson and James M. McCormick, "Foreign Policy by Executive
    Fiat," *Foreign Policy*, no. 28 (Fall 1977), pp. 117–23.

83. Princeton Seminar Transcript, February 13–14, 1954, Box 66, Acheson
    Papers.

84. Quoted in Graber, *Public Opinion*, p. 340. See also Schlesinger, *Impe-
    rial*.

CHAPTER 8. SUSPICIOUSNESS: STALIN AND
SOVIET FOREIGN POLICY

1. Whitney, *Russia*, p. 98; Kennan, *Memoirs*, pp. 240–44.

2. Elbridge Durbrow to White House, January 22, 1945, 861.00/1-2245,
   DSR.

3. Stephen F. Cohen, *Rethinking the Soviet Experience: Politics and History Since 1917* (New York, 1985), p. 19.
4. For various interpretations, see Alexander Dallin, ed., *Soviet Conduct in World Affairs* (New York, 1960); Morton Schwartz, *The "Motive Forces" of Soviet Foreign Policy: A Reappraisal* (Denver, 1971); Daniel Bell, "Ten Theories in Search of Reality," *World Politics*, X (April 1958), 327–65; William A. Glaser, "Theories of Soviet Foreign Policy: A Classification of the Literature," *World Affairs Quarterly*, XXVII (1956–1957), 128–52.
5. Charles W. Thayer, *Diplomat* (New York, 1959), p. 179.
6. Smith, *My Three Years*, p. 55.
7. William Welch, *American Images of Soviet Foreign Policy: An Inquiry into Recent Appraisals from the Academic Community* (New Haven, 1970); Israel Shenker, "Hats Are Off to Kremlinologists," *New York Times*, September 20, 1974.
8. Konstantin V. Pleshakov, "The Pacific War, 1945: American and Soviet Decisionmaking," Seminar on the Origins of the Cold War, pp. 5, 7; Konstantin V. Pleshakov, "Joseph Stalin's World View," in Paterson and McMahon, *Origins*, pp. 61–73; David Reynolds, "The 'Big Three' and the Division of Europe, 1945–48: An Overview," *Diplomacy & Statecraft*, I (July 1990), 114–15.
9. Viktor Levonovich Israelyan, "Notes for a History of the 'Cold War,' " *Ekonomika, Politika, Ideologiya*, no. 9 (September 1989), translated in *Joint Publications Research Service*, January 2, 1990, p. 17.
10. Quoted (1946) in Mayers, *Kennan*, pp. 109–10.
11. Quoted (1950) in Watt, "British Military," p. 336.
12. "Notes on Conversation in Moscow with Maxim Litvinov," December 6, 1944, by Edgar Snow, Box 68, President's Secretary File, Franklin D. Roosevelt Papers, Roosevelt Library. See also Molotov, *Problems*, pp. 96, 106; Vera Micheles Dean, *The United States and Russia* (Cambridge, Mass., 1948), p. 132; James L. Gormly, *The Collapse of the Grand Alliance, 1945–1948* (Baton Rouge, 1987), pp. 30–31.
13. *FRUS, Berlin*, I, 32.
14. Ross, *Foreign Office*, p. 239.
15. Quoted in Yergin, *Shattered*, p. 118.
16. See, for example, "Analysis of Soviet Strength and Weakness," by Joint Working Committee of the American Embassy, Moscow, September 1, 1946, 861.00/9-946, Box 6462, DSR; James Forrestal to Clarence D. Dillion, February 11, 1947, Box 125, Forrestal Papers; "The USSR and United States Foreign Policy," May 5, 1949, Office of Public Affairs Information Memorandum No. 45, RP #106, Reports of Foreign Policy Studies Branch, Division of Historical Policy Research, DSR.

17. New York State Chamber of Commerce, *Monthly Bulletin*, XLI (June 1949), 52.
18. Elbridge Durbrow in *FRUS, 1946*, VI, 798.
19. Constantine Simonov in *Literaturnaia Gazeta*, November 23, 1946, reprinted in House of Representatives, Committee on Foreign Affairs, *The Strategy and Tactics of World Communism*, 80th Cong., 2d sess. (Washington, D.C., 1948), House Document 619, Supplement I, p. 182.
20. V. Svetlov, "The Ideological Training of Students Must Be Improved," *Izvestia*, December 14, 1946, in *Soviet Press Translations*, II (March 15, 1947), 23.
21. John W. Spanier, *Games Nations Play* (New York, 1972), pp. 274–75; Alfred G. Meyer, "The Functions of Ideology in the Soviet Political System," *Soviet Studies*, XVII (January 1966), 273–85.
22. Herbert S. Dinerstein, *The Making of a Missile Crisis: October 1962* (Baltimore, 1976), p. 62.
23. For expressions of Communist ideological tenets, see Molotov, *Problems;* Eugene Varga, "Anglo-American Rivalry and Partnership: A Marxist View," *Foreign Affairs*, XXV (July 1947), 583–95; B. Ponomaryov, A. Gromyko, and V. Khvostov, *History of Soviet Foreign Policy, 1917–1945* (Moscow, 1969), pp. 9–28; speeches and writings by Marx, Lenin, Stalin, Zhdanov, Molotov, and Vyshinsky in House, *Strategy;* and various Communist statements in LaFeber, *Eastern Europe*, pp. 191–381. For discussions of the ideology, see Tucker, *Soviet Political Mind;* Waldemar Gurian, "Permanent Features of Soviet Foreign Policy," *Year Book of World Affairs, 1947* (London, 1947), pp. 1–39; William Zimmerman, "The Soviet Union," in Steven L. Spiegel and Kenneth N. Waltz, eds., *Conflict in World Politics* (Cambridge, Mass., 1971), pp. 38–54; Paul E. Zinner, "The Ideological Bases of Soviet Foreign Policy," *World Politics*, IV (July 1952), 489–511; Zbigniew Brzezinski, "Communist Ideology and International Affairs," *Journal of Conflict Resolution*, IV (September 1960), 266–90; Schwartz, *"Motive Forces"*; Frederick C. Barghoorn, *The Soviet Image of the United States* (New York, 1950).
24. Quoted in Robert C. Tucker, *The Soviet Political Mind: Stalinism and Post-Stalin Change*, rev. ed. (New York, 1971), p. 229. See also House, *Strategy*, pp. 209, 216.
25. N. Voznesensky in Barrington Moore, Jr., *Soviet Politics—The Dilemma of Power* (Cambridge, Mass., 1950), p. 372.
26. Speech of September 10, 1947, in House, *Strategy*, p. 184.
27. Harriman and Abel, *Special*, p. 541.
28. Konstantin V. Pleshakov, "Soviet Union and United States," *Ekonomika, Politika, and Ideologiya*, no. 9 (September 1989), translated in *Joint Publications Research Service*, January 2, 1990, pp. 10–17.

29. *New York Times*, March 14, 1946. See also Andrei Zhdanov, *The International Situation* (Moscow, 1947); Embassy of the USSR, *Information Bulletin*, VI (March 26, 1946), 252–53; Smith, *My Three Years*, p. 52; *FRUS, 1946*, VI, 785.

30. Quoted in Deutscher, *Stalin*, p. 537; Djilas, *Conversations*, p. 114.

31. Pleshakov, "Stalin's World View."

32. *FRUS, 1946*, VI, 763.

33. Ibid., 769–70. Edgar Snow wrote about the Russian "consciousness of vulnerability." Edgar Snow, *The Pattern of Soviet Power* (New York, 1945), p. 211.

34. For security as a fundamental ingredient of Soviet foreign policy, see Becker, *How New*, pp. 68–70; Memorandum for William Leahy from the British Joint Staff Mission, September 18, 1946, Folder 46, William Leahy Papers, Naval Historical Office; Blum, *Price*, p. 503; Vera Micheles Dean, *Russia: Menace or Promise* (New York, 1947), pp. 61–62; Diary, July 14, 1945, Box 17, Davies Papers; Philip E. Mosely, *Kremlin and World Politics* (New York, 1960), pp. 42–66; Ivo J. Lederer, "Russia and the Balkans," in Ivo J. Lederer, ed., *Russian Foreign Policy* (New Haven, 1962), pp. 417–51; Moore, *Soviet Politics*, pp. 350–94.

35. Louis J. Halle, *The Cold War as History* (New York, 1967), p. 17.

36. W. Averell Harriman, *Peace with Russia?* (New York, 1959), p. 12. See also Hull, *Memoirs*, II, 1299.

37. Quoted in Vojtech Mastny, "The Cassandra in the Foreign Commissariat: Maxim Litvinov and the Cold War," *Foreign Affairs*, LIV (January 1976), 374.

38. Molotov in *FRUS, 1945*, V, 238–39; Stalin in *The Tehran, Yalta, and Potsdam Conferences: Documents* (Moscow, 1969), pp. 93–94.

39. Ministry of Foreign Affairs of the USSR, *Correspondence Between the Chairman of the Council of Ministers of the U.S.S.R. and the Presidents of the U.S.A. and the Prime Ministers of Great Britain During the Great Patriotic War of 1941–1945* (New York, Capricorn Books edition, 1965): *Stalin's Correspondence with Roosevelt and Truman, 1941–1945*, p. 220.

40. *FRUS, Berlin*, I, 39. See also Joseph Stalin, *The Great Patriotic War* (New York, 1945), pp. 152–53.

41. *New York Times*, March 14, 1946.

42. Ross, *Foreign Office*, p. 178.

43. *FRUS, Yalta*, p. 903.

44. Quoted in Smith, *My Three Years*, p. 53.

45. Quoted in Milovan Djilas, *Wartime* (New York, 1977), p. 438.

46. Quoted in Eduard Taborsky, "Beneš and Stalin—Moscow, 1943 and 1945," *Journal of Central European Affairs*, XIII (July 1953), 179.

47. Dean, *United States and Russia*, p. 136.
48. Quoted in Yergin, *Shattered*, p. 298. See also Truman's talk with Mackenzie King, in J. W. Pickersgill and D. F. Forster, *The Mackenzie King Record* (Toronto, 1960–1970; 4 vols.), III, 361.
49. White House Summary, September 19, 1946, DSR.
50. Paterson, *Soviet-American*, ch. 5.
51. Quoted in Gormly, *Collapse*, p. 30.
52. Quoted in Robert Slusser, ed., *Soviet Economic Policy in Postwar Germany* (New York, 1953), p. 49.
53. Paterson, *Soviet-American*, chs. 5, 11.
54. For Iran and oil, see ibid., pp. 177–83; Yergin, *Shattered*, pp. 179–90. As for Africa and uranium, at least Secretaries Byrnes and Bevin thought that the Soviet request for a trusteeship in Tripolitania was designed to afford the USSR access to the uranium (essential to atomic development) of the Belgian Congo. Indigenous Soviet sources of uranium were apparently low-grade. Quoted in Herkin, *Winning*, p. 50.
55. Thomas B. Inglis to James Forrestal, January 21, 1946, Box 24, Forrestal Papers.
56. Molotov, *Problems*, pp. 83–84. See also pp. 94, 224, 251.
57. *FRUS, 1946*, VI, 764. See also Robert R. McNeal, "Roosevelt through Stalin's Spectacles," *International Journal*, XVIII (Spring 1963), 202–04.
58. Quoted in Yergin, *Shattered*, p. 118.
59. "Joint Basic Outline War Plan ('Pincher')," by Joint War Plans Committee, JWPC 423/3, April 27, 1946, Geographic File 381-USSR, JCS Records.
60. LaFeber, *Eastern Europe*, p. 194.
61. The following discussion of the Soviet military is especially indebted to Matthew A. Evangelista, "Stalin's Postwar Army Reappraised," *International Security*, VII (Winter 1982–1983), 110–38. See also Thomas W. Wolfe, *Soviet Power and Europe, 1945–1970* (Baltimore, 1970).
62. Edgar O'Ballance, *The Red Army* (New York, 1964), p. 192.
63. Inglis to Forrestal, January 21, 1946. For similar views, see Ambassador Smith in C. L. Sulzberger, *A Long Row of Candles* (New York, 1969), p. 313; Memorandum by the Chief of Staff, U.S. Army, to JCS, July 28, 1947, Box 166, Central File 471.6, JCS Records; Truman in Pickersgill and Forster, *Mackenzie King*, IV, 3; *FRUS, 1948*, III, 157; Yergin, *Shattered*, p. 467; Eayers, *In Defence*, p. 334.
64. *FRUS, 1946*, VI, 707.
65. Diary, November 27, 1948, Lippmann Papers.
66. Zbigniew Brzezinski, "The Competitive Relationship," in Charles Gati,

ed., *Caging the Bear: Containment and the Cold War* (Indianapolis, 1974), p. 161; *The Soviet Army* (Moscow, 1971), p. 313.

67. The *New York Times*, May 12, 1947, for example, gave a figure of five million for Soviet troop strength.

68. Djilas, *Conversations*, p. 182.

69. "Analysis of Soviet Strength and Weakness," Joint Working Committee of the American Embassy, Moscow, September 1, 1946, 861.00/9-946, DSR.

70. Quoted in Truman, *Truman*, p. 306.

71. Whitney, *Russia*, p. 105.

72. "American Foreign Policy," transcript of proceedings, June 4, 1947, Box 93, Records of the U.S. Mission to the United Nations.

73. *Washington Post*, May 6, 1947. See also "X," "Sources"; Schwartz, *"Motive Forces,"* pp. 34–37; Ulam, *Expansion*, pp. 398–403; Harriman and Abel, *Special*, p. 521; Stimson and Bundy, *On Active*, p. 639; Louis Fischer, *The Great Challenge* (London, 1947), p. 254.

74. Harriman and Abel, *Special*, pp. 214, 308, 317, 547; Ulam, *Stalin*, pp. 633–34; Whitney, *Russia*, p. 23.

75. Speech by Wayne Morse, January 8, 1947, Box 0-3, Morse Papers.

76. Djilas, *Conversations*, p. 132.

77. See Joseph R. Starobin, "Origins of the Cold War: The Communist Dimension," *Foreign Affairs*, XLVII (July 1969), 681–96.

78. Memorandum of Conversation with Harriman, July 17, 1945, Box 18, Davies Papers; *FRUS, 1944*, IV, 989.

79. Harriman and Abel, *Special*, p. 316.

80. See Slusser, *Soviet Economic Policy*.

81. See Mastny, "Cassandra."

82. Shulman, *Stalin's*, pp. 32–33; *Soviet Views on the Post-War World Economy* (Washington, 1948); Frederick C. Barghoorn, "The Varga Discussion and Its Significance," *American Slavic and East European Review*, III (October 1948), 214–36.

83. Hahn, *Postwar Soviet Politics;* Ulam, *Expansion*, p. 402; Deutscher, *Stalin*, p. 579.

84. *FRUS, 1946*, VI, 722.

85. *PPP, Truman, 1948*, p. 329. See also notes from interview with Harry S. Truman, August 30, 1949, Box 85, Daniels Papers.

86. Smith, *My Three Years*, p. 55.

87. Campbell and Herring, *Diaries*, p. 440 (October 22, 1945).

88. Edward R. Stettinius, Jr., *Roosevelt and the Russians* (New York, 1949), p. 309; Harriman and Abel, *Special*, pp. 344, 444.

89. As general secretary of the party he seldom consulted with the Central Committee (it convened only once in 1946, once in 1947, and then not

again until 1952), and the Politburo met irregularly and apparently only occasionally. Robert H. McNeal, *Stalin: Man and Ruler* (New York, 1988), pp. 271–72. For the suggestion that the 1946 Novikov telegram became part of an internal policy debate in Moscow, see George F. Kennan, "Commentary," *Diplomatic History*, XV (Fall 1991), 539–43, and Melvyn P. Leffler, "Commentary," ibid., 548–53.

90. Harriman and Abel, *Special*, p. 377.

91. Svetlana Alliluyeva, *Twenty Letters to a Friend* (New York, 1967), p. 196.

92. For the paranoia thesis, see Schlesinger, "Origins"; Tucker, *Soviet Political Mind*. For criticism of this view, see William A. Williams, "The Cold War Revisionists," *The Nation*, CCV (November 13, 1967), 492–95; Yergin, *Shattered*, pp. 51–52; Melvin Croan in "Origins of the Post-War Crisis—A Discussion," *Journal of Contemporary History*, III (April 1968), 233–37; Adomeit, *Soviet Risk-Taking*, pp. 144–47.

93. Anthony Eden, *The Reckoning* (Boston, 1965), pp. 336–37; Harriman in *FRUS, Berlin*, I, 61; Truman, *Memoirs*, I, 263; Blum, *Price*, pp. 172, 347; Philip E. Mosely, "Across the Green Table from Stalin," *Current History*, XV (September 1948), 129–33, 167; Dixon, *Double*, p. 140.

94. George F. Kennan, "The United States and the Soviet Union, 1917–1976," *Foreign Affairs*, LIV (July 1976), 681.

95. Authors of the *Diplomatichesky Slovar* in W. Gottlieb, "A Self-Portrait of Soviet Foreign Policy," *Soviet Studies*, III (October 1951), 187.

96. Clement Attlee on Molotov in Williams, *Twilight*, p. 59. See also Campbell and Herring, *Diaries*, p. 449; Pickersgill and Forster, *Mackenzie King*, I. 432.

97. Quoted in Donovan, *Conflict*, p. 209.

98. *FRUS, Berlin*, I, 61.

99. Quoted in Bohlen, *Witness*, p. 220.

100. For the Soviet diplomatic style, see Raymond Dennett and Joseph E. Johnson, eds., *Negotiating with the Russians* (Boston, 1951); Mosely, *Kremlin*, pp. 3–41; Mosely, "Across"; Stephen Kertesz, "Reflections on Soviet and American Negotiating Behavior," *Review of Politics*, XIX (January 1957), 3–36; Gordon A. Craig, "Techniques of Negotiation," in Lederer, *Russian Foreign Policy*, pp. 351–73; James B. Reston, "Negotiating with the Russians," *Harper's Magazine*, CXCV (August 1947), 97–106; House of Representatives, Committee on Government Operations, *The Soviet Approach to Negotiation: Selected Writing* (Washington, D.C., 1969).

101. Teddy J. Uldricks, "The Impact of the Great Purges on the People's Commissariat of Foreign Affairs," *Slavic Review*, XXXVI (June 1977), 187–203.

102. Dean Acheson, *Sketches from Life* (Westport, Conn., 1974). pp. 91–92.

103. Quoted in Walton, *Wallace*, p. 41.
104. Harry S. Truman to Eleanor Roosevelt, May 10, 1945, Box 4560, Eleanor Roosevelt Papers.
105. Leslie Hollis, *One Marine's Tale* (London, 1956), pp. 144–45.
106. Lie, *In the Cause*, p. 223.
107. Quoted in Alfred Steinberg, *The Man from Missouri* (New York, 1962), p. 259.
108. Quoted in Truman, *Truman*, p. 279. See also Salisbury, *Russia*, p. 381.
109. Vyshinsky in Campbell and Herring, *Diaries*, p. 453.
110. See Isador Lubin's comments in "American-Soviet Relations," Discussion Meeting Report, October 2, 1947, Records of Groups, vol. XIV, Council on Foreign Relations Files; General Osborn, ibid., April 5, 1948; Charles Bohlen in Memorandum of Background Press and Radio Conference, May 11, 1948, Box 8, Bohlen Files.
111. Blum, *Price*, p. 245.
112. Harriman and Abel, *Special*, p. 412.
113. *FRUS, 1948*, V, Part 1, 164.
114. For contemporary comments on Soviet diplomats as dishonest, see Truman in Donovan, *Conflict*, p. 62; Leahy in Journal, August 1, 1945, Box 19, Davies Papers; John R. Deane, "Negotiating on Military Assistance, 1943–1945," in Dennett and Johnson, *Negotiating*, pp. 8, 27; Baruch in Bernstein, "Quest," p. 1042; *FRUS, 1948*, V, 164.
115. Smith, *My Three Years*, p. 60.
116. Hugh Dalton Diary, October 5, 1946, Hugh Dalton Papers, London School of Economics. For other comments, mostly critical, on the Soviet diplomatic style, see Harry S. Truman to Eleanor Roosevelt, December 21, 1948, Box 4560, Eleanor Roosevelt Papers; Blum, *Price*, p. 451; Memorandum of telephone conversation, December 6, 1946, Box 30, Warren Austin Papers, University of Vermont Library, Burlington; William Leahy, *I Was There* (New York, 1950), p. 349; Cabinet Meeting, October 11, 1946, Notes on Cabinet Meetings, Connelly Papers; Dean, *United States and Russia*, p. 49; "An American's Opinion on Iran," June 20, 1946, 891.00/6-2046, DSR; Acheson in *New York Times*, October 13, 1971; Digest of Meeting, April 10, 1947, Records of Meetings, vol. VIII, Council of Foreign Relations Files; Walter Johnson, ed., *Papers of Adlai Stevenson* (Boston, 1972–1977; 7 vols.), II, 301; Sulzberger, *Long Row*, p. 364.
117. Senate, *Legislative Origins*, p. 95.

CHAPTER 9. DECLINE: THE EROSION OF POWER AND
THE APPEAL OF DÉTENTE, 1950s–1980s

1. *FRUS, 1952–1954*, II, part 2, 1684–85.
2. Data and trends on the United States, including comparisons with other nations, were drawn from U.S. government publications, including the annual *Statistical Abstract of the United States;* Arms Control and Disarmament Agency, *World Military Expenditures and Arms Transfers* (annual); Agency for International Development, *U.S. Overseas Loans and Grants* (1988); Central Intelligence Agency, *Handbook of Economic Statistics* (annual). Also helpful were Thelma Liesner, *One Hundred Years of Economic Statistics* (New York, 1989); Allan R. Millett and Peter Maslowski, *For the Common Defense* (New York, 1984); George T. Kurian, *The New Book of World Rankings* (New York, 1988); Herbert Block, *The Planetary Product in 1980* (Washington, D.C., 1981); Robert Gilpin, *The Political Economy of International Relations* (Princeton, N.J., 1987); Barry P. Bosworth and Robert Z. Lawrence, "America in the World Economy," *The Brookings Review*, VII (Winter 1988–1989), 39–48; Council on Competitiveness, *Gaining New Ground* (Washington, D.C., 1991).
3. Zbigniew Brzezinski, "Limited War, Maximum Advantage," *New York Times*, February 4, 1991.
4. Aaron Friedberg, "In Search of the Peace Dividend," *Wilson Quarterly*, XIV (Autumn 1990), 78–79; Lloyd J. Dumas, *The Overburdened Economy* (Berkeley, 1986), pp. 208–17.
5. Quoted in Michael A. Genovese, *The Nixon Presidency* (Westport, Conn., 1990), p. 69.
6. Quoted in Nye, *Bound*, p. 2.
7. Henry Kissinger, *White House Years* (Boston, 1979), p. 57.
8. *PPP, Kennedy, 1961*, p. 1.
9. Quoted in *Washington Post National Weekly Edition*, February 26–March 4, 1990, p. 9.
10. Gerald Epstein, "Mortgaging America," *World Policy Journal*, VIII (Winter 1990–1991), 27–59.
11. Susan Strange, "The Persistent Myth of Lost Hegemony," *International Organization*, XLI (Autumn 1987), 551–74, argues that America's structural power, the power that decides "outcomes," has on balance increased (p. 553).
12. "Discussion at the 309th Meeting of the National Security Council, Friday, January 11, 1957," Box 7, NSC Summaries of Discussion, NSC Series, Ann Whitman File, Dwight D. Eisenhower Papers, Dwight D. Eisenhower Library, Abilene, Kan.

13. *FRUS, 1952–1954*, II, 317.
14. Quoted in Stephen E. Ambrose, *Eisenhower: The President* (New York, 1984), p. 434.
15. *PPP, Eisenhower, 1953*, pp. 182–83.
16. Ibid., p. 421.
17. Seymour Melman, *Our Depleted Society* (New York, 1965).
18. Their views and others are represented in James L. Clayton, ed., *The Economic Impact of the Cold War* (New York, 1970).
19. Quoted in Harvard Sitkoff, *The Struggle for Black Equality, 1954–1980* (New York, 1981), p. 219. See also Adam Fairclough, "Martin Luther King, Jr., and the War in Vietnam," *Phylon*, XLV (March 1984), 27.
20. George F. Kennan, *The Cloud of Danger* (Boston, 1977), p. 26.
21. Mayers, *Kennan*, p. 325.
22. Quoted in *New York Times*, May 4, 1983.
23. Strange, "Persistent Myth," p. 570.
24. Walter Goldstein, "The Erosion of the Superpowers: The Military Consequences of Economic Distress," *SAIS Review*, VIII (Summer–Fall 1988), 54, 60.
25. Henry Allen, "Give Us This Day Our Daily Bread," *Washington Post National Weekly Edition*, December 17–23, 1990, p. 11.
26. For Soviet data and trends, see Anders Åslund, *Gorbachev's Struggle for Economic Reform* (Ithaca, N.Y., 1991); Christopher M. Davis, "Economic Influence on the Decline of the Soviet Union as a Great Power: Continuity Despite Change," *Diplomacy & Statecraft*, I (November 1990), 81–109; Paul R. Gregory and Robert C. Stuart, *Soviet Economic Structure and Performance*, 3d ed. (New York, 1986); Roger Munting, *The Economic Development of the USSR* (New York, 1982); Alec Nove, *An Economic History of the U.S.S.R.* (London, 1969); Harry Schwartz, *An Introduction to the Soviet Economy* (Columbus, Ohio, 1968); Wolfe, *Soviet Power;* Kennedy, *Rise;* and statistical sources cited in note 2 above.
27. Douglas Pike, *Vietnam and the Soviet Union* (Boulder, Colo., 1987), p. 139.
28. *FRUS, 1955–1957*, II, 253–54.
29. Memorandum for the President, "Harriman Visit to Moscow," April 30, 1963, Box 30, President's Office File, John F. Kennedy Library, Boston.
30. Daniel P. Moynihan, "How America Blew It," *Newsweek*, CXVI (December 10, 1990), 14.
31. Quoted in Sidney Blumenthal, "Coming In from the Cold," *Washington Post National Weekly Edition*, June 27–July 3, 1988, p. 6; Stephen F. Cohen and Katrina Vanden Heuvel, *Voices of Glasnost: Interviews with Gorbachev's Reformers* (New York, 1989), p. 326.

32. Quoted in *New York Times,* February 26, 1986.
33. Robert G. Kaiser, *Why Gorbachev Happended: His Triumphs and His Failures* (New York, 1991), p. 115.
34. Quoted in Foreign Policy Association, *Great Decisions 1988* (New York, 1988), p. 43.
35. McCormick, *America's Half-Century,* p. 216.
36. Hoffmann, "A View," p. 468.
37. Kissinger, *White House,* p. 55.
38. See Ulam, *Expansion;* Gaddis, *Russia;* LaFeber, *America.*
39. Gordon H. Chang, *Friends and Enemies: The United States, China, and the Soviet Union* (Stanford, 1990); John Gittings, *Survey of the Sino-Soviet Dispute* (London, 1968); Donald S. Zagoria, *The Sino-Soviet Conflict, 1956–1961* (Princeton, N.J., 1962); Spence, *Search.*
40. Central Intelligence Agency, "The Deterioration of Sino-Soviet Relations: 1956–1966," April 22, 1966, Lyndon B. Johnson Library, Austin, Texas.
41. S. R. Ashton, *In Search of Détente: The Politics of East-West Relations since 1945* (New York, 1989), p. 183.
42. For some of America's troubles with European allies, see "Anti-Americanism: Origins and Context," *The Annals,* CDXCVII (May 1988); Stanley Hoffmann, *Decline or Renewal? France since the 1930s* (New York, 1974); Kaplan, *NATO and the United States;* David N. Schwartz, *NATO's Nuclear Dilemmas* (1983); Frank Costigliola, *France and the United States: The Cold Alliance since World War II* (Boston, 1992); Joseph Lepgold, *The Declining Hegemon: The United States and European Defense, 1960–1990* (Westport, Conn., 1990); A. W. DePorte, *Europe between the Superpowers* (New Haven, 1979); Alfred Grosser, *The Western Alliance: European-American Relations since 1945* (New York, 1980); Jean-Baptiste Duroselle, *France and the United States* (Chicago, 1978); Diane B. Kunz, *The Economic Diplomacy of the Suez Crisis* (Chapel Hill, 1991); Sheldon Anderson, "Poland and the Marshall Plan, 1947–1949," *Diplomatic History,* XV (Fall 1991), 493.
43. Psychological Strategy Board (1953) in *FRUS, 1952–1954,* I, part 2, 1483, 1484.
44. Quoted in DePorte, *Europe,* p. 240.
45. Frank Costigliola, "The Pursuit of Atlantic Community: Nuclear Arms, Dollars, and Berlin," in Thomas G. Paterson, ed., *Kennedy's Quest for Victory: American Foreign Policy, 1961–1963* (New York, 1989), p. 25.
46. Quoted (1963) in Grosser, *Western Alliance,* p. 209.
47. Quoted in *New York Times,* December 21, 1981.
48. Kissinger, *White House,* pp. 403, 409.
49. Ethan B. Kapstein, *The Insecure Alliance: Energy Crises and Western Politics since 1944* (New York, 1990), pp. 97, 136–39, 195–96, 205–06.
50. See Abraham F. Lowenthal, *Partners in Conflict,* rev. ed. (Baltimore,

1990); Stephen G. Rabe, *Eisenhower and Latin America* (Chapel Hill, N.C., 1988); Richard H. Immerman, *The CIA in Guatemala* (Austin, 1982); Walter LaFeber, *The Panama Canal*, updated ed. (New York, 1989); Walter LaFeber, *Inevitable Revolutions: The United States in Central America* (New York, 1984); Thomas G. Paterson, "Fixation with Cuba: The Bay of Pigs, Missile Crisis, and Covert War Against Castro," in Paterson, *Kennedy's Quest*, pp. 123–55; Lester D. Langley, *America and the Americas* (Athens, Ga., 1989); Marvin R. Zahniser and W. Michael Weis, "A Diplomatic Pearl Harbor?: Richard Nixon's Goodwill Mission to Latin America in 1958," *Diplomatic History*, XIII (Spring 1989), 163–90; Jorge G. Castañeda, "Latin America and the End of the Cold War," *World Policy Journal*, VII (Summer 1990), 467–92; Guy Poitras, *The Ordeal of Hegemony* (Boulder, Colo., 1990).

51. Richard Rosecrance, ed., *America as an Ordinary Country* (Ithaca, N.Y., 1976), p. 205.
52. Ethan B. Kapstein, "The Brazilian Defense Industry and the International System," *Political Science Quarterly*, CV (Winter 1990–1991), 579–96.
53. Abraham F. Lowenthal, "The United States and Latin America: Ending the Hegemonic Presumption," *Foreign Affairs*, LV (October 1976), 199–213.
54. On this point, see Thomas G. Paterson, "The Defense-of-Cuba Theme and the Missile Crisis," *Diplomatic History*, XIV (Spring 1990), 249–56.
55. Jorge A. Domínguez, Jr., *To Make the World Safe for Revolution: Cuba's Foreign Policy* (Cambridge, Mass., 1989).
56. *PPP, Nixon, 1971*, p. 806.
57. Quoted in James Chace, *Endless War* (New York, 1984), p. 86.
58. Studies of this phenomenon and the U.S. response include Merrill, *Bread and the Ballot*; Stavrianos, *Global Rift*; Kolko, *Confronting*; Stephen D. Krasner, *Structural Conflict: The Third World Against Global Liberalism* (Berkeley, 1985); Robert A. Packenham, *Liberal America and the Third World* (Princeton, N.J., 1973); Melvin Gurtov, *The United States Against the World: Anti-Nationalism and Intervention* (New York, 1974); *Barnet, Intervention*; Brands, *Specter*; and works on specific countries cited previously.
59. George W. Ball, *The Past Has Another Pattern* (New York, 1982), p. 175
60. United Nations, General Assembly, *Official Records*, 22d sess., August 18, 1967, Agenda Item 92, Annexes, Document A/6695, p. 1.
61. Miguel Marín-Bosch, "How Nations Vote in the General Assembly of the United Nations," *International Organization*, XLI (Autumn 1987), 705–24; Charles W. Kegley, Jr., and Steven W. Hook, "U.S. Foreign Aid and U.N. Voting: Did Reagan's Linkage Strategy Buy Deference or Defiance?," *International Studies Quarterly*, XXXV (1991), 296n.
62. Quoted (1979) in Karl P. Sauvant, *The Group of 77* (New York, 1981),

pp. 131–36. See also R. K. Sinha, ed., *New International Economic Order* (New Delhi, India, 1985); Jagdish N. Bhagwati, ed., *The New International Economic Order: The North-South Debate* (Cambridge, Mass., 1977).

63. Quoted (1974) in Lowenthal, *Partners*, p. 42.
64. Quoted in Robert K. Olson, *U.S. Foreign Policy and the New International Economic Order: Negotiating Global Problems, 1974–1981* (Boulder, Colo., 1981), p. 17.
65. Quoted in Edmund Stillman and William Pfaff, *The New Politics* (New York, 1961), p. 127.
66. *PPP, Nixon, 1970*, p. 409.
67. J. William Fulbright, *The Arrogance of Power* (New York, 1966).
68. Michael Mandelbaum, "The Bush Foreign Policy," *Foreign Affairs: America and the World 1990/91*, LXX (No. 1, 1990–1991), 20–21.
69. Quoted in John Lewis Gaddis, *Strategies of Containment* (New York, 1982), p. 345.
70. Coral Bell, "*Détente* and the American National Interest," in Rosecrance, *America*, p. 45.
71. U.S. Department of State, *Dispatch*, I (October 22, 1990), 201.

CHAPTER 10. END: TOWARD A POST-COLD WAR ORDER

1. Henry Kissinger, *Years of Upheaval* (Boston, 1982), p. 238.
2. Quotation from Thomas W. Simons, Jr., *The End of the Cold War* (New York, 1990), p. 31. See also Kenneth A. Oye, "International Systems Structure and American Foreign Policy," in Kenneth A. Oye et al., eds., *Eagle Defiant: United States Foreign Policy in the 1980s* (Boston, 1983), p. 13.
3. Editorial, "Soviet-American Relations in Perestroika," *International Affairs* (Moscow), no. 7 (July 1990), 65.
4. John E. Mroz, "Soviet Foreign Policy and New Thinking," ibid., no. 5 (May 1990), 23–33; Fernando Bustamante, "Soviet Policy toward Latin America: Time for Renewal," *Journal of Interamerican Studies and World Affairs*, XXXII (Winter 1990), 35–65; Robert A. Pastor, "Forging a Hemispheric Bargain: The Bush Opportunity," *Journal of International Affairs*, XLIII (Summer–Fall 1989), 69–81.
5. Robert G. Kaiser, "The End of the Soviet Empire," *Washington Post National Weekly Edition*, January 1–7, 1990, p. 23.
6. Fred Kaplan, "Time to Bring the Boys Home," *Boston Globe*, March 18, 1990.

7. Quoted in *Newsweek*, CXV (February 26, 1990), 17.

8. Lance Morrow, "The Russian Revolution," *Time*, CXXXVIII (September 2, 1991), 20.

9. See, for example, John Lewis Gaddis, *Russia, the Soviet Union, and the United States*, 2d ed. (New York, 1990), pp. 337–38. For a contrary, persuasive view that President Ronald Reagan's confrontational anti-Sovietism actually delayed *perestroika*, see Michael MccGwire, *Perestroika and Soviet National Security* (Washington, D.C., 1991), pp. 381–93.

10. *PPP, Reagan, 1983*, I, 265; *Weekly Compilation of Presidential Documents*, XXVI (September 17, 1990), 1359, 1360. For a critique of America's "yearning for a refurbished national identity," see Michael T. Klare, "Policing the Gulf—and the World," *Nation*, CCLI (October 15, 1990), 40 ff.

11. *Wall Street Journal*, January 18, 1991. For a rebuttal that argues that the United States could best restore its reputation not by winning on the battlefield but by addressing its serious domestic needs, see Paul Kennedy, "A Declining Empire Goes to War," ibid., January 24, 1991.

12. Michael Novak quoted in *New York Times*, March 4, 1991.

13. Christopher Layne, "Why the Gulf War Was Not in the National Interest," *Atlantic Monthly*, CCLXVIII (July 1991), 70. See also Morton Kondrake, "The Democracy Gang: A Movement in Search of a Leader," *New Republic*, CCI (November 6, 1989), 18–23; Charles William Maynes, "America without the Cold War," *Foreign Policy*, no. 78 (Spring 1990), 3–25. For minimal success in the past, see Abraham F. Lowenthal, ed., *Exporting Democracy: The United States and Latin America* (Baltimore, 1991; 2 vols.).

14. Quoted in Bernard Gwertzman and Michael T. Kaufman, eds., *The Collapse of Communism* (New York, 1990), p. 289.

15. Richard Nixon, *In the Arena: A Memoir of Victory, Defeat, and Renewal* (New York, 1990), p. 323.

16. Senator George J. Mitchell quoted in *New York Times*, March 4, 1991.

17. Quoted in Strobe Talbott, "The Delicate Balancing Act," *Time*, CXXXVIII (July 29, 1991), 32.

18. A point well made in Ronaldo Sardenberg, "Changing International Context for United States-Latin America Relations," workshop paper, May 23–25, 1990, Inter-American Dialogue of the Aspen Institute, Washington, D.C.

19. Ronald Steel, "Europe after the Superpowers," in Nicholas X. Rizopoulos, ed., *Sea-Changes: American Foreign Policy in a World Transformed* (New York, 1990), p. 9.

20. Stanley Hoffmann, "A New World and Its Troubles," ibid., pp. 279–80; Thomas G. Paterson, "Defining and Doing the History of American For-

eign Relations: A Primer," in Hogan and Paterson, *Explaining*, pp. 39, 47–52.

21. Robert J. Samuelson, "Superpower Swan Song?," *Newsweek*, CXVI (December 24, 1990), 35; Marshall D. Shulman, "The Superpowers: Dance of the Dinosaurs," *Foreign Affairs: America and the World 1987/1988*, LXVI (no. 3, 1988), 494.

22. For examples, see Joshua Muravchik, "At Last, Pax Americana," *New York Times*, January 24, 1991, and Charles Krauthammer, "The Unipolar Moment," *Foreign Affairs: America and the World 1990/91*, LXX (no. 1, 1991), 23–33. For contrary views, see William Pfaff, "Redefining World Power," ibid., 34–48, and Anthony Lewis, "Is It Our Leaders, or Is It Us?," *New York Times*, February 11, 1991.

23. *Congressional Record*, CXXXVII (January 29, 1991), S1216–19.

24. Quoted in *New York Times*, March 7, 1991.

25. Quoted in *Hartford Courant*, January 14, 1992.

26. Washington pundit Ben Wattenberg quoted in ibid., January 30, 1991.

27. *Congressional Record*, CXXXVII (January 29, 1991), S1216–19; *New York Times*, February 10, 1991.

28. For a suggestive study of the stresses that produced the fall of past societies, including the Roman Empire, see Joseph A. Tainter, *The Collapse of Complex Societies* (Cambridge, Eng., 1988).

29. Quoted in *Time*, CXXXV (June 4, 1990), 30.

INDEX